Words of Life 2009

Words of Life 2009

Daily Reflections for Your Spirit

Edited by *Caryl Green*

NOVALIS

© 2009 Novalis, Saint Paul University, Ottawa, Canada

Cover design: Audrey Wells
Cover illustration: Sue Todd
Layout: Audrey Wells

Business Offices:

Novalis Publishing Inc.
10 Lower Spadina Avenue, Suite 400
Toronto, Ontario, Canada
M5V 2Z2

Novalis Publishing Inc.
4475 Frontenac Street
Montréal, Québec, Canada
H2H 2S2

Phone: 1-800-387-7164
Fax: 1-800-204-4140
E-mail: books@novalis.ca
www.novalis.ca

Library and Archives Canada Cataloguing in Publication

Words of life 2009 daily reflections for your spirit / edited by Caryl
Green.

ISBN 978-2-89646-038-0

    1. Bible–Meditations. 2. Spiritual life–Christianity–
Meditations. 3. Devotional calendars. I. Green, Caryl

BS491.5.W862 2008   242'.5   C2008-903980-7

Printed in Canada.

We acknowledge the financial support of the Government of Canada through
the Book Publishing Industry Development Program (BPIDP) for our publishing
activities.

I would like to welcome you to *Words of Life: Daily Reflections for Your Spirit – 2009.* Since its launch in 1998 as a monthly magazine, *Words of Life* has provided readers with passages drawn from Scripture, along with reflections and prayers for every day. This book draws from those reflections and prayers, and is based on the Scripture readings for Year B of the church's lectionary.

Life's stories

The reflections in *Words of Life* draw their inspiration from Scripture *and* from everyday life experiences. They describe how real people continue to seek God in a real way within their lives and their communities. The stories in *Words of Life* describe situations when authors have chosen to live according to the teachings of Jesus in matters both large and small. The choice to live with God's Word in their hearts influenced not only their own lives, but also the lives of family members, friends and colleagues and their communities.

I would like to take this opportunity to thank the many individuals who have contributed to this publication especially the authors, editors, proofreaders, photographers and graphic designers. (The names of authors whose reflections appear in this book are listed on pages 374-375.)

Our journey of life

I'd also like to express my deep appreciation to the many subscribers who, after receiving their final issue of *Words of Life*, wrote to tell me how much they would miss its presence in their lives. As one subscriber wrote: "I've always regarded *Words of Life* like a friend who shares his or her 'secrets' with me, whether they be personal or family-based, work-related or within the public sphere. Sharing stories from different perspectives builds community, even if that community is somewhat artificial. It's like listening to a wonderful piece of music on the radio – the fact that others are listening to it at the same time increases the pleasure by being able to share it within a community of listeners. So it has been with *Words of Life* – a constructed community of friends. And when a friend decides to move away, you grieve for a while knowing that the intimacy of shared experiences goes with them, but also knowing that the opportunity to have shared provided real context within our common journey of life." Many subscribers said that they wanted something that would continue to sustain their daily prayer life. It was that feedback and encouragement that made this book possible. Thank you.

Word Made Flesh

If you are beginning to read this book in January, you will have celebrated the birth of Jesus recently. Many of us struggle to keep alive the spirit of Emmanuel or God-with-us throughout the year. Jesus, as the Word-Made-Flesh, brings healing to the brokenness we experience within ourselves and in our world. *Words of Life* offers us a still point in our busy lives to be with God's Word on a daily basis. I hope you are able to take a quiet moment with *Words of Life* each day – to centre yourselves in God and to be aware of God working in your lives to transform your burdens into opportunities for change, for growth. And to know the deep peace that God's love brings.

I wish you peace, hope and the knowledge of God's abiding love.

Caryl Green

Editor

So they hurried off and found Mary and Joseph and saw the baby lying in the manger. When the shepherds saw him, they told them what the angel had said about the child. All who heard it were amazed at what the shepherds said. Mary remembered all these things and thought deeply about them. The shepherds went back, singing praises to God for all they had heard and seen; it had been just as the angel had told them. A week later, when the time came for the baby to be circumcised, he was named Jesus, the name which the angel had given him before he had been conceived.

Luke 2: 16-21

> "Mary remembered all these things…"

A new journey

When our daughter was born, I remember a roller-coaster rhythm of guests coming and going. These visits were punctuated by moments of remarkable stillness – when we were alone with our newborn. In those moments, it was as if our baby was inviting us simply to *be* with her, to ponder the new journey we were beginning.

Was Mary overwhelmed with the shepherds' unexpected arrival, and their stories of angels and bright stars? If she was, today's reading reminds me that she still took time to pause and reflect deeply.

There is something sacred in new beginnings: new ideas, new friendships, new jobs and challenges. As I step into this new year, I want to remember to look for the sacred, and rejoice in the mystery of each new day.

**God, help me celebrate this new beginning
without worrying about what will be.**

The Jewish authorities in Jerusalem sent some priests and Levites to John to ask him, "Who are you?" John spoke out openly and clearly, saying: "I am not the Messiah."

"Who are you, then?" they asked. "Are you Elijah?" "No, I am not," John answered. "Are you the Prophet?" they asked. "No," he replied.

"Then tell us who you are," they said. "We have to take an answer back to those who sent us. What do you say about yourself?" John answered by quoting the prophet Isaiah: "I am 'the voice of someone shouting in the desert: Make a straight path for the Lord to travel!' ... I baptize with water, but among you stands the one you do not know. He is coming after me, but I am not good enough even to untie his sandals." *John 1: 19-28*

"John spoke out openly and clearly..."

Knowing who I am

If there's anything we know about John the Baptist, it's that he's fearless and determined. But today's reading shows a side of him I've always found appealing and challenging: his modesty. John knows who he is and, more importantly, he knows who he's not.

At times I think that what I do is not good enough, or important enough, or recognized enough; and I'm tempted to puff myself up to look more significant in the eyes of others. Though I never truly convince myself, the temptation remains.

What does John do when the spotlight shines on him? He's quick to say that what he does and who he is are not that important. How clearly he sees reality. How I wish I could see as clearly!

Lord, you have made me.
Help me to see clearly who I am, and to live my life fully.

S ing a new song to the Lord;
he has done wonderful things!
By his own power and holy strength
he has won the victory....
He kept his promise to the people of Israel
with loyalty and constant love for them.
All people everywhere have seen the victory of our God.
Sing for joy to the Lord, all the earth;
praise him with songs and shouts of joy!
Sing praises to the Lord!
Play music on the harps!
Blow trumpets and horns,
and shout for joy to the Lord, our king.
Psalm 98: 1-6

"Sing for joy to the Lord…"

Reason to sing

It's the first week of the New Year. I'm grateful to have survived the chaotic days of Christmas; but now that they're over, I want to lie low and enjoy the peace that follows the holiday season.

In these early days of January, I am not thinking about singing for joy. I know the bills will start streaming in any day now; I've already broken a resolution or two; and I'm worn out from all the shopping, wrapping and visiting that have consumed the last few weeks.

I have to remind myself why I've put myself through all this activity – not just to prepare for family gatherings, not just to give to others, but to celebrate the birth of Jesus. When I think of it that way, how can I help but sing for joy?

Lord, help me remember to sing for joy each day – when I'm celebrating and when I'm recovering from celebrating.

J esus was born in the town of Bethlehem in Judea, during the time when Herod was king. Soon afterward, some men who studied the stars came from the East to Jerusalem and asked, "Where is the baby born to be the king of the Jews…?"

When King Herod heard about this, he was very upset. He called together all the chief priests and the teachers of the Law and asked them, "Where will the Messiah be born…?"

So Herod called the visitors from the East to a secret meeting and found out from them the exact time the star had appeared. Then he sent them to Bethlehem with these instructions: "Go and make a careful search for the child; and when you find him, let me know, so that I too may go and worship him."   *Matthew 2: 1-12*

"When King Herod heard about this, he was very upset."

Terrors of children

When our two oldest children were toddlers, we went to a theatre production of the Christmas story. About 100 parents and children sat on the floor of the community centre while the play of puppets – many of them literally larger than life-size – took place all around us.

When the part about Herod being very upset was read, Herod and his soldiers marched through the audience playing loud drums. Most kids in the room burrowed into their parents' laps. Who could blame them? Herod was fearsome to children even as a puppet character.

I see modern-day Herods – leaders of nations who initiate war or who fail to prevent it – still filling children with terror today.

**Lord, help me to hear the needs of all children.
May their cries prompt me to do your work.**

When Jesus heard that John had been put in prison, he went away to Galilee. He went to live in Capernaum, a town by Lake Galilee, in the territory of Zebulun and Naphtali. This was done to make come true what the prophet Isaiah had said, "Land of Zebulun and land of Naphtali, on the road to the sea, on the other side of the Jordan, Galilee, land of the Gentiles! The people who live in darkness will see a great light. On those who live in the dark land of death the light will shine." From that time Jesus began to preach his message: "Turn away from your sins, because the kingdom of heaven is near!"

Matthew 4: 12-17, 23-25

"...the light will shine."

The light of Christ

"The people who live in darkness" – there's an image a hardy northerner like myself can identify with. It's so hard to get out of bed on these dark winter mornings. My body is heavy, my eyes unwilling to greet the gloom. Coming home to dine in the dark is little better. Even the cold is easier to bear in the light. Everything seems menacing when it's night.

But night gives way to day, and day brings with it energy and animation. Winter melts into spring, and I am filled with hope and new resolve.

And the darkness of my confusion, uncertainty and sin is redeemed by the "great light," the light of Christ. This light banishes fear, promises forgiveness, and fills me with life.

When darkness threatens to overwhelm me,
Lord, give me the patience to wait for your promised light.

T he disciples came to Jesus and said, "Send the people away, and let them go to the nearby farms and villages in order to buy themselves something to eat."

"You yourselves give them something to eat," Jesus answered. They asked, "Do you want us to go and spend two hundred silver coins on bread in order to feed them?" So Jesus asked them, "How much bread do you have? Go and see." When they found out, they told him, "Five loaves and also two fish...."

Then Jesus took the five loaves and the two fish, looked up to heaven, and gave thanks to God. He broke the loaves and gave them to his disciples to distribute to the people. He also divided the two fish among them all. Everyone ate and had enough.   *Mark 6: 34-44*

> "You yourselves give them something to eat."

Waiting for the miracle

Reading today's passage, I notice that it is called the "Miracle of the Loaves and Fishes." This sub-title reminds me of a slogan one hears in Alcoholics Anonymous: "Don't quit before the miracle happens." This slogan is an encouragement to avoid falling into the temptation of the disciples – to set ourselves up to do nothing because the situation looks impossible.

Sometimes it takes a miracle – and sometimes that miracle happens – if we persevere. But if we don't wait... no miracle.

Now for someone like me who wants everything *right now,* that waiting is difficult. Some things haven't changed all that much since the time of Jesus and his disciples! "Don't quit before the miracle," indeed.

**God, remind me that I don't have to do it all by myself.
There are others who can help.**

Dear friends, if this is how God loved us, then we should love one another. No one has ever seen God, but if we love one another, God lives in union with us, and his love is made perfect in us…. We have seen and tell others that the Father sent his Son to be the Saviour of the world. If we declare that Jesus is the Son of God, we live in union with God and God lives in union with us. And we ourselves know and believe the love which God has for us.

1 John 4: 11-18

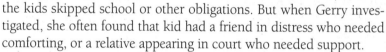

"…if we love one another…"

Tough love

My friend Gerry lived and worked with Native kids in the bleak inner core of Winnipeg. People complained to her that the kids skipped school or other obligations. But when Gerry investigated, she often found that kid had a friend in distress who needed comforting, or a relative appearing in court who needed support.

And if a family got evicted from its home, some other family in the community would usually let the family "crash" at their place, even if it meant everyone was crowded and uncomfortable.

"Yes, there's violence and addiction," Gerry would say. "But I've also found more love and generosity here than in any middle-class neighbourhood I've ever known. This is where you find God."

Lord, help me realize that love is far more important than schedules, or money, or marks.

We love because God first loved us. If we say we love God, but hate others, we are liars. For we cannot love God, whom we have not seen, if we do not love others, whom we have seen. The command that Christ has given us is this: whoever loves God must love others also.

Whoever believes that Jesus is the Messiah is a child of God; and whoever loves a father loves his child also. This is how we know that we love God's children: it is by loving God and obeying his commands.

1 John 4: 19 – 5: 4

> "Whoever loves God must love others also."

Small acts of love

An absent co-worker being dissected… An adolescent facing hard choices for the first time, negotiating the issues… It is so easy to take on the values of the group; so hard to go it alone.

I'm reminded of Gandhi: one man committed to a non-violent way of love. Who would not participate in something unjust. Who would not hate those who hated him. One small man changed the British Empire. And Mother Teresa, caring for one person at a time. And Jesus, the son of a carpenter, who changed the world.

What of us? When I feel small and alone, it helps to know that it is what's inside that counts. That each small act of love transforms me. The world cannot defeat me.

**Lord, let me have faith in you, and in me
– that I can do what I know to be right.**

Once Jesus was in a town where there was a man who was suffering from a dreaded skin disease. When he saw Jesus, he threw himself down and begged him, "Sir, if you want to, you can make me clean!"

Jesus reached out and touched him. "I do want to," he answered. "Be clean!" At once the disease left the man. Jesus ordered him, "Don't tell anyone, but go straight to the priest and let him examine you; then to prove to everyone that you are cured, offer the sacrifice as Moses ordered."

But the news about Jesus spread all the more widely, and crowds of people came to hear him and be healed from their diseases. But he would go away to lonely places, where he prayed.

Luke 5: 12-16

"But he would go away to lonely places…"

Time to heal

Each day people approach me for a healing word, a healing touch – my child, my family, my friends, my co-workers. I try to respond to them, even though it may be painful or difficult. And I know that reaching out to others is a huge risk; there's a chance they might reject my offer.

When I respond to the needs of other people, I give something of myself. To regain my strength, I need to get away by myself – even for half an hour – just to be quiet, to be renewed. If I don't, I can't continue to give others what they need.

And so I retreat and find the strength to offer a healing word, a healing touch, to those who ask each day.

**Jesus, may I remember that to help heal others,
I need to spend healing time alone.**

Some of John's disciples began arguing with a Jew about the matter of ritual washing. So they went to John and told him, "Teacher, you remember the man who was with you on the east side of the Jordan, the one you spoke about? Well, he is baptizing now, and everyone is going to him!"

John answered, "No one can have anything unless God gives it. You yourselves are my witnesses that I said, 'I am not the Messiah, but I have been sent ahead of him.' The bridegroom is the one to whom the bride belongs; but the bridegroom's friend, who stands by and listens, is glad when he hears the bridegroom's voice. This is how my own happiness is made complete. He must become more important while I become less important."

John 3: 22-30

> "...while I become less important."

Keeping focused

As a parent sitting in the stands, I cringed to see my son's coach yelling and gesturing wildly – drawing attention to himself, and away from the players on the ice. In contrast, the visiting team's coach spoke in a way that made him "invisible" – leaving the focus and the spotlight on the players themselves.

It would have been easy for John the Baptist to agree with Jesus' detractors, thus securing their loyalty and attention for himself. But he didn't.

How easy to get drawn into our society's emphasis on individuality and self-fulfillment. John's words challenge me to consider where I look for signs of success and how I measure happiness; to clarify who and what truly matters in life, and to keep focused on that.

**Lord, help me to keep focused on what matters in life:
truth, honesty and integrity.**

"Listen now, my people, and come to me;
come to me, and you will have life....
My thoughts," says the Lord, "are not like yours,
and my ways are different from yours.
As high as the heavens are above the earth,
so high are my ways and thoughts above yours.
My word is like the snow and the rain
that come down from the sky to water the earth.
They make the crops grow
and provide seed for planting and food to eat.
So also will be the word that I speak –
it will not fail to do what I plan for it;
it will do everything I send it to do."

Isaiah 55: 1-11

> "My word is like the snow and the rain..."

Words of life

One of the earliest and most telling photographs of me shows a toddler standing on a chair at a kitchen table, looking closely at a newspaper spread before him.

Since then, I have rarely been without a book nearby. I read the newspaper daily to see what's going on. And, for almost thirty years, I have made my living by moving words around on paper, trying to find exactly the right word to express what needs to be expressed.

You would be right if you concluded that I have a hunger for words and their meanings. But most words are fluff – without real sustenance, and my restless appetite is rarely satisfied.

The Lord promises better, and I wonder, "Are these the words that will nourish?"

Lord, I am hungry. Nourish me with your words.

J esus went to Galilee and preached the Good News from God. "The right time has come," he said, "and the kingdom of God is near! Turn away from your sins and believe the Good News!"

As Jesus walked along the shore of Lake Galilee, he saw two fishermen, Simon and his brother Andrew, catching fish with a net. Jesus said to them, "Come with me, and I will teach you to catch people." At once they left their nets and went with him.

He went a little farther on and saw two other brothers, James and John, the sons of Zebedee. They were in their boat getting their nets ready. As soon as Jesus saw them, he called them; they left their father Zebedee in the boat with the hired men and went with Jesus.

Mark 1: 14-20

> "...they left their nets and went with him."

Recognizing the call

Up early, lunches made, last sleepyhead awakened, breakfast assembly line operating at full speed. Any e-mails overnight? How are we for milk? Who's got the newspaper? Is there enough in the fridge to make dinner, or will it be leftovers again? Out the door, out the door. Don't be late.

The familiar start of an ordinary day, and my work hasn't even begun yet!

Life is full of small, plucking fingers that pull at the sleeves of my life. How will I recognize the hand on my shoulder signalling not the urgent, but the important? Will I have the wisdom of Simon and Andrew? Or will I miss the call because, oh, this net has a knot that needs untangling?

Lord, teach me silence so I can hear your call.

O Lord, our Lord,
your greatness is seen in all the world!
Your praise reaches up to the heavens;
it is sung by children and babies....
When I look at the sky, which you have made,
at the moon and the stars,
which you set in their places –
what are human beings, that you think of them;
mere mortals, that you care for them?
Yet you made them inferior only to yourself;
you crowned them with glory and honour.
You appointed them rulers
over everything you made.

Psalm 8: 1-8

"When I look at the sky, which you have made…"

Words that last

The sky was big, the night was dark, and
I was afraid. I stood on the shore of the lake, surrounded by dense
forest, myriad stars reflecting on the water. Unfortunately, I was less
aware of the beauty around me than of my fear of the walk through
the bush to get back to the cabin.

I was with a friend who was everything I wasn't: big, strong and
powerful. As we looked out at the lake, he said, "I'm scared of the
dark." His words were a gift to me. If he was scared, I could be, too.

Like light still visible from stars long dead, his words remain
though he does not. Often when I'm scared, I remember his words,
and they help me believe that I'm stronger than I feel.

**Lord, help me to accept myself as I am
– with my strengths and fears alike.**

S ince the children, as he calls them, are people of flesh and blood, Jesus himself became like them and shared their human nature. He did this so that through his death he might destroy the Devil, who has the power over death, and in this way set free those who were slaves all their lives because of their fear of death. For it is clear that it is not the angels that he helps. Instead, he helps the descendants of Abraham. This means that he had to become like his people in every way, in order to be their faithful and merciful High Priest in his service to God, so that the people's sins would be forgiven. And now he can help those who are tempted, because he himself was tempted and suffered. *Hebrews 2: 14-18*

> "...it is not the angels that he helps."

If I fall...

It's one of those songs that lodged itself in my memory the first time I heard it. "What if I stumble? What if I fall? What if I lose my step and make fools of us all?"*

Today's reading reminds me that when I lose my step, it's not foolishness. I merely find myself once more amid the fragile community of those who have faltered. I seek their helping hand, not sure that I even have the courage or humility to accept their offer.

It is comforting to know that Jesus understands those who are tempted – because of the temptations he himself experienced. I may feel unangelic, but I am not abandoned.

Dear God, help me learn that experience becomes wisdom and blossoms into compassion.

*"What if I Stumble" written by Toby McKeehan and Daniel Joseph, from the D.C. Talk album: *Jesus Freak*.
© Up in the Mix Music/BMI (ForeFront Records, 1995).

A s the Holy Spirit says, "If you hear God's voice today, do not be stubborn, as your ancestors were when they rebelled against God, as they were that day in the desert when they put him to the test.... I was angry with those people and said, 'They are always disloyal and refuse to obey my commands.' I was angry and made a solemn promise: 'They will never enter the land where I would have given them rest!'"

My friends, be careful that none of you have a heart so evil and unbelieving that you will turn away from the living God. Instead, in order that none of you be deceived by sin and become stubborn, you must help one another every day.

Hebrews 3: 7-14

"If you hear God's voice today, do not be stubborn..."

Listening for God's voice

I hear many voices throughout the day.
At breakfast, my daughter whines so that she will get her own way. On my way out the door, a neighbour phones to ask for a favour. En route to work, the driver in the next lane mouths something that is probably best left unheard. At the photocopier, my co-worker insists that I pick up more responsibilities. On the message machine, my husband apologizes that he has to work late... again!

My instinct is to harden my heart, if not stop up my ears. Yet somewhere in all these voices is the echo of God's voice. May I have the wisdom to hear it.

God, I am listening. Let me hear your voice.

Jesus was preaching the message to them when four men arrived, carrying a paralyzed man. Because of the crowd, however, they could not get the man to him. So they made a hole in the roof right above the place where Jesus was. When they had made an opening, they let the man down, lying on his mat. Seeing how much faith they had, Jesus said, "My son, your sins are forgiven."

Some teachers of the Law thought to themselves, "This is blasphemy! God is the only one who can forgive sins!" Jesus knew what they were thinking, so he said, "Is it easier to say to this paralyzed man, 'Your sins are forgiven,' or to say, 'Get up, pick up your mat, and walk'?" … So he said, "I tell you, get up, pick up your mat, and go home!" The man got up, picked up his mat, and hurried away.

Mark 2: 1-12

> "So they made a hole in the roof…"

Risking it all

Thomas Merton once wrote in his journal: "Suddenly there is a point where religion becomes laughable. Then you decide you are nevertheless religious."

It is almost comical to think of a couple of men cutting a hole in the roof – because they were unable to push through the crowd around Jesus. I imagine the look on the face of the house's owner when he sees his roof broken, and the other, more decorous bystanders who have to step aside – to avoid being hit on the head by falling roofing tiles! It could just as well be a scene from a Laurel and Hardy movie.

These roof-breakers will do anything to get to Jesus – even risk ridicule. But the point is that Jesus is happy to see them, even more so because of their laughable means of entry!

**Lord, give me the grace to become even laughable,
so long as it brings me closer to you.**

As Jesus walked along, he saw a tax collector, Levi son of Alphaeus, sitting in his office. Jesus said to him, "Follow me." Levi got up and followed him.

Later on Jesus was having a meal in Levi's house. A large number of tax collectors and other outcasts was following Jesus, and many of them joined him and his disciples at the table. Some teachers of the Law, who were Pharisees, saw that Jesus was eating with these outcasts and tax collectors, so they asked his disciples, "Why does he eat with such people?"

Jesus heard them and answered, "People who are well do not need a doctor, but only those who are sick. I have not come to call respectable people, but outcasts."

Mark 2: 13-17

"I have not come to call respectable people..."

Who gets called?

My friend is a teacher in a very difficult school. Every day she calls up one of the parents. She makes a point of calling up the parents of the children who are the most difficult of all. At first, the parents were dismayed, expecting the worst: What had Johnny or Lizzie done now?

But that's not why my friend calls. She never calls about the bad things. Instead, she tells them something good their child has done. All day long she takes special care to watch for signs of something positive in the most difficult of her kids, so she can report it back to their parents.

Perhaps the parents of the well-behaved kids don't get that same kind of encouragement. But isn't that what Jesus is talking about?

Lord, help me to see your light in everyone I meet.

25

J ohn was standing with two of his disciples, when he saw Jesus walking by. "There is the Lamb of God!" he said. The two disciples heard him say this and went with Jesus. Jesus asked, "What are you looking for?" They answered, "Where do you live, Rabbi?" (This word means "Teacher.") "Come and see," he answered.... So they went with him and saw where he lived, and spent the rest of that day with him. One of them was Andrew, Simon Peter's brother. At once he found his brother Simon and told him, "We have found the Messiah." (This word means "Christ.") Then he took Simon to Jesus. Jesus looked at him and said, "Your name is Simon son of John, but you will be called Cephas." (This is the same as Peter and means "a rock.")   *John 1: 35-42*

"What are you looking for?"

The true rock

When I first met my husband-to-be, I did not know what I was looking for. Yet, like the disciples, I responded to the invitation to "Come and see." Over the weeks and months that followed, we discovered a deep love – a love that brought healing to past hurts, a love that opened us to the future.

Eight years into our marriage, my husband was diagnosed with cancer. When he died, I felt as if I'd lost everything. Our shared love, the rock upon which I'd built my life, had been shattered.

With time, I've come to recognize the true rock – the source of any love – is, in fact, God's love. Turning to God in my despair, I find the courage to love again.

**Lord, when my life seems to have lost all meaning,
gather me up in your deep and unshakable love.**

Some people came to Jesus and asked him, "Why is it that the disciples of John the Baptist and the disciples of the Pharisees fast, but yours do not?"

Jesus answered, "Do you expect the guests at a wedding party to go without food? Of course not…. But the day will come when the bridegroom will be taken away from them, and then they will fast.

"No one uses a piece of new cloth to patch up an old coat, because the new patch will shrink and tear off some of the old cloth, making an even bigger hole. Nor does anyone pour new wine into used wineskins, because the wine will burst the skins, and both the wine and the skins will be ruined. Instead, new wine must be poured into fresh wineskins."

Mark 2: 18-22

"New wine must be poured into fresh wineskins."

Changes

I like the idea of change; it's just that I don't like *changes*. At the office, we recently came up with a well-thought-out plan for changing the positions of our workstations. It made sense, but in my heart of hearts, I would have much preferred that things stay the way they were. Or better yet, that everyone else change, and I stay the same.

New is good, but old is so comfortable. Now that computers are a familiar, even automatic way of putting my thoughts on paper, I forget the resistance I initially felt to giving up my typewriter. I still hoard yellow pads, but rarely use them. But I keep them… just in case.

Change is necessary; change is good. However, change is not always comfortable.

Lord, when the very thought of doing things differently leaves me fearful, help me stay open to your word.

Jesus was walking through some wheat fields on a Sabbath. As his disciples walked along with him, they began to pick the heads of wheat. So the Pharisees said, "Look, it is against our Law for your disciples to do that on the Sabbath!"

Jesus answered, "Have you never read what David did that time when he needed something to eat? He and his men were hungry, so he went into the house of God and ate the bread offered to God.... According to our Law only the priests may eat this bread – but David ate it and even gave it to his men."

Jesus concluded, "The Sabbath was made for the good of human beings; they were not made for the Sabbath. So the Son of Man is Lord even of the Sabbath."   *Mark 2: 23-28*

> "It is against our Law... to do that on the Sabbath!"

Sabbath time

I love the idea of the Sabbath. But modern life (or, at least, my life) does not really lend itself to a day of rest. My Sundays are full of activity. I try to catch up on all the things I didn't get around to during the week: errands, cleaning, laundry, phone calls.... How can I combine the ideal of the Sabbath with real life?

Maybe I can scale back on some of the chores, and spend more time being aware of God's presence in my life as I do the chores that can't wait. Someone I know prays while she's vacuuming – a mindless task becomes a moment for reflection and conversation with God. I can make time to rest and to worship God within the busyness of my day.

**Lord, help me find moments of rest
and praise even in the most mundane tasks.**

Jesus went back to the synagogue, where there was a man who had a paralyzed hand. Some people were there who wanted to accuse Jesus of doing wrong; so they watched him closely to see whether he would cure the man on the Sabbath. Jesus said to the man, "Come up here to the front." Then he asked the people, "What does our Law allow us to do on the Sabbath? To help or to harm? To save someone's life or to destroy it?"

Jesus was angry as he looked around at them, but at the same time he felt sorry for them, because they were so stubborn and wrong. Then he said to the man, "Stretch out your hand." He stretched it out, and it became well again. So the Pharisees left the synagogue.

Mark 3: 1-6

"…because they were so stubborn and wrong."

True healing

I have medical problems with my hands. But it's not the man with paralysis I identify with in today's reading; it's those people who sit in judgment of Jesus.

Like the Pharisees, I spend a lot of time observing and commenting from the sidelines on all manner of things. I get preoccupied with style over substance. The people in the synagogue saw Jesus healing people, but still didn't understand. Like them, I can be blinded to the spirit of what is happening around me. Maybe it's my eyes and not my hands that need the attention!

Meanwhile, Mark says Jesus actually feels sorry for people like me – who look without seeing, who can be both stubborn and wrong in equal measure. Jesus gently calls me to change my ways.

Dear God, may I learn to let go of my instinct to judge others. Help me open my eyes to your presence in your world.

J esus and his disciples went away to Lake Galilee, and a large crowd followed him…. All these people came to Jesus because they had heard of the things he was doing. The crowd was so large that Jesus told his disciples to get a boat ready for him, so that the people would not crush him. He had healed many people, and all the sick kept pushing their way to him in order to touch him. And whenever the people who had evil spirits in them saw him, they would fall down before him and scream, "You are the Son of God!"

Jesus sternly ordered the evil spirits not to tell anyone who he was.   *Mark 3: 7-12*

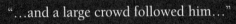

"…and a large crowd followed him…"

Looking for…?

Thousands of fans gather on the sidewalk all night, waiting for the box office to open. Morning comes, and ticket sales begin. There's a wild crush, people screaming, pushing. Someone collapses from exhaustion; the police arrive on horseback.

I am part of the crowd. What am I looking for, out there on the sidewalk? Escape from ordinary life, excitement, friendship, fun? Instead, I am caught in a seething mass of uncontrollable humanity. It's not fun at all.

Today's reading features Jesus Christ Superstar, the focus of mad hysteria. What do his fans hope to find – those who push and shove, screaming and shouting? Miracles? Entertainment? Answers? Following Jesus through the gospel stories, what do I hope to hear? Answers, of course. Sometimes all I hear are more questions.

**Son of God, fill my restless searching heart
with your stillness and peace.**

J esus went up a hill and called to himself those he wanted. They came to him, and he chose twelve, whom he named apostles. "I have chosen you to be with me," he told them. "I will also send you out to preach, and you will have authority to drive out demons."

These are the twelve he chose: Simon (Jesus gave him the name Peter); James and his brother John, the sons of Zebedee (Jesus gave them the name Boanerges, which means "Men of Thunder"); Andrew, Philip, Bartholomew, Matthew, Thomas, James son of Alphaeus, Thaddaeus, Simon the Patriot, and Judas Iscariot, who betrayed Jesus.

Mark 3: 13-19

"Jesus gave him the name Peter…"

Called by name

When my daughter was only a few hours old, a nurse came into my room, took the baby in her arms, and stood by the window gazing at her. I lay in the bed looking at the winter light falling on the two of them. The nurse said, "This child is very peaceful, and very strong." I have marvelled ever since at that nurse's perception of my daughter's character.

When Jesus called the apostles to him, he gave some of them new names that characterized their gifts. He named them with deep love and faith in them.

I had already named my daughter as soon as she was born, but in some sense the nurse was giving her that new name. What is God's loving name for me?

Lord, help me to hear the loving name you call me by, and to be true to it throughout my life.

Then Jesus went home. Again such a large crowd gathered that Jesus and his disciples had no time to eat. When his family heard about it, they set out to take charge of him, because people were saying, "He's gone mad!" *Mark 3: 20-21*

"...people were saying, 'He's gone mad!'"

Mad or holy?

All parents hope their children grow up kind and compassionate – within reason. Jesus, however, seemed unreasonably compassionate. In fact, the crowds considered him mad because his compassion exceeded their imaginations.

Saint Francis initially was locked up by his father. Mother Teresa's superiors first tried to talk her out of living among the poor. Dorothy Day had friends who thought she was foolish for devoting her life to the "worthless" poor. And some people considered both Oscar Romero and Martin Luther King "mad" for the risks they took.

Compassion, I guess, is a good thing – until it hinders personal success or challenges social norms. Then it starts to look like madness – or holiness – depending on whether your perspective is the world's or God's.

**God, inspire me today, even if only in small ways,
to be madly compassionate.**

Teach me your ways, O Lord; make them known to me.
Teach me to live according to your truth,
for you are my God, who saves me. I always trust in you.
Remember, O Lord, your kindness and constant love
which you have shown from long ago.
Forgive the sins and errors of my youth.
In your constant love and goodness, remember me, Lord!
Because the Lord is righteous and good,
he teaches sinners the path they should follow.
He leads the humble in the right way and
teaches them his will.

Psalm 25: 4-9

"He leads the humble in the right way..."

Humility and truth

Years ago, an immigrant family moved to
our neighbourhood. As with most children,
sports was the forum whereby we came to know ourselves and one
another. Carl, one of this immigrant family's sons, couldn't play most
of the games we played, and he was often teased. His response? "I try.
I'm not good now, but I'm learning. I am strong."

Carl was neither self-deprecatory nor self-congratulatory; he was
humble. He accepted himself with neither shame nor false pride. He
faced his mistakes and went on, willing to be taught. He became, as
you might have guessed, the best of us all.

Carl taught me an important lesson about humility and truth.
If I'm humble, how much I can learn! How good I can be!

**Lord, lead me to humility and acceptance of who I am.
Teach me your ways, O Lord.**

The Lord chose another seventy-two men and sent them out two by two, to go ahead of him to every town and place where he himself was about to go. He said to them, "I am sending you like lambs among wolves.... Whenever you go into a house, first say, 'Peace be with this house.' If someone who is peace-loving lives there, let your greeting of peace remain on that person; if not, take back your greeting of peace. Stay in that same house, eating and drinking whatever they offer you, for workers should be given their pay.... Whenever you go into a town and are made welcome, eat what is set before you, heal the sick in that town, and say to the people, 'The kingdom of God has come near you.'"   *Luke 10: 1-9*

> "Peace be with this house."

The gift of peace

"Peace be with this house." Could there ever be a more warm and welcome blessing?

I have lived in many different houses in my life. The one I grew up in, where I became the person I am today, and that now lives only in memory. A lonely rented room, where an insecure young man lived in a house full of solitary men who seemed to have no one in their lives but themselves. A small rented house where I learned to be a husband. And a slightly bigger one where I learned to be a father. All with their own character and their own stories. But in all of them, God's presence and peace could be found. I just had to look.

**You have offered me peace all my life, O Lord.
I am grateful.**

34

Then Jesus' mother and brothers arrived. They stood outside the house and sent in a message, asking for him. A crowd was sitting around Jesus, and they said to him, "Look, your mother and your brothers and sisters are outside, and they want you."

Jesus answered, "Who is my mother? Who are my brothers?" He looked at the people sitting around him and said, "Look! Here are my mother and my brothers! Whoever does what God wants is my brother, my sister, my mother."

Mark 3: 31-35

"They stood outside the house…"

Moving away

A mother looking for her son. Her strange and wonderful son, who was moving away from her, towards his destiny. Why was she looking for him? Why did she wait outside the house? Did she feel that he was hanging around with the wrong crowd?

And now it's my turn to stand and watch as my children move off into the world. They've had friends who've had troubles – with school, with parents, with drugs. And sometimes it scares me. How can I say that everyone is a child of God and is worthy of their friendship, but also protect my own children?

I can't imagine what Mary went through as she saw the dangers mounting. I admit to hoping that, when my children reach out to others, it doesn't cost them as much.

**Dear God, help my children live their destiny.
Give them the strength to do it well.**

Again Jesus began to teach beside Lake Galilee. The crowd that gathered around him was so large that he got into a boat and sat in it. The boat was out in the water, and the crowd stood on the shore at the water's edge. He used parables to teach them many things....

When Jesus was alone, some of those who had heard him came to him with the twelve disciples and asked him to explain the parables. "You have been given the secret of the kingdom of God," Jesus answered. "But the others, who are on the outside, hear all things by means of parables, so that, 'They may look and look, yet not see; they may listen and listen, yet not understand. For if they did, they would turn to God, and he would forgive them.'"   *Mark 4: 1-20*

"He used parables to teach them many things..."

Between the words

Who talks in parables these days? People pride themselves on saying what they mean. Media reports give graphic details. Everything is in-your-face. There's little subtlety left in our lives.

One day my four-year-old complained that he couldn't hear God's voice. "I must be talking too much," he said. Jesus says the same thing to me through the parables. The stories he chooses are drawn from daily life, and he tells me to be quiet and listen anew to God's voice in small, simple acts.

The subtlety I desire *is* there. It's just that I've been too busy talking, too concerned with "reality," to see how the parables point me to what is true and real in my life.

You challenge me, Lord, to find the parables in my own life.
May I listen with new ears to your ever-present voice.

We have, then, my friends, complete freedom to go into the Most Holy Place by means of the death of Jesus. He opened for us a new way, a living way, through the curtain – that is, through his own body.... So let us come near to God with a sincere heart and a sure faith.... Let us hold on firmly to the hope we profess, because we can trust God to keep his promise. Let us be concerned for one another, to help one another to show love and to do good. Let us not give up the habit of meeting together, as some are doing. Instead, let us encourage one another all the more, since you see that the Day of the Lord is coming nearer.

Hebrews 10: 19-25

> "...hold on firmly to the hope we profess..."

Holding on to hope

My aunt's health has gone from bad to worse. She is unable to walk, except short distances, and she cannot read because of failing sight. Her mind remains sharp, but her spirits frequently sag. "What use am I?" she asks me. "I just sit in this chair all day long."

I tell her how much we, as a family, value her presence in our lives. But even more important is the example she gives us of patient suffering and trust in God's promises. In these last years of her life, she has a precious opportunity to witness to a hope that defies human logic. It is not easy to do, but it is very valuable for the rest of us.

Dear Jesus, when trouble threatens to overwhelm me, help me remember your promises.

" The kingdom of God is like this. A man scatters seed in his field. He sleeps at night, is up and about during the day, and all the while the seeds are sprouting and growing…. The soil itself makes the plants grow and bear fruit…. When the grain is ripe, the man starts cutting it with his sickle, because the harvest time has come.

"What shall we say the kingdom of God is like?" asked Jesus. "It is like this. A man takes a mustard seed, the smallest seed in the world, and plants it in the ground. After a while it grows up and becomes the biggest of all plants. It puts out such large branches that the birds come and make their nests in its shade."

Mark 4: 26-34

"The kingdom of God is like… a mustard seed."

Small acts of kindness

When I read the story *Les Misérables*, I was moved by the way the Bishop's single act of kindness transforms the life of the escaped convict, Jean Valjean. When Valjean is caught stealing the Bishop's candlesticks, the Bishop simply says to the police, "He didn't steal them; I gave them to him." That moment turns Valjean's life around. He finds hope and new meaning in life and goes on to do good for others.

That single act of kindness is like the mustard seed.

My forgiveness towards someone who has wronged me, my word of encouragement to someone in despair, my gesture of welcome to a stranger: these can be the mustard seed that will grow and bear fruit in that person's life in ways that I may never know.

**O God, may I be aware of how important
my small gestures of love can be for someone else.**

To have faith is to be sure of the things we hope for, to be certain of the things we cannot see. It was by their faith that people of ancient times won God's approval.

It is by faith that we understand that the universe was created by God's word, so that what can be seen was made out of what cannot be seen....

It was faith that made Abraham obey when God called him to go out to a country which God had promised to give him. He left his own country without knowing where he was going. By faith he lived as a foreigner in the country that God had promised him.... For Abraham was waiting for the city which God has designed and built, the city with permanent foundations. *Hebrews 11: 1-3, 8-19*

> "To have faith is to be sure of the things we hope for..."

Faith in the unknown

Abraham's journey of faith may be fact or legend. But it is certainly symbolic.

Joan and I began one such journey when we got married. Neither of us had any idea what we were in for. But we believed God had called us into this union, and would be with us whatever happened.

Having children was another unknown destination. We could not have anticipated that one of our children would have an incurable genetic illness. Three times, we gave up our home to move to new jobs – each time to places that were foreign lands to us.

Like Abraham and Sarah, we set out on these journeys in the conviction that whatever difficulties we might encounter, things would be better in the long run.

**Let my fears never cause me to back away
from the new challenges you call me to, God.**

A man with an evil spirit came into the synagogue and screamed, "What do you want with us, Jesus of Nazareth? Are you here to destroy us? I know who you are – you are God's holy messenger!" Jesus ordered the spirit, "Be quiet, and come out of the man!" The evil spirit shook the man hard, gave a loud scream, and came out of him. The people were all so amazed that they started saying to one another, "What is this? Is it some kind of new teaching? This man has authority to give orders to the evil spirits, and they obey him!"

Mark 1: 21-28

"...you are God's holy messenger!"

Recognizing the divine

Recently I visited an exhibit of Vincent van Gogh's paintings, "Irises." I was surprised to learn that van Gogh had painted these flowers while at an asylum for the mentally ill. What prompted him to paint such beauty? What did he see that others missed?

The man with the evil spirits in today's reading recognized Jesus for who he was and called out to him. Similarly, van Gogh, tormented by his own demons, saw divinity in those flowers, and he was moved to paint them.

I often struggle with demons of loneliness, anger and depression. Can I accept that these "evil spirits" have the power to reveal the divine? Do I have the courage to look, to recognize God acting in my life, and to respond?

God, help me recognize you in the people
and places I might otherwise want to dismiss.

There was a man named Simeon living in Jerusalem. He was a good, God-fearing man and was waiting for Israel to be saved. The Holy Spirit was with him and had assured him that he would not die before he had seen the Lord's promised Messiah. Led by the Spirit, Simeon went into the Temple. When the parents brought the child Jesus into the Temple to do for him what the Law required, Simeon took the child in his arms and gave thanks to God: "Now, Lord, you have kept your promise, and you may let your servant go in peace. With my own eyes I have seen your salvation, which you have prepared in the presence of all peoples: A light to reveal your will to the Gentiles and bring glory to your people Israel."

Luke 2: 22-40

"Now, Lord, you have kept your promise..."

Times of waiting

When I was little, it was so hard to wait: for dinner, for a friend to come and play, for my birthday, for Christmas morning. As an adult, I find it's still hard to wait. But now I find myself waiting for different things: for insight, for understanding, for hope.

Often, it's not clear to me why one friend's marriage ends, why another friend becomes HIV positive through tainted blood, why I've ended up on the path I'm on. And then, out of the blue, I'll have a moment of great insight, where all the pieces of the puzzle fit together.

I marvel at what each period of waiting brings me. Then, renewed by a moment of insight, I am strengthened – for the next round of uncertainty and searching.

**Lord, give me hope when I can't see clearly,
and patience to wait for promises to be fulfilled.**

T he Lord does not neglect the poor
    or ignore their suffering;
    he does not turn away from them,
but answers when they call for help.
The poor will eat as much as they want;
those who come to the Lord will praise him....
All nations will remember the Lord.
From every part of the world they will turn to him;
all races will worship him.
The Lord is king, and he rules the nations.
All proud people will bow down to him;
all mortals will bow down before him.
Future generations will serve him;
they will speak of the Lord.   *Psalm 22:24-31*

> "All nations will remember the Lord."

Too comfortable?

I sat on my comfortable sofa in my warm living room, listening to a radio commentary on the Olympic Games. The reporter spoke of how the host city had poured new cement armrests on the park benches – making it hard for the homeless to sleep comfortably in the parks. He described how the street people were being moved out of the city parks to temporary shelters in the suburbs – out of sight of the reporters and camera crews.

The city defended its actions by pointing to the potential revenue through increased tourism in the years following the Games. After all, the entire world would be watching the Olympics. What would they see? What would they remember?

Today's reading says the Lord does not neglect the poor. I wonder, do we?

**Lord, when I want to remain on my comfortable perch,
unsettle me.**

J esus went back to his hometown, followed by his disciples. On the Sabbath he began to teach in the synagogue. Many people were there; and when they heard him, they were all amazed. "Where did he get all this?" they asked. "What wisdom is this that has been given him? How does he perform miracles? Isn't he the carpenter, the son of Mary, and the brother of James, Joseph, Judas and Simon? Aren't his sisters living here?" And so they rejected him.

Jesus said to them, "Prophets are respected everywhere except in their own hometown and by their relatives and their family." He was not able to perform any miracles there, except that he placed his hands on a few sick people and healed them. *Mark 6: 1-6*

"And so they rejected him."

Finding our path

There was a lot of unspoken jealousy and competition in the neighbourhood where I grew up. It wasn't about possessions and social status. It focused more on the children: whose children would turn out well and whose would not. Even now, when I return home, I get an update on how everyone is doing – as though there's some kind of scorecard.

I hear the same jealousy and competitiveness in today's reading. Jesus' neighbours wanted to pull him down because he seemed to have moved beyond them.

Growing up, we were told: "Be the best you can be," and "Follow your dreams." Often, when we tried to follow that advice, we were ostracized by our peers. It's not always easy to let our true light shine.

**Lord, give me the confidence to let my own light shine.
Help me when I am jealous of others.**

Jesus called the twelve disciples together and sent them out two by two. He gave them authority over the evil spirits and ordered them, "Don't take anything with you on the trip except a walking stick – no bread, no beggar's bag, no money in your pockets. Wear sandals, but don't carry an extra shirt." He also told them, "Wherever you are welcomed, stay in the same house until you leave that place. If you come to a town where people do not welcome you or will not listen to you, leave it and shake the dust off your feet. That will be a warning to them!"

So they went out and preached that people should turn away from their sins. They drove out many demons, and rubbed olive oil on many sick people and healed them. *Mark 6: 7-13*

> "Don't take anything with you…"

Learning to trust

I might as well admit it: I'll never be ready on time. My husband says that watching me leave the house is like watching some strange Olympic event! I sprint in and out, looking for things that seem so essential. Deep down, I think I'm terrified of depending on someone else. I'd rather be proudly self-sufficient than humble myself and ask for help.

Perhaps Jesus was suggesting that it's far better to trust in the generosity of others than to try to carry the whole load alone. By going empty-handed, the disciples had to rely on the goodness of others. Besides, with free hands, they could reach out more readily to offer assistance.

I'll try to remember that when I leave the house today.

God, as I move through this day,
help me to carry less and to trust others more.

Herodias held a grudge against John and wanted to kill him, but she could not because of Herod. Herod was afraid of John because he knew that John was a good and holy man....

Finally Herodias got her chance. It was on Herod's birthday, when he gave a feast for all the top government officials, the military chiefs, and the leading citizens of Galilee. The daughter of Herodias came in and danced, and pleased Herod and his guests. So the king said to the girl, "What would you like to have? I will give you anything you want...." So the girl went out and asked her mother, "What shall I ask for?"

"The head of John the Baptist," she answered.... This made the king very sad, but he could not refuse her because of the vows he had made in front of all his guests.

Mark 6: 14-29

> "...he knew that John was a good and holy man ..."

Knowing the truth, but...

Blinded by lust – one can imagine him leering as the young girl dances before him – Herod commits the ultimate crime. And yet, Herod knew in his heart "that John was a good and holy man."

Herod not only lacked the will to do what he knew was right (welcome to the club!), but he also was blind to what would really make him happy.

Today, in a society that worships consumption and that treats women as commodities, I am bombarded with messages that tell me: "You'll be happy if you look like this..., or drive this car..., or buy this product...."

Herod did not listen to the voice in his heart. I must try to listen to mine and to act accordingly.

Lord, let me hear your voice within me and follow it.

The apostles returned and told Jesus all they had done and taught. There were so many people coming and going that Jesus and his disciples didn't even have time to eat. So he said, "Let us go off by ourselves to some place where we will be alone and you can rest a while." So they started out in a boat by themselves to a lonely place.

Many people, however, saw them leave and knew at once who they were; so they went from all the towns and ran ahead by land and arrived at the place ahead of Jesus and his disciples. When Jesus got out of the boat, he saw this large crowd, and his heart was filled with pity for them, because they were like sheep without a shepherd. So he began to teach them many things.

Mark 6: 30-34

> "...his heart was filled with pity for them..."

Finding the balance

This is one of my favourite readings. An exhausted Jesus wants some solitude for himself and his disciples. But when faced with the choice between the crowd's desire for his teaching and healing presence, and his own needs, he chooses the crowd. He has pity on them.

I like this reading because I struggle to find the balance between solitude and family, work and community activities. Part laziness, part natural temperament, I am frequently tempted to withdraw from the fray, to not get involved.

I have to remind myself that, once I'm out and involved, I so often get a second wind, and wonderful things happen. I like to think that's what happened to Jesus that day: his hunger and exhaustion gone, he had a great time.

Dear Jesus, you lived the way of love.
Help me respond with generosity to the needs of others.

have no right to boast just because I preach the gospel. After all, I am under orders to do so…. If I did my work as a matter of free choice, then I could expect to be paid; but I do it as a matter of duty, because God has entrusted me with this task. What pay do I get, then? It is the privilege of preaching the Good News without charging for it, without claiming my rights in my work for the gospel.

I am a free man, nobody's slave; but I make myself everybody's slave in order to win as many people as possible…. Among the weak in faith I become weak like one of them, in order to win them. So I become all things to all people, that I may save some of them by whatever means are possible. All this I do for the gospel's sake, in order to share in its blessings.   *1 Corinthians 9: 16-23*

"…in order to win as many people as possible."

Super salesman

I spent four years in sales. I did fairly well. But I was relieved when a different career opened up, because I didn't like myself much as a sales representative. After a while, I no longer saw the people I called on as individuals. Rather, they became *prospects*. They mattered only because they might, someday, sign a contract for my company's services. And if they didn't, I dumped them.

Perhaps that's why I don't like Paul very much. I respect him. I admire him. But I feel that sometimes he didn't see people as individuals either – he saw only potential converts.

Paul carried Christianity to what we now call Europe. Without Paul, I probably would not be Christian today. But I don't necessarily have to like him.

You love everyone unconditionally, Lord.
I want to try harder to act like you.

They crossed the lake and came to land at Gennesaret, where they tied up the boat. As they left the boat, people recognized Jesus at once. So they ran throughout the whole region; and wherever they heard he was, they brought to him the sick lying on their mats. And everywhere Jesus went, to villages, towns, or farms, people would take their sick to the marketplaces and beg him to let the sick at least touch the edge of his cloak. And all who touched it were made well.

Mark 6: 53-56

"And all who touched it were made well."

True faith

But what about those who didn't get to touch the edge of his cloak? Two days ago Kayci's mother died after routine surgery. She experienced complications – and Jesus' cloak was nowhere in sight. Why are some healed while others are not? I don't know.

Honestly, I don't think today's reading will comfort those who grieve Mary Beth's death right now. But I do know this much. When tragedy strikes – without warning or explanation – and when healing doesn't happen, faith cannot be the blind conviction that this tragedy was somehow for the best.

Sometimes all you can do is reach out with compassion to the family and friends who are grieving. That reaching out is the real faith – even when it doesn't find a cloak to touch.

Dear Jesus, help me touch one person with compassion today – and let that touch bring some healing into the world.

When I look at the sky, which you have made,
at the moon and the stars, which you set in their places
– what are human beings, that you think of them;
mere mortals, that you care for them?
Yet you made them inferior only to yourself;
you crowned them with glory and honour.
You appointed them rulers over everything you made;
you placed them over all creation:
sheep and cattle, and the wild animals too;
the birds and the fish
and the creatures in the seas.

Psalm 8: 3-8

"…you crowned them with glory and honour."

A child's wonder

During the morning rush out the door, my five-year-old daughter exclaims, "This is amazing!" It is February, and it is cold. We are in a hurry. It is beyond me what might prompt her to find anything amazing about February mornings.

I look her way, but don't see anything remarkable, so I try to hurry her along. She persists. "Here, Mama! Look here!" I follow the tilt of her gaze and there they are: small squirrel tracks under the bird feeder have made a lovely pattern. They dance in the February sunlight.

My tendency would be to see the tracks and curse the squirrels for scaring the birds. My daughter saw something else, and marvelled at it.

God, give me eyes to see the signs of your greatness.

Jesus said to the crowd, "There is nothing that goes into you from the outside which can make you ritually unclean. Rather, it is what comes out of you that makes you unclean."

When he left the crowd and went into the house, his disciples asked him to explain this saying. Jesus said, "Don't you understand? Nothing that goes into you from the outside can really make you unclean, because it does not go into your heart but into your stomach and then goes on out of the body." (In saying this, Jesus declared that all foods are fit to be eaten.)

And he went on to say, "It is what comes out of you that makes you unclean. For from the inside, from your heart, come the evil ideas which lead you to do immoral things."   *Mark 7: 14-23*

"It is what comes out of you that makes you unclean."

Unclean words

When we purchased our new van, we wanted to keep it nice and clean. One day, after driving around doing errands, I thought we'd pull into a drive-through restaurant and pick up a snack. As I pulled away, one of my sons reached for his drink and accidentally spilt most of it on the floor! I was so angry. I immediately yelled at my son, then kept berating him about his clumsiness.

After a minute or two I calmed down. I apologized to him for my outburst. I realized that I had put more value on the cleanliness of the van than I did on my relationship with him. Upon further reflection, I could see that it was I who had sullied the van with my angry words.

Jesus, help me to clean up my words and actions.

J esus went away to the territory near the city of Tyre…. A woman, whose daughter had an evil spirit in her, heard about Jesus and came to him at once and fell at his feet. The woman was a Gentile, born in the region of Phoenicia in Syria. She begged Jesus to drive the demon out of her daughter. But Jesus answered, "Let us first feed the children. It isn't right to take the children's food and throw it to the dogs." "Sir," she answered, "even the dogs under the table eat the children's leftovers!" Jesus said to her, "Because of that answer, go back home, where you will find that the demon has gone out of your daughter!" She went home and found her child lying on the bed; the demon had indeed gone out of her. *Mark 7: 24-30*

"Sir… even the dogs under the table eat the children's leftovers!"

Courage to persevere

The human heart has many longings, and few of those longings are satisfied without some effort. An old adage says: "There's a cost to everything!" Often, when I've had to struggle to reach a goal, I find that I treasure what I've gained even more.

Because she loved her daughter, the Phoenician woman struggled to overcome barriers. First she found the courage to make her way through the crowd. Then, in spite of rejection, she humbled herself before Jesus and persevered with her request for healing for her daughter.

When a colleague criticizes me, or a friend rejects me, or my family fails to understand me, I am called to overcome these obstacles as I try to grow in faith and love.

Lord, give me courage to set my goal
– and the stubbornness to achieve it.

Some people brought Jesus a man who was deaf and could hardly speak, and they begged Jesus to place his hands on him. So Jesus took him off alone, away from the crowd, put his fingers in the man's ears, spat, and touched the man's tongue. Then Jesus looked up to heaven, gave a deep groan, and said to the man, "Ephphatha," which means, "Open up!"

At once the man was able to hear, his speech impediment was removed, and he began to talk without any trouble. Then Jesus ordered the people not to speak of it to anyone; but the more he ordered them not to, the more they told it. And all who heard were completely amazed. "How well he does everything!" they exclaimed. "He even causes the deaf to hear and the dumb to speak!"

Mark 7: 31-37

"...gave a deep groan..."

The miracle

I teach at a school for adults. Many of my students have problems that make it difficult for them to learn. Sometimes, no matter how hard they try, no matter how hard I try, it doesn't seem to work.

On one occasion a young woman said to me, "I guess I'm just too stupid." And she began to cry. What I would have given to be able to give a deep groan and perform a miracle, as Jesus did. But I couldn't, and her situation remained the same.

Eventually she had to lower her sights and switch programs. She seemed to accept her limitations. It always amazes me how people forge bravely on in a world that has not been generous to them. Maybe that's the miracle.

**Dear God, help me to recognize and
tear down obstacles that stand in the way of others.**

A nother large crowd came together. When the people had nothing left to eat, Jesus called the disciples to him and said, "I feel sorry for these people, because they have been with me for three days and now have nothing to eat...."

His disciples asked him, "Where in this desert can anyone find enough food to feed all these people?" "How much bread do you have?" Jesus asked. "Seven loaves," they answered.

He ordered the crowd to sit down on the ground. Then he took the seven loaves, gave thanks to God, broke them, and gave them to his disciples to distribute to the crowd; and the disciples did so. They also had a few small fish. Jesus gave thanks for these and told the disciples to distribute them too. Everybody ate and had enough.

Mark 8: 1-10

> "Everybody ate and had enough."

Love received and shared

While I don't worry much about my ability to feed my children, I do worry about my ability to "nourish" their souls. As a single working parent, I find that I have little energy to share with my three children at the end of the day.

Today's reading reminds me that Jesus fed the crowds from the few fish and loaves that the disciples scrounged from among the people themselves.

I think of the times when my youngest child makes me laugh at a joke, or my middle son gives me his "bear hug," or my oldest asks, "How was your day, Mum?" Somehow, their small gestures of love give me the energy to go on, to continue giving when there seems little left to give.

Thank you, God, for the gift of love – both received and given.

Happy are those whose sins are forgiven,
whose wrongs are pardoned.
Happy is the one whom the Lord does not accuse
of doing wrong
and who is free from all deceit....
I confessed my sins to you;
I did not conceal my wrongdoings.
I decided to confess them to you,
and you forgave all my sins....
The wicked will have to suffer,

but those who trust in the Lord
are protected by his constant love.
You that are righteous, be glad and rejoice
because of what the Lord has done.

Psalm 32: 1-2, 5, 10-11

"I did not conceal my wrongdoings..."

Coming clean

Last year someone stole my watch from my classroom. It was a difficult moment for me. As a teacher, I look for the "teachable moment." But what did I want to teach, at that moment?

Certainly I was upset, and I wanted to teach that stealing was wrong. My anger and disappointment must have been obvious. Little wonder that no one ever came forward! Perhaps it would have been wiser to teach about forgiveness. But I was in no mood to forgive, either.

Looking back, I realize that I missed the opportunity to teach that forgiveness is possible. This is what we hope for when we face God. And yet it is so difficult to give when we are faced with each other.

**God, give me the confidence to ask for forgiveness,
and the courage to be forgiving.**

Adam had intercourse with his wife, and she bore a son... and she named him Cain. Later she gave birth to another son, Abel. Abel became a shepherd, but Cain was a farmer.... Cain brought some of his harvest and gave it as an offering to the Lord. Then Abel brought the first lamb born to one of his sheep, killed it, and gave the best parts of it as an offering. The Lord was pleased with Abel and his offering, but he rejected Cain and his offering. Cain became furious, and he scowled in anger. Then the Lord said to Cain, "Why are you angry? Why that scowl on your face...?"

Cain said to his brother Abel, "Let's go out in the fields." When they were out in the fields, Cain turned on his brother and killed him.   *Genesis 4: 1-15, 25*

"Cain turned on his brother..."

Brotherly love

"Mom always liked you best!" was one of the standard lines of the Smothers Brothers comedy team. It always got a big (and nervous) laugh.

I always felt inferior to my older brother. It seemed that he could do everything better than I could – and Mom, I was sure, liked him best. In adulthood I continued to crave his approval, and when he was critical of my efforts I could have "killed" him.

Today's reading touches something deep in people's experience. I see the same sibling rivalry in my own sons. I tell them that they each have their own special gifts, but they continue to compare and compete – just like I did.

"Brotherly love" is a great gift, but sometimes it comes slowly.

Lord, heal whatever jealousies linger from my childhood, and help me see my unique gifts.

The disciples had forgotten to bring enough bread and had only one loaf with them in the boat…. [and] they started discussing among themselves…. Jesus knew what they were saying, so he asked them, "Why are you discussing about not having any bread? Don't you know or understand yet? Are your minds so dull? You have eyes – can't you see? You have ears – can't you hear? Don't you remember when I broke the five loaves for the five thousand people? How many baskets full of leftover pieces did you take up?" "Twelve," they answered. "And when I broke the seven loaves for the four thousand people," asked Jesus, "how many baskets full of leftover pieces did you take up?" "Seven," they answered. "And you still don't understand?" he asked them.   *Mark 8: 14-21*

> "Don't you know or understand yet?"

An unseen God

At a workshop, I asked the participants to remember times when God had intervened in their lives. One woman told about being an abused child and being moved into a loving foster home. When she ran away from home, strangers gave her shelter. She got hooked on booze and drugs, and a caring counsellor helped her break her addiction. Eventually she met a man who loved her, married her, and gave her a good home.

"But those were all *people* that did that," she finished. "I don't see where God has done anything in my life."

Jesus must have felt as frustrated as I did. He kept demonstrating, symbolically, how much God cared. But his disciples kept seeing only literal meanings.

**God, give me eyes to see and ears to hear you behind
the camouflage of commonplace things.**

After forty days Noah opened a window and sent out a raven. It did not come back, but kept flying around until the water was completely gone. Meanwhile, Noah sent out a dove to see if the water had gone down, but since the water still covered all the land, the dove did not find a place to light. It flew back to the boat, and Noah reached out and took it in. He waited another seven days and sent out the dove again. It returned to him in the evening with a fresh olive leaf in its beak. So Noah knew that the water had gone down. Then he waited another seven days and sent out the dove once more; this time it did not come back.

Genesis 8: 6-13, 20-22

Keep searching

A plain, rather unromantic bird, the raven is often overlooked in this story. What did she see when she perched on Noah's hand? Only water. And yet she flew off into uncharted territory, with no guarantees.

I think of the many women and men who have dedicated their lives to working with those in search of peace in places like Afghanistan, Palestine, Israel, Sierra Leone, Sri Lanka.... They were there long before the news made the headlines, and will remain there long after. God bless them. God bless their work in hospitals, schools, refugee camps, on the streets, in slums and shantytowns. God bless those who continue to work for peace – with no land in sight.

God bless the raven who teaches us to keep searching – until the water subsides.

**God, I don't always know where I'm going.
Give me the strength to continue.**

J esus asked the disciples, "Tell me, who do people say I am?" "Some say that you are John the Baptist, others say that you are Elijah, while others say that you are one of the prophets."

"What about you?" he asked them. "Who do you say I am?" Peter answered, "You are the Messiah." Then Jesus ordered them, "Do not tell anyone about me…. The Son of Man must suffer much and be rejected by the elders, the chief priests, and the teachers of the Law. He will be put to death, but three days later he will rise to life." Peter took him aside and began to rebuke him. But Jesus turned around, looked at his disciples, and rebuked Peter. "Get away from me, Satan," he said. "Your thoughts don't come from God but from human nature!"

Mark 8: 27-33

"Who do you say I am?"

A question of identity

As a child I thought of Jesus as the dutiful son portrayed in sacred art: yellow halo around his head, performing small household tasks before beaming parents. When I was a teenager, he was a social revolutionary: angry at the greed and hypocrisy of the authorities, calling for the overthrow of the status quo. Still later, he was a mystic: providing enigmatic answers to questions of meaning and morality, telling Zen-like stories to wondering crowds.

Hmmm. I detect a pattern: Jesus was who I wanted or needed him to be. But now I'm middle-aged, married, and a father of three, which makes it difficult to bend Jesus into the shape I want. I'm left facing the question Jesus asked his other followers: "Who do you say I am?"

Lord, you have been with me my whole life.
Help me know you, as you are.

The Lord frustrates the purposes of the nations;
he keeps them from carrying out their plans.
But his plans endure forever;
his purposes last eternally.
Happy is the nation whose God is the Lord;
happy are the people he has chosen for his own!
The Lord looks down from heaven
and sees all of us humans.
From where he rules, he looks down
on all who live on earth.
He forms all their thoughts
and knows everything they do.

Psalm 33: 10-15

> "Happy is the nation whose God is the Lord."

Nations at war

"Happy is the nation whose God is the Lord." Oh really? Tell that to the Palestinian family whose house was just bulldozed by the Israelis. Tell that to the Israelis shattered by yet another suicide bomber. Tell that to the children still grieving a parent killed in 9/11. Tell that to the Irish who buried loved ones killed by car bombs. Tell that to the mother in Afghanistan whose child just lost a limb to a landmine. Tell that to the father in Iraq who holds his dying child in his arms.

I have great trouble seeing God at work in the nations that march under a banner of God. If, as this psalm says, God frustrates the plans of nations, what is my role as citizen?

**God, help me to discover your plan for me
as citizen of the world.**

J esus took with him Peter, James and John, and led them up a high mountain, where they were alone. As they looked on, a change came over Jesus, and his clothes became shining white – whiter than anyone in the world could wash them. Then the three disciples saw Elijah and Moses talking with Jesus. Peter spoke up and said to Jesus, "Teacher, how good it is that we are here! We will make three tents, one for you, one for Moses, and one for Elijah." He and the others were so frightened that he did not know what to say.

Then a cloud appeared and covered them with its shadow, and a voice came from the cloud, "This is my own dear Son – listen to him!"   *Mark 9: 2-13*

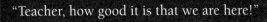

"Teacher, how good it is that we are here!"

Seeing the wonders of today

Not only are the disciples dazzled by the remarkable sight on the mountain, they are confused. In Peter's befuddlement, perhaps his desire to preserve a magical moment, he suggests making camp there.

I've known that same temptation, especially when something momentous has happened. To hang onto the moment: a profound religious experience, falling in love, standing before death, or the birth of a child. After a period of great intensity – be it great joy or great suffering – I realize, however, I must return to my day-to-day life. Changed, yes, but return I must.

Peter, too, had to return to Galilee, to the long, dusty treks to distant towns, following and learning from Jesus. And Peter, the doubter, had to learn that the cross – experienced in life's daily challenges – comes before the joy of the resurrection.

Lord, you dwell in the simple and the ordinary.
Give me eyes of wonder for this day.

esus was preaching when four men arrived, carrying a paralyzed man. Because of the crowd, however, they could not get the man to him. So they made a hole in the roof right above the place where Jesus was…. They let the man down, lying on his mat. Seeing how much faith they had, Jesus said to the paralyzed man, "My son, your sins are forgiven."

Some teachers of the Law who were sitting there thought to themselves, "This is blasphemy! God is the only one who can forgive sins!" At once Jesus knew what they were thinking, so he said to them, "Is it easier to say to this paralyzed man, 'Your sins are forgiven,' or to say, 'Get up, pick up your mat, and walk…'?" So he said, "Get up, pick up your mat, and go home!"   *Mark 2: 1-12*

> "Seeing how much faith they had…"

"With a little help from my friends"

Years ago I was very ill. For the first time since childhood, I was completely helpless. Even if I'd wanted to, I could not have gotten up and left. My friends rallied, looking after my family and me. It was truly overwhelming.

This man, this paralyzed man, is cured by Jesus. A miracle, sure. But what has always amazed me is the friends this man had. Today's reading highlights their faith. What is also striking is their friendship and persistence on behalf of their friend. No room? Okay – they climb up on the roof.

Reading this story, I ask: What can I do? Heal people with a word? No, but perhaps I can try, with love and dogged persistence, to participate in the miracle of friendship.

Lord, help me to be a good friend.

Aman said, "Teacher, I brought my son to you, because he has an evil spirit in him...." As soon as the spirit saw Jesus, it threw the boy into a fit, so that he fell on the ground and rolled around, foaming at the mouth. "How long has he been like this?" Jesus asked the father. "Ever since he was a child," he replied. "Have pity on us and help us, if you possibly can!"

"Everything is possible for the person who has faith," Jesus said. The father cried out, "I do have faith, but not enough. Help me have more!"

Jesus gave a command to the spirit: "Deaf and dumb spirit, I order you to come out of the boy and never go into him again!" The spirit screamed, threw the boy into a bad fit, and came out.

Mark 9: 14-29

"Everything is possible for the person who has faith..."

A person of faith

The first time I asked Colin to answer a question in class, I was shocked by the severity of his stuttering. His face contorted, and he struggled fiercely with every sound. Afterward I always felt awkward, even a little intimidated, around Colin because, despite his stuttering, he seemed to have a faith in himself that I lacked.

One night I heard him sing a solo in the school production of *Godspell*. He sang with no stutter at all – right from his heart. It was as though his whole personality and spirit had been freed.

After the performance, I saw him in the hall and gave him a huge hug. "You were fantastic!" Colin wasn't cured that night: I was – of my blindness.

**Lord, free me from all my demons. Let me take courage
from others who have overcome theirs.**

Tuesday | FEBRUARY 24

My child, if you are going to serve the Lord, be prepared for times when you will be put to the test. Be sincere and determined. Keep calm when trouble comes. Stay with the Lord; never abandon him, and you will be prosperous at the end of your days. Accept whatever happens to you. Even if you suffer humiliation, be patient. Gold is tested by fire, and human character is tested in the furnace of humiliation. Trust the Lord, and he will help you. Walk straight in his ways, and put your hope in him.

All you that fear the Lord, wait for him to show you his mercy. Do not turn away from him, or you will fall. All you that fear the Lord, trust him, and you will certainly be rewarded. All you that fear the Lord, look forward to his blessings of mercy and eternal happiness.

Sirach 2: 1-11

> "Stay with the Lord…"

Believing

Every week a sign in front of a local church offers passersby an inspirational or provocative thought. Recently, it read, "What to do when you pray and God says No." I was amused when the next day, it was revised, "What to do when you pray and nothing changes." Someone must have complained that the first sign gave the wrong message!

The notion that God says No to our prayers, or that God tests us, makes many people uncomfortable. It also misses the point. My attitude, not God's, is the issue.

The challenge for me is to not over-analyze these things, to keep focused and to accept whatever happens. God knows me intimately and will protect me, in good times and bad.

Lord, I look to you and trust in your love and mercy.

"**M**ake certain you do not perform your religious duties in public…. When you give something to a needy person, do it in such a way that even your closest friend will not know about it….

"When you pray, do not be like the hypocrites! They love to pray in the houses of worship and on the street corners, so that everyone will see them…. But when you pray, go to your room, close the door, and pray to your Father, who is unseen. And your Father, who sees what you do in private, will reward you."

Matthew 6: 1-6, 16-18

"When you pray, go to your room…"

An unseen God?

One grey afternoon, the house is silent all around me. In the quiet twilight I reflect on the activities of my day. One special moment stands out: a long distance telephone call to a friend. She cheered me up when I was gloomy, changing the day from sad to glad for me.

Now, quietly grateful for my friend's kind words, I read Jesus' words about prayer. In the silent stillness of my empty house, deep in the privacy of my heart and my mind, I am newly conscious of my blessings, humbly grateful for God's presence all around me.

An unseen God? Yes, but a presence as real, as alive, as immediate as my unseen friend on the other end of the telephone.

O unseen God, hear my prayer: when you look into my heart, may you find gratitude and peace dwelling there.

J esus also told them, "The Son of Man must suffer much and be rejected by the elders, the chief priests, and the teachers of the Law. He will be put to death, but three days later he will be raised to life."

And he said to them all, "If you want to come with me, you must forget yourself, take up your cross every day, and follow me. For if you want to save your own life, you will lose it, but if you lose your life for my sake, you will save it. Will you gain anything if you win the whole world but are yourself lost or defeated? Of course not!"

Luke 9: 22-25

> "...he will be raised to life."

New life

It is only February, but I am already dream-
ing about my garden. In my mind's eye,
I see daisies, peonies and lilies. The forget-
me-nots are spreading a blue haze and the roses are fragrant in their
scarlet glory. Briefly, I forget about the howling blizzard outside my
house today as I remember purple clusters of clematis on the trel-
lis. How hard to truly understand the mystery of a frozen earth that
bursts into life!

The rebirth of my garden every year reminds me of the resurrection. All of God's nature is restored in spring. So, too, we are reborn
through God's gift of life beyond the grave. Some day I, like Jesus, will
be raised to eternal life.

**Dear God, thank you for my renewal in your creation,
a reminder of your promise of new life!**

Threpeople ask, "Why should we fast if the Lord never notices?" The Lord says to them, "The truth is that at the same time you fast, you pursue your own interests and oppress your workers. Your fasting makes you violent, and you quarrel and fight. Do you think this kind of fasting will make me listen to your prayers? When you fast, you make yourselves suffer…. Is that what you call fasting? Do you think I will be pleased with that?

"The kind of fasting I want is this: Remove the chains of oppression and the yoke of injustice, and let the oppressed go free. Share your food with the hungry and open your homes to the homeless poor. Give clothes to those who have nothing to wear, and do not refuse to help your own relatives."   *Isaiah 58: 1-9*

> "…do not refuse to help your own relatives."

Closer to home

I notice that today's reading ends with "…do not refuse to help your own relatives." When I hear about feeding the hungry and giving shelter to the homeless, I feel overwhelmed. The problems "out there" seem so big, and my efforts seem so insignificant.

I agree that I must not forget the needs of the hungry and the homeless. But neither can I overlook the needs of those closer to home. I must be honest with myself and acknowledge when I've been defensive or self-righteous with members of my family. When I've quarrelled needlessly. When I've not tried to find a peaceful settlement of our differences.

Today, I will try to lift the burden of misunderstanding that I've placed on someone's shoulders and bring peace to that relationship.

**Lord, today I will look at my relationships within my family.
I will reach out to one person in a gesture of peace.**

After this, Jesus went out and saw a tax collector named Levi, sitting in his office. Jesus said to him, "Follow me." Levi got up, left everything, and followed him.

Then Levi had a big feast in his house for Jesus, and among the guests were a large number of tax collectors and other people. Some Pharisees and some teachers of the Law who belonged to their group complained to Jesus' disciples. "Why do you eat and drink with tax collectors and other outcasts?" they asked.

Jesus answered them, "People who are well do not need a doctor, but only those who are sick. I have not come to call respectable people to repent, but outcasts."

Luke 5: 27-32

> "I have not come to call respectable people…"

Today's outcasts

Anna is a well-known figure in our community. She owns and runs two rooming houses in my neighbourhood. Now age eighty-eight, she has spent her life taking in and caring for those who have been given up as "lost causes" by other social agencies. Many of the men and women she shelters are mentally ill, broken by years of alcoholism or drug abuse, prone to anti-social behaviour, and often in trouble with the courts.

What Anna offers is much more than just a place to eat and sleep. To her "tenants," she is friend and advocate and family; often, she is their last hope.

Anna turns no one away. For her, everyone – no matter what their situation – is deserving of dignity and respect.

**Lord, help me to recognize your face
in each person I meet today.**

God said to Noah and his sons, "I am now making my covenant with you and with your descendants, and with all living beings – all birds and all animals – everything that came out of the boat with you. With these words I make my covenant with you: I promise that never again will all living beings be destroyed by a flood; never again will a flood destroy the earth. As a sign of this everlasting covenant that I am making with you and with all living beings, I am putting my bow in the clouds. It will be the sign of my covenant with the world. Whenever I cover the sky with clouds and the rainbow appears, I will remember my promise."   *Genesis 9: 8-15*

"...never again will a flood destroy the earth."

When bad things happen

I think many people, still clearing the wreckage from the latest devastating flood, would side initially with Mrs. Noah. In the medieval play based on the story of Noah's ark, she resists stepping into a boat laden with smelly animals. Her husband has heard God's warning but she's more concerned with her life as she knows it. As the waters rise she's dragged unwillingly into the boat while her friends and her world are swept away.

It is easy to "like" God when all is calm. But disasters do happen, and when they do, they shake us to the core. Mrs. Noah came to realize that storms, floods and other terrible events are not tests from a vengeful God. Rather, they offer an opportunity to discover the true face of God.

**Dear God, in times of trouble,
may I learn to believe in your promise.**

"The King will say to the people on his right, 'Come, you that are blessed by my Father! I was hungry and you fed me, thirsty and you gave me a drink; I was a stranger and you received me in your homes, naked and you clothed me; I was sick and you took care of me, in prison and you visited me.' The righteous will then answer him, 'When, Lord, did we ever see you hungry and feed you, or thirsty and give you a drink? When did we ever see you a stranger and welcome you in our homes, or naked and clothe you? When did we ever see you sick or in prison, and visit you?' The King will reply, 'I tell you, whenever you did this for one of the least important of these followers of mine, you did it for me!'"

Matthew 25: 31-46

> "...in prison and you visited me."

Closer to God

I just saw my sister off at the bus station, on her way back to Central Africa. For nearly ten years she worked with a big NGO where she had a computer, a cell phone, a vehicle, a salary, benefits and an annual flight back home.

This time she went back to a verbal job offer with a fragile African church, and none of the above. All she knows about her new job is that it will involve visiting people in prison and helping people with AIDS.

Everything in me wanted to dissuade her from returning. But she said, "God is close to the broken-hearted. When I am with the broken-hearted I feel close to God." I have only to read today's gospel to understand her words.

Help me to be inspired by the passion of those who long, above all else, to be in your presence.

Tuesday | **MARCH 3**

R emember, O Lord, your kindness and constant love
which you have shown from long ago.
Forgive the sins and errors of my youth.
In your constant love and goodness,
remember me, Lord!
Because the Lord is righteous and good,
he teaches sinners the path they should follow.
He leads the humble in the right way
and teaches them his will.

Psalm 25: 4-9

"Forgive the sins and errors of my youth."

Forgiving kindness

When I remember mistakes I have made
and harm I have caused, I am filled with
regret and self-blame. "You should have
known better," I tell myself. "You should
have done better." And it's often true; I should have.

But the sharpness of self-condemnation causes the deepest
wounds. Wounds that never heal. And the soothing balm of forgiveness, a salve perhaps best applied by another's hand, seems mine not
to have.

I feel paralyzed and helpless at these times, and unsure of where
to turn. It takes all my strength to remember that there is someone
who knows the darkest place within me. And that someone has not
abandoned me, the way I sometimes have abandoned myself.

Only then can I think of myself with more kindness.

Lord, when I am in despair, speak louder so that I can hear you.

"How evil are the people of this day! They ask for a miracle, but none will be given them except the miracle of Jonah. In the same way that the prophet Jonah was a sign for the people of Nineveh, so the Son of Man will be a sign for the people of this day. On the Judgment Day the Queen of Sheba will stand up and accuse the people of today, because she travelled all the way from her country to listen to King Solomon's wise teaching; and there is something here, I tell you, greater than Solomon. On the Judgment Day the people of Nineveh will stand up and accuse you, because they turned from their sins when they heard Jonah preach; and I assure you that there is something here greater than Jonah!"

Luke 11: 29-32

> "...the Son of Man will be a sign for the people..."

Signs of God's love

How immune I have become to the little miracles happening all around me! Weighed down by the concerns of the day, I miss the signs of God's love that cross my path each day, even many times a day.

I need to savour the sun today, feel its increasing strength and recognize its promise of springtime warmth. I need to hear in my son's "I'm sorry, Mum" his faltering attempt at reconciliation, and believe that love does indeed transform our lives.

People asked Jesus for a sign but did not recognize, or chose to ignore, the sign he gave them. Can I pause in my busyness to look – with eyes of love, patience and openness – and see the miracle before me and allow it to change my life?

Loving God, open my eyes that I may see the signs of your presence all around me. Open my heart to your constant love.

Thursday | **MARCH 5**

"Ask, and you will receive; seek, and you will find; knock, and the door will be opened to you. For everyone who asks will receive, and anyone who seeks will find, and the door will be opened to those who knock. Would any of you who are fathers give your son a stone when he asks for bread? Or would you give him a snake when he asks for a fish? As bad as you are, you know how to give good things to your children. How much more, then, will your Father in heaven give good things to those who ask him!

"Do for others what you want them to do for you: this is the meaning of the Law of Moses and of the teachings of the prophets."

Matthew 7: 7-12

"For everyone who asks will receive..."

Asking for...

Several years ago, a friend of mine prayed that her husband's life be spared. But it wasn't. If I were to ask God to remove my friend's Alzheimer's disease, would God?

There is an old conundrum: Can God create a rock so big God can't pick it up? This may seem a little glib, but it resonates with me. Maybe God can't create the laws of physics and then revoke them, simply because I ask. Maybe God can't answer every prayer the way we want them answered. So what can I ask of God, knowing I'll receive it?

Perhaps I can ask for the strength to change what's inside of *me*. And for the courage and wisdom to find my salvation in the life I have received.

**Dear God, help me to live with unanswered questions.
Help me to accept my life.**

"You have heard that people were told in the past, 'Do not commit murder; anyone who does will be brought to trial.' But now I tell you: if you are angry with your brother you will be brought to trial, if you call your brother 'You good-for-nothing!' you will be brought before the Council, and if you call your brother a worthless fool you will be in danger of going to the fire of hell. So if you are about to offer your gift to God at the altar and there you remember that your brother has something against you, leave your gift there in front of the altar, go at once and make peace with your brother, and then come back and offer your gift to God."

Matthew 5: 20-26

> "...go at once and make peace..."

Reaching out

Jason isn't close to his in-laws at the best of times. But when his youngest daughter landed a role in her school play, he suggested inviting them to her opening performance.

After the play, even before they'd left the auditorium, he found himself arguing with his father-in-law. Fuming, he turned to his wife and muttered angrily, "That's the last time I'll ever invite them to an event!"

With time, Jason's anger has abated. But he finds he can't shake the resentment he feels towards his in-laws. He knows that this last fight is merely one in a long string of arguments. He wants to bridge the gap between them and mend their strained relationship. It's just that he doesn't know where to start.

Lord, give me the courage to reach out to those with whom I am in conflict, and the wisdom to know how.

"You have heard that it was said, 'Love your friends, hate your enemies.' But now I tell you: love your enemies and pray for those who persecute you, so that you may become the children of your Father in heaven. For he makes his sun to shine on bad and good people alike, and gives rain to those who do good and to those who do evil. Why should God reward you if you love only the people who love you? Even the tax collectors do that! And if you speak only to your friends, have you done anything out of the ordinary? Even the pagans do that! You must be perfect – just as your Father in heaven is perfect."

Matthew 5: 43-48

"Love your enemies…"

Love your enemies

Is Jesus *really* asking me to love Adolf Hitler? To love the people who flew the planes into the Twin Towers on 9/11? To love those who kill innocent civilians in the many war-torn cities around the world?

All who visit – or even think about – Ground Zero find themselves moved to pray for the thousands of people who were killed in that attack. And some pray for those who flew the planes that day.

Jesus seems to be asking me to do the near impossible. But he knows (from personal experience, in fact) that it is the only way to peace – in ourselves and in our world.

O God, do you understand the demands you make on those who want to follow you? Help me accept that kind of demand.

What can I offer the Lord
for all his goodness to me?
I will bring a wine offering to the Lord,
to thank him for saving me.
In the assembly of all his people
I will give him what I have promised.
How painful it is to the Lord
when one of his people dies!
I am your servant, Lord;
I serve you just as my mother did.
You have saved me from death.
I will give you a sacrifice of thanksgiving
and offer my prayer to you.

Psalm 116: 10-19

"How painful it is to the Lord when one of his people dies!"

Faith and science

During his lifetime, Jesuit theologian Pierre Teilhard de Chardin was forbidden to publish his ground-breaking synthesis of mysticism and science. This profound treatise united spirituality and natural evolution at a time when many Christians were becoming lost in a combative closed-mindedness about science, creation and evolution.

Teilhard found a path through this confusion, but Rome was not ready to step onto it. With his death in 1955, however, his work burst upon the world.

For Teilhard, Christ is our evolutionary destiny where spirit and matter converge. Today Teilhard's vision feels more necessary than ever: a starting point for discovery in a world that has evolved technologically to the brink of its own destruction.

**Lord, help me to see the potential for joy
in the mystery of my own death.**

"**B**e merciful just as your Father is merciful. Do not judge others, and God will not judge you; do not condemn others, and God will not condemn you; forgive others, and God will forgive you. Give to others, and God will give to you. Indeed, you will receive a full measure, a generous helping, poured into your hands – all that you can hold. The measure you use for others is the one that God will use for you."

Luke 6: 36-38

"…forgive others, and God will forgive you."

Hope in forgiveness

I am tired of forgiving him, of listening to his excuses, of giving him another chance. Why? Because nothing changes. Forgiveness just lets him off the hook so he can go back to his old ways: breaking his promises, ignoring my needs. He's hopeless.

Forgiving. Giving in. Giving up. What's the difference?

God, do you take my repeated failures as personally as I take his? Do you feel as hurt and ignored as I do? Do you look on me with disdain? Do you shake your head and want to give up on me and walk away?

Please do not look on me as hopeless. Maybe that's the difference: giving up implies no hope. Forgiveness is grounded in hope – that the best in me can shine.

**God, help me to forgive others –
believing in their best selves – as often as you forgive me.**

Jerusalem, pay attention to what our God is teaching you.... "Wash yourselves clean. Stop all this evil that I see you doing. Yes, stop doing evil and learn to do right. See that justice is done – help those who are oppressed, give orphans their rights, and defend widows."

The Lord says, "Now, let's settle the matter. You are stained red with sin, but I will wash you as clean as snow.... If you will only obey me, you will eat the good things the land produces. But if you defy me, you are doomed to die. I, the Lord, have spoken...."

Because the Lord is righteous, he will save Jerusalem and everyone there who repents. But he will crush everyone who sins and rebels against him; he will kill everyone who forsakes him.

Isaiah 1: 10-31

> "See that justice is done..."

Hungry for justice

During the long struggle for civil rights, Martin Luther King often voiced his conviction that "the arc of the universe bends slowly, but it bends in the direction of justice." I like this image because of its certitude that the ultimate triumph of justice does not depend on God's anger.

I know firsthand the temptation to wish that God's wrath be released against the unjust. But King suggests that there is an abiding hunger – not for vengeance but for justice – woven subtly and lovingly into the very fabric of creation.

I share that hunger for justice. King's imagery helps me stay focused on the creative power of God's compassion, reminding me that all of creation accompanies me in this struggle for justice.

**God, as I seek justice in my own small way,
let me sense the universe bending alongside me.**

Be merciful to me, Lord,
for I am in trouble....
I hear many enemies whispering;
terror is all around me.
They are making plans against me,
plotting to kill me.
But my trust is in you, O Lord;
you are my God.
I am always in your care;
save me from my enemies,
from those who persecute me.

Psalm 31: 4-5, 9, 13-15

"I hear many enemies whispering..."

Facing "the enemy"

I could barely believe my ears! What I expected to be a straightforward and overall positive job review had turned into a confrontation. To my complete surprise, two senior colleagues had expressed some serious reservations about my job performance. Worst of all, my superiors had discussed this three months earlier, but no one had spoken with me.

I felt caught in a web of office politics. And, because my job depended on working – and working well – with these persons, I faced the daunting task of approaching them and trying to resolve the issue.

But how could I do this with persons whom I saw – at least at that moment – as my enemies? Only, as the psalmist says, by placing myself fully in God's care.

**God, in the midst of situations that threaten me,
calm me with the comfort of your care.**

"There was once a rich man who dressed in the most expensive clothes and lived in great luxury every day. There was also a poor man named Lazarus, covered with sores, who used to be brought to the rich man's door, hoping to eat the bits of food that fell from the rich man's table.... The poor man died and was carried by the angels to sit beside Abraham at the feast in heaven. The rich man died and was buried, and in Hades, where he was in great pain.... He called out, 'Father Abraham! Take pity on me, and send Lazarus to dip his finger in some water and cool off my tongue....' But Abraham said, 'Remember, my son, that in your lifetime you were given all the good things, while Lazarus got all the bad things. But now he is enjoying himself here, while you are in pain. Besides all that, there is a deep pit lying between us, so that those who want to cross over from here to you cannot do so.'"   *Luke 16: 19-31*

> "...there is a deep pit lying between us..."

All by myself

Jean-Paul Sartre once wrote that "Hell is other people." I think the pain of *isolation* is far worse.

How terrible it is for the rich man to know that he cannot undo the past. Worse still, that he cannot change the future by warning others of the consequences of his selfishness. A gulf now separates him from those he loves. His isolation is complete.

Our culture encourages me to fend for myself and to live by the creed "No compromise." When I get caught up in my own needs and neglect the needs of others, I live by that creed. When I shut the door on the poor, I live by that creed. After all, who is there to compromise with when I'm only concerned with myself?

Lord, help me to reach out to others with compassion today.

"There was once a landowner... who rented the vineyard to tenants and left home on a trip. When the time came to gather the grapes, he sent his slaves to receive his share of the harvest. The tenants grabbed his slaves, beat one, killed another, and stoned another.... Last of all he sent his son to them. But when the tenants saw the son, they said, 'Come on, let's kill him, and we will get his property!'

"Now, when the owner of the vineyard comes, what will he do to those tenants?" Jesus asked. "He will certainly kill those evil men," they answered.

Jesus said, "Haven't you ever read what the Scriptures say? 'The stone which the builders rejected as worthless turned out to be the most important of all.'"   *Matthew 21: 33-46*

> "The stone which the builders rejected as worthless..."

Rejecting the stone

The chief priests reject "the most important stone of all" because they don't like what they hear Jesus saying. They don't want to recognize what he is doing.

I wonder how often the same thing happens to me. To all of us. I remember sitting at meetings in which someone has a suggestion so novel that it is immediately rejected – without real consideration. Or someone who says what they think – and it goes against what we all want to believe – and is left a little outside the circle.

When I hear things I don't want to hear, especially about me, it's hard to really hear the truth. How often do I reject "the most important stone" because I can't recognize it, or don't *want* to?

**God, give me the openness to hear the truth,
and the strength to accept it.**

Saturday | MARCH 14

"There was once a man who had two sons.... [The older son] called one of the servants: 'What's going on?' 'Your brother has come back home, and your father has killed the prize calf....' The older brother was so angry.... 'Look, all these years I have worked for you like a slave, and I have never disobeyed your orders. What have you given me? Not even a goat for me to have a feast with my friends! But this son of yours wasted all your property on prostitutes, and when he comes back home, you kill the prize calf for him!' 'My son,' the father answered, 'you are always here with me, and everything I have is yours. But we had to celebrate, because your brother was dead, but now he is alive; he was lost, but now he has been found.'"

Luke 15: 11-32

"What have you given me?"

The value of kindness

I left England when I was 22, returning only for the occasional holiday, and most recently for my father's funeral. As the visitor, I'd get special treatment, such as meals in restaurants that we never went to in the years before I left. Often my father would tuck bank notes into my pocket. "Get yourself something you want," he'd say.

"He does a lot for the others because they're here. He's just trying to be fair," my mother would explain. The measured fairness of parents – aware of the often precarious balance between brothers and sisters.

As Jesus reminds me in today's parable, it's the recipients who get it wrong. How easy it is to be blind to the true meaning of kindness: to know its price, but not its real value.

Dear Lord, help me learn to receive as well as to give with unstinting generosity.

n the Temple Jesus found people selling cattle, sheep and pigeons, and also the moneychangers sitting at their tables. So he made a whip from cords and drove all the animals out; he overturned the tables of the moneychangers and scattered their coins; and he ordered those who sold the pigeons, "Take them out of here! Stop making my Father's house a marketplace!"

The Jewish authorities came back at him with a question, "What miracle can you perform to show us that you have the right to do this?" Jesus answered, "Tear down this Temple, and in three days I will build it again."

"Are you going to build it again in three days?" they asked him. "It has taken forty-six years to build this Temple!" But the temple Jesus was speaking about was his body.   *John 2: 13-25*

> "…the temple Jesus was speaking about was his body."

The body as temple

Jesus spoke of the temple as his own body, and he angrily drove out any corrupting market influences. Recently I have been struck by stories in the newspapers about men who have hair transplants and hormone treatments, women who have operations to remove fat or increase their breast size, and both men and women who have botox injections to paralyze their facial muscles and take away age lines. They have allowed the market to influence what they think their bodies should look like.

At times those influences get to me, too, and I become ashamed of my body. But when I think of how angry Jesus got with the market booths in the temple, I realize my body is a holy place, and that Jesus loves it and is distraught when I disrespect it.

**Lord, you hold my body dear.
Teach me to respect it until the day we meet in the flesh.**

"Prophets are never welcomed in their hometown. Listen to me: it is true that there were many widows in Israel during the time of Elijah, when there was no rain for three and a half years and a severe famine spread throughout the whole land. Yet Elijah was not sent to anyone in Israel, but only to a widow living in Zarephath. And there were many people suffering from a dreaded skin disease who lived in Israel during the time of the prophet Elisha; yet not one of them was healed, but only Naaman the Syrian."

When the people in the synagogue heard this, they were filled with anger.

Luke 4: 24-30

"Prophets are never welcomed in their hometown."

Prophets

Today, decades after he was shot, Martin Luther King continues to rise in people's esteem. A new generation is discovering his message of Christian nonviolence while they learn new ways to face his challenge to a system that perpetuates racism and war at the expense of the poor.

For many, Dr. King has become an inspiration, a prophet and a saint. But, in his own time, a paranoid FBI hounded him relentlessly, attempting to undermine his work and to destroy his character.

Today we know better whose legacy deserves to endure – Martin Luther King's or J. Edgar Hoover's. But we have to ask the question of our own time: Who are today's prophets? Are we listening to them, or are we tacitly permitting their persecution?

Lord, you were chased from your own hometown.
Open my heart and my mind to today's prophets.

"Once there was a king who decided to check on his servants' accounts... one of them was brought in who owed him millions of dollars.... The servant fell on his knees before the king. 'Be patient with me,' he begged, 'and I will pay you everything!' The king felt sorry for him, so he forgave him the debt and let him go.

"The man went out and met one of his fellow servants who owed him a few dollars. 'Pay back what you owe me!' he said. His fellow servant begged him, 'Be patient with me, and I will pay you back!' But he refused.... When the other servants saw what had happened, they were very upset and went to the king and told him everything. So he called the servant in. 'You worthless slave!' he said. 'You should have had mercy on your fellow servant, just as I had mercy on you.'"

Matthew 18: 21-35

> "You should have had mercy..."

Bill collectors

Many stock traders, bill collectors, soldiers and political leaders behave as if the forgiving of debts – if left unchecked – would bring the world to a halt. The problem about debt is not the need to collect it; it is the need to *forgive* it.

Jesus calls me to forgive the debt of a relative or a neighbour – or the debt I feel is owed me by members of another religion, race or country. He calls me to forgive even the worst kind of debt: the debt of an enemy.

If I insist on collecting these debts, I am, says Jesus, heading for trouble. That is, unless I am so certain I am able to pay off all my own debts.

**Lord, in gratitude I experience your mercy in my life –
mercy that is meant to be spread around.**

"Do not think that I have come to do away with the Law of Moses and the teachings of the prophets. I have not come to do away with them, but to make their teachings come true. Remember that as long as heaven and earth last, not the least point nor the smallest detail of the Law will be done away with – not until the end of all things. So then, whoever disobeys even the least important of the commandments and teaches others to do the same, will be least in the kingdom of heaven. On the other hand, whoever obeys the Law and teaches others to do the same, will be great in the kingdom of heaven."

Matthew 5: 17-19

"...to make their teachings come true."

The purpose of the law

When I got my first job, I wanted to impress my boss. I arrived before starting time; I never took my full lunch hour; and, even if I had finished all my assigned tasks, I found something meaningless to keep me occupied until it was quitting time.

As I became more involved in my work – and more confident – I stopped worrying about the clock and began to concentrate more on what we were trying to do as a team. I hadn't done away with my timetable. Instead, I got better at fulfilling its purpose.

My life is richer when I stop worrying about the details of God's law and concentrate on its purpose: to guide me towards a life of truth, justice and love.

**Lord, help me to commit myself
to your holy purpose for my life.**

When Jesus was twelve years old, they went to the festival.... When the festival was over, they started back home, but the boy Jesus stayed in Jerusalem. His parents did not know this... so they travelled a whole day and then started looking for him.... On the third day they found him in the Temple... and his mother said, "Son, why have you done this to us? Your father and I have been terribly worried trying to find you." He answered them, "Why did you have to look for me? Didn't you know that I had to be in my Father's house?" But they did not understand his answer. Jesus went back with them to Nazareth.... His mother treasured all these things in her heart. Jesus grew both in body and in wisdom, gaining favour with God and people.   *Luke 2: 41-51*

"But they did not understand his answer."

Understanding with hindsight

"I've been worried sick" is one of my mother's favourite sayings. For as long as I can remember, I've been the cause of her frequent use of this phrase. As a child I would roll my eyes, laugh or get angry.

Now, in my middle age and with no children of my own, I look back in amazement at her generosity. I marvel at all the years she withstood not being taken seriously.

The exchange between the twelve-year-old Jesus and his parents is all too recognizable. Like my mother, Mary and Joseph were "worried sick." And Jesus' brief explanation of his behaviour doesn't really settle matters. It takes years before they – and we – are able to look back with a deeper understanding.

Dear God, may the memories parents treasure in their hearts outweigh the worries their children bring them.

A teacher of the Law came to Jesus with a question: "Which commandment is the most important of all?"

Jesus replied, "The most important one is this: 'Listen, Israel! The Lord our God is the only Lord. Love the Lord your God with all your heart, with all your soul, with all your mind, and with all your strength.' The second most important commandment is this: 'Love your neighbour as you love yourself.' There is no other commandment more important than these two."

The teacher of the Law said to Jesus, "Well done, Teacher! It is true as you say: it is more important to obey these two commandments than to offer on the altar animals and other sacrifices to God."

Mark 12: 28-34

"Love your neighbour as you love yourself."

The greatest commandment

It's easy to love God whom you can't see; whom you don't live with. But my neighbour? What if my neighbour is a child molester? Or the guy who stole my girlfriend? Or the woman at work who sees me as a stepping stone in her career? Or the girl who won the school presidency I wanted so badly? What does Jesus really expect?

Seconds after I write this, I am interrupted. My anger begins to rise: anger at the interruption, at my son, at myself. Jesus' teaching is so true, but it's so hard to weave the *doing* into my life. Maybe, like Jesus on the way to Calvary, I must continue to get up when I fall.

Lord, give me understanding. When that fails, give me strength to muddle through, and pureness of heart not to become cynical.

"Once there were two men who went up to the Temple to pray: one was a Pharisee, the other a tax collector. The Pharisee stood apart by himself and prayed, 'I thank you, God, that I am not greedy, dishonest, or an adulterer, like everybody else. I thank you that I am not like that tax collector over there....' But the tax collector stood at a distance and would not even raise his face to heaven, but beat on his breast and said, 'God, have pity on me, a sinner!'

"I tell you," said Jesus, "the tax collector, and not the Pharisee, was in the right with God when he went home. For those who make themselves great will be humbled, and those who humble themselves will be made great."

Luke 18: 9-14

> "God, have pity on me, a sinner."

The Pharisee in me

When things are going smoothly in my life, it's easy to congratulate myself on how well I'm doing. Then, it seems, God finds subtle ways to deflate my inflated notions of self.

Just when I think I am better than one of my relatives, I discover how kind she's been to others in the family. Or when I look down on my neighbour, he does something unbelievably generous. I've been aloof with a co-worker until I find out what a heroic life she's led.

That's when I realize that I have a lot more of the Pharisee in me than I thought. God lets me know that I need to place myself alongside the tax collector and ask for grace and mercy.

Lord, help me to be humble in spirit and generous in deed.

As Moses lifted up the bronze snake on a pole, in the same way the Son of Man must be lifted up, so that everyone who believes in him may have eternal life. For God loved the world so much that he gave his only Son, so that everyone who believes in him may not die but have eternal life. For God did not send his Son into the world to be its judge, but to be its saviour....

The light has come into the world, but... those who do evil things hate the light and will not come to the light, because they do not want their evil deeds to be shown up. But those who do what is true come to the light in order that the light may show that what they did was in obedience to God.   *John 3: 14-21*

"For God loved the world so much..."

Love in action

"How much do you love me?" I asked my toddler. He stretched out his arms as wide as possible and said, "Thiiiiiiiiis much!" That exchange is one of those "family things" we've done ever since our children were babies.

But that's not the only way our family demonstrates love. Love also means taking out the garbage, giving up an afternoon nap to play baseball, stumbling out of bed at two a.m. to banish nightmares, letting someone else have that last piece of chocolate cake.... Love in action.

Once I heard the saying, "I asked Jesus, 'How much do you love me?' and he said, 'This much,' and stretched out his arms on a cross and died for me." Love in action.

**Jesus, help me to follow my declarations of love
with concrete acts of love.**

The Lord says, "I am making a new earth and new heavens. The events of the past will be completely forgotten. Be glad and rejoice forever in what I create. The new Jerusalem I make will be full of joy, and her people will be happy. I myself will be filled with joy because of Jerusalem and her people. There will be no weeping there, no calling for help. Babies will no longer die in infancy, and all people will live out their life span.... People will build houses and get to live in them – they will not be used by someone else. They will plant vineyards and enjoy the wine – it will not be drunk by others. Like trees, my people will live long lives."   *Isaiah 65: 17-21*

"The new Jerusalem I make will be full of joy…"

The big city

Visions of prophets. Of things not there. Of things yet to come. Cries within the heart. Longings for cities full of joy.

I went down to the city. I was a young man in a big city in a rich country. And what did I see? A man sleeping on a grate at 10 below zero. "And her people will be happy." Hands out on every corner. "No calling for help." A headline: "Baby found in dumpster." "Babies will no longer die." Shaky hands clenching bottles in paper bags. "They will plant the vineyards and enjoy the wine."

And so we struggle, and work, and cry. And fall down, and get up. And long, and hope, and pray for the new Jerusalem.

God, help me to bring about the new Jerusalem, today.

Tuesday | MARCH 24

Jesus went to Jerusalem for a religious festival. Near the Sheep Gate in Jerusalem there is a pool with five porches; in Hebrew it is called Bethzatha. A large crowd of sick people were lying on the porches – the blind, the lame and the paralyzed. A man was there who had been sick for thirty-eight years. Jesus saw him lying there, and he knew that the man had been sick for such a long time; so he asked him, "Do you want to get well?"

The sick man answered, "Sir, I don't have anyone here to put me in the pool when the water is stirred up; while I am trying to get in, somebody else gets there first."

Jesus said to him, "Get up, pick up your mat, and walk." Immediately the man got well; he picked up his mat and started walking.

John 5: 1-16

"Do you want to get well?"

True healing

This seems a strange question for Jesus to ask someone who has been crippled for 38 years. But the moment of true healing is perhaps in how the man answers.

I tend to rush in 20 different directions at once, and my efforts end up scattered and diffuse. But do I want to change? I'm attached to the identity of a busy person. Doing important things. Never idle. Part of me dreads the intense focus that God wants my work to have; I'm afraid of failure.

Perhaps the man in today's reading needs to let go of his vision of himself as a man cursed by fate never to make it into the healing pool. Jesus is asking him to take this first step.

Holy Spirit, tear down the barriers that I've built against your healing love.

You do not want sacrifices and offerings;
you do not ask for animals burned whole on the altar
or for sacrifices to take away sins.
Instead, you have given me ears to hear you,
and so I answered, "Here I am;
your instructions for me are in the book of the Law.
How I love to do your will, my God!
I keep your teaching in my heart."
In the assembly of all your people, Lord,
I told the good news that you save us.

Psalm 40: 6-10

"You do not want sacrifices and offerings…"

Known as I am

There's a famous scene in *The Wizard of Oz* where Dorothy's dog, Toto, pulls on a curtain to reveal the nondescript little man behind all the magic and power of "the Great and Powerful Oz." The whole Emerald City has been fooled by the machinery and the noise… and their own wishes.

Sometimes I see that little man in myself. I hide my doubts and fears behind a big show, trying to convince the world of my significance, yet worried all the time that someone will pull back the curtain.

It's all to no avail. God knows the secrets of my heart and says, "No grand displays, please. No public demonstrations. I know who you are. All I want is your ears to hear my words and your voice to say Yes."

Lord, help me to resist the temptation to seem more than I am.

The Lord said to Moses, "Hurry and go back down, because your people, whom you led out of Egypt, have sinned and rejected me.... I am angry with them, and I am going to destroy them. Then I will make you and your descendants into a great nation."

But Moses pleaded with the Lord his God and said, "Lord, why should the Egyptians be able to say that you led your people out of Egypt, planning to kill them in the mountains and destroy them completely? Stop being angry; change your mind and do not bring this disaster on your people...." So the Lord changed his mind and did not bring on his people the disaster he had threatened.

Exodus 32: 7-14

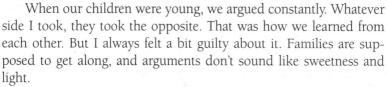

"So the Lord changed his mind..."

Seeking the truth

I love arguing – not because I want to be difficult, but because it's a way of getting at the truth. It lets me probe for flaws in reasoning, in logic, in facts.

When our children were young, we argued constantly. Whatever side I took, they took the opposite. That was how we learned from each other. But I always felt a bit guilty about it. Families are supposed to get along, and arguments don't sound like sweetness and light.

It's a relief to find that it's okay to argue – even with God. Moses did. He showed God that destroying a stubborn and disobedient people would damage God's reputation. Amazingly, God yielded. Maybe God learns from arguments, too.

**I'm glad you're willing to listen to other viewpoints, God.
May I learn from your example.**

Some of the people of Jerusalem said, "Isn't this the man the authorities are trying to kill? Look! He is talking in public, and they say nothing against him! Can it be that they really know that he is the Messiah? But when the Messiah comes, no one will know where he is from. And we all know where this man comes from."

As Jesus taught in the Temple, he said in a loud voice, "Do you really know me and know where I am from? I have not come on my own authority. He who sent me, however, is truthful. You do not know him, but I know him, because I come from him and he sent me."

Then they tried to seize him, but no one laid a hand on him, because his hour had not yet come.

John 7: 1-2, 10, 25-30

"Do you really know me...?"

Standing with

Today's reading reminds me of the old spiritual "Nobody knows the trouble I've seen. Nobody knows my sorrow." And I think of people I know, of friends....

Some have lost spouses – suddenly or after long, horrific struggles. Some have walked into bedrooms to find their babies dead in cribs. Some have had marriages go sour and spent years living like strangers in their own homes. Some have worries over children whom they feel they're losing to drugs and alcohol. Some, as adolescents, were abused by adults they trusted.

I try not to say, "Yes, I know how you feel," because I don't. How can I truly know how someone else feels? But I can stand with them, and try. Perhaps, just for a moment, I can help them feel less alone.

Dear Lord, at times we feel so alone. May I reach out to others and stand with them, and in so doing, come to know you.

Some of the people in the crowd said, "This man is really the Prophet!" Others said, "He is the Messiah!" But others said, "The Messiah will not come from Galilee! The scripture says that the Messiah will be a descendant of King David and will be born in Bethlehem, the town where David lived." So there was a division in the crowd because of Jesus. Some wanted to seize him, but no one laid a hand on him….

One of the Pharisees there was Nicodemus, the man who had gone to see Jesus before. He said, "According to our Law we cannot condemn people before hearing them and finding out what they have done."

"Well," they answered, "are you also from Galilee? Study the Scriptures and you will learn that no prophet ever comes from Galilee."

John 7: 40-53

> "…and finding out what they have done."

Open to the unexpected

While they knew where Jesus lived, the people in today's reading wrongly assumed they knew where he'd been born. In refusing to consider all the information before them, they missed seeing God's presence in their lives.

Similarly, I've tended to cling to what I know (or what I think I know), rejecting anything that challenges my sense of order and timing. It was only when my life was turned upside down – when I had to confront the reality of illness and death – that I came to see God more clearly.

I still need to hear Nicodemus' words: let the events and the people in my life speak to me, find out all I can, before I dismiss what may in fact reveal God's presence in my life.

God, you reveal your truth in unexpected ways. May I always be open to new questions, and to surprising answers!

Some Greeks said, "Sir, we want to see Jesus." … Jesus answered them, "The hour has now come for the Son of Man to receive great glory…. Now my heart is troubled – and what shall I say? Shall I say, 'Father, do not let this hour come upon me'? But that is why I came – so that I might go through this hour of suffering. Father, bring glory to your name!"

Then a voice spoke from heaven, "I have brought glory to it, and I will do so again." The crowd standing there heard the voice, and some of them said it was thunder, while others said, "An angel spoke to him!" But Jesus said to them, "It was not for my sake that this voice spoke, but for yours." *John 12: 20-33*

"Then a voice spoke from heaven…"

A voice from above

The airport was a madhouse. Crowds milled around baggage carousels; equipment clanked and clattered; announcements echoed off the walls. I couldn't find the two people I was supposed to meet. In desperation, I asked the information counter staff to make an announcement. About a half hour later, when the crowds cleared, I spied a couple standing helplessly by their baggage. "What announcement?" they asked. "We didn't hear any announcement!"

A group of Greeks wanted to meet Jesus. A voice spoke from heaven. But it was no more intelligible to them than airport announcements. Some attributed the sound to thunder, others to an angel.

I can identify with that. It's so easy to explain away unexpected insights. I wonder how often I too have missed God's messages.

God, your voice is often blurred by the bustle around me.
Open my ears so I may hear.

"Teacher, this woman was caught in the very act of committing adultery. In our Law Moses commanded that such a woman must be stoned to death. Now, what do you say?" They said this to trap Jesus, so that they could accuse him. But he bent over and wrote on the ground with his finger. ... He said to them, "Whichever one of you has committed no sin may throw the first stone at her." ... When they heard this, they all left, one by one, the older ones first. Jesus was left alone, with the woman still standing there. He said to her, "Where are they? Is there no one left to condemn you?" "No one, sir," she answered. "Well, then," Jesus said, "I do not condemn you either. Go, but do not sin again."

John 8: 1-11

> "Is there no one left to condemn you?"

A love that heals

Once a young teenager came for counselling because she had been caught shoplifting. She came from a "good family," and her parents could afford to give her anything she wanted. But, as we talked, it became clear that she lacked something money couldn't buy: her parents' time and affection.

This young girl's desperate cry for love and attention was expressed in her act of stealing. With some guidance, she realized she had other choices and, in time, she was able to talk to her parents about what she needed most from them.

Getting "caught" can often be the first step to changing a destructive pattern of behaviour: the first step towards finding the love that truly satisfies. The love that heals those deep, often hidden wounds.

Lord, when someone "catches" me today, let me listen – with openness to their words that challenge me to change.

J esus said, "I will go away; you will look for me, but you will die in your sins. You cannot go where I am going."

So the Jewish authorities said, "He says that we cannot go where he is going. Does this mean that he will kill himself?" Jesus answered, "You belong to this world here below, but I come from above…. That is why I told you that you will die in your sins. And you will die in your sins if you do not believe that 'I Am Who I Am.'"

"Who are you?" they asked him. Jesus answered, "I have much to say about you, much to condemn you for. The one who sent me, however, is truthful, and I tell the world only what I have heard from him."

John 8: 21-30

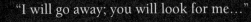

"I will go away; you will look for me…"

Blind to God's truth

How obtuse the Pharisees seem to me… with the benefit of hindsight. Trapped in their own view of things, they cannot see beyond their immediate concerns or reality. But in this exchange, the Pharisees seem more puzzled than conniving. They are trying to understand Jesus' reality. They struggle to see, to understand… but they can't. Am I so different from them?

Not so long ago, a dear friend faced a life-threatening illness. I struggled to see, to understand why he might be going to die… but I couldn't understand. I asked God "Why?" and couldn't grasp the answer.

When all the news is bad, I can't see anything good, much less God's presence. Yes, I'm often like the Pharisees: blinded by my own notions of how things should be.

**Lord, let me see with new eyes, so that I may feel you
even when the night is dark.**

The king flew into a rage and said, "Is it true that you refuse to worship my god and to bow down to the gold statue I have set up? Now then, as soon as you hear the sound of the trumpets, oboes, lyres, zithers, harps, and all the other instruments, bow down and worship the statue. If you do not, you will immediately be thrown into a blazing furnace. Do you think there is any god who can save you?"

Shadrach, Meshach and Abednego answered, "If the God whom we serve is able to save us from the blazing furnace and from your power, then he will. But even if he doesn't, Your Majesty may be sure that we will not worship your god, and we will not bow down to the gold statue that you have set up."   *Daniel 3: 13-20, 24, 49-50, 91-95*

"Do you think there is any god who can save you?"

The courage to say "no"

For eight years Mary lived in an abusive marriage. She erased whole parts of herself trying to keep peace in the family. She explained away her aches and pains, and covered up the bruises her body harboured. She didn't know what else to do. Whenever "the music played," she found herself bowing down to violence and aggression.

Until one day, like Shadrach, Meshach and Abednego, she looked straight at the king and said, "No more." Mary's moment of courage didn't mean immediate freedom. She spent many months in a fiery furnace, disentangling herself from that relationship.

But the roots of her present freedom run back to that first day she found the faith to stand on her feet – even when the music began to play.

Dear God, when "the music plays" in my life, keep my ears focused on your promise to keep me in your care.

Thursday | **APRIL 2**

G o to the Lord for help;
and worship him continually.
You descendants of Abraham, his servant;
you descendants of Jacob, the man he chose:
remember the miracles that God performed
and the judgments that he gave....
He will keep the agreement he made with Abraham
and his promise to Isaac.
The Lord made a covenant with Jacob,
one that will last forever.

Psalm 105: 4-10

"He will keep the agreement he made..."

A faithful God

I become bored when the folks start "sorting out" relatives. What does this have to do with the lives of the people around the table? It helps if I remember that Abraham, Isaac and Jacob were very ordinary, human, sinful people. In their day there were just as many broken families, heroic mothers, faithful fathers, kind hard-working grandmothers and drunken uncles as there are today.

God's covenant did not mean that we would all be perfect. It meant that we would always have a God who cares and is faithful – to that first couple who came to Canada to make a new life, to the girl down at the end of the table who is going to raise her baby even if there's no father in sight.

**God, help me to be as faithful to you as you are to me.
It's tempting to forget your promise; but you never forget.**

Jesus said, "I have done many good deeds in your presence which the Father gave me to do; for which one of these do you want to stone me?"

They answered, "We do not want to stone you because of any good deeds, but because of your blasphemy! You are only a man, but you are trying to make yourself God!"

Jesus answered, "It is written in your own Law that God said, 'You are gods.' ... The Father chose me and sent me into the world. How, then, can you say that I blaspheme because I said that I am the Son of God? Do not believe me, then, if I am not doing the things my Father wants me to do. But if I do them, even though you do not believe me, you should at least believe my deeds."

John 10: 31-42

"...at least believe my deeds."

Good intentions

Throughout the day I carry a list of good intentions. I should phone so-and-so... It's been ages since I've seen... I should drop by.... But I rarely follow through. Instead, I busy myself with trying to maintain the precarious balance of daily living. Clear the dishes, make the lunches, sweep the floor, fold the laundry....

The end of the day comes and, like the music that plays in the grocery store – ever-present but easily ignored – my list has all but faded away.

They say that we make time for what we believe is really important. If that is true, what do my deeds say about what I believe is important? A cleaner fridge or closer friendships? Everything in its place or a place for everyone?

God, may my actions today reflect what I truly value most.

Many who had come to visit Mary saw what Jesus did, and they believed in him. But some of them returned to the Pharisees and told them what Jesus had done. So the Pharisees and the chief priests met with the Council and said, "What shall we do? Look at all the miracles this man is performing! If we let him go on in this way, everyone will believe in him, and the Roman authorities will take action and destroy our Temple and our nation!"

One of them, named Caiaphas, who was High Priest that year, said, "What fools you are! Don't you realize that it is better for you to have one man die for the people, instead of having the whole nation destroyed?"

John 11:45-57

"What shall we do?"

Faced with a choice

Recently a friend confided in me that she'd fallen in love. Unfortunately, the man she loved was married. She found herself in a "no-win" situation: if she cut off the relationship, she risked losing a dear friend, a soulmate; if she chose to have an affair, she would hurt others and betray her very core. She agonized over the decision. The answer is obvious, you say. But is it?

Most difficult decisions that we face are over two "good" things. That's what makes them so hard.

"What shall we do?" the Pharisees and chief priests ask. Should they believe in Jesus and his message of healing and forgiveness, or should they defend and protect their nation? An obvious choice. Or was it?

**Lord, in times of turmoil and questioning,
keep my heart and mind open to your word.**

Jesus' disciples asked him, "Where do you want us to go and get the Passover meal ready for you?" Then Jesus sent two of them off with instructions…. The disciples left, went to the city, and found everything just as Jesus had told them; and they prepared the Passover meal….

While they were eating, Jesus took a piece of bread, gave a prayer of thanks, broke it, and gave it to his disciples. "Take it," he said, "this is my body."

Then he took a cup, gave thanks to God, and handed it to them; and they all drank from it. Jesus said, "This is my blood which is poured out for many, my blood which seals God's covenant. I tell you, I will never again drink this wine until the day I drink the new wine in the kingdom of God."

Mark 14: 1 – 15: 47

> "…and they all drank from it."

Living the passion

That was all so long ago. Who drinks from the cup now?

My friend, a widow, raises three children alone. Another friend gave one of his kidneys to his brother. My wife poured out her youth, nursing dying children. "Take it – this is my body…."

Immigrants I have met: victims of torture, who have spoken out for justice. "This is my blood which is poured out for many…."

All of these people have given of themselves when it really cost them. I think that each, in their own way, is joined with Jesus and drinks from his cup.

**Lord, help me give of myself –
especially in those times when it's so hard.**

S ix days before the Passover, Jesus went to Bethany, the home of Lazarus, the man he had raised from death. They prepared a dinner for him there…. Then Mary took a whole pint of a very expensive perfume made of pure nard, poured it on Jesus' feet, and wiped them with her hair. The sweet smell of the perfume filled the whole house. One of Jesus' disciples, Judas Iscariot – the one who was going to betray him – said, "Why wasn't this perfume sold for three hundred silver coins and the money given to the poor…?"

But Jesus said, "Leave her alone! Let her keep what she has for the day of my burial. You will always have poor people with you, but you will not always have me."   *John 12: 1-11*

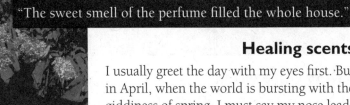

"The sweet smell of the perfume filled the whole house."

Healing scents

I usually greet the day with my eyes first. But in April, when the world is bursting with the giddiness of spring, I must say my nose leads the way. The fresh smell of earth after April rain, the fragile fragrance of new tulips and the extravagant explosion of hyacinths awaken an energy that has slept through the long winter months.

I don't often think of Jesus as someone who delighted in the small pleasures of the senses. This passage reminds me that, like the rest of us, he was touched by the world around him.

I think Mary knew something about both the power and soothing abilities of smell. Her gesture and Jesus' response are both a delight and a surprise to me.

**God, as I go through this day, remind me to delight
in the gifts that you place right under my nose.**

A fter Judas had left, Jesus said, "My children, I shall not be with you very much longer. You will look for me; but I tell you now what I told the Jewish authorities, 'You cannot go where I am going....'"

"Where are you going, Lord?" Simon Peter asked him.

"You cannot follow me now where I am going," answered Jesus; "but later you will follow me."

"Lord, why can't I follow you now?" asked Peter. "I am ready to die for you!"

Jesus answered, "Are you really ready to die for me? I am telling you the truth: before the rooster crows you will say three times that you do not know me."

John 13: 21-33, 36-38

Fear and denial

When I was in my teens, my mother bought an adult tricycle. She liked to ride it to the store for groceries because she could stop and rest whenever she wanted.

And me? Was I proud of my mother's independence – that in a place and time when people her age didn't do that kind of thing, my mother walked (or rode) her own path? No, I was ashamed. I was frightened that I'd be associated with "the weird lady with the tricycle."

Peter, I can't judge you for being scared and cowardly. In fact, it's comforting to know that I'm in such good company. What can I learn from you? When I fall down, get up. And don't judge others when they fall. They're just like you and me.

God, give me strength to stand up when I know I should. Forgive me when I don't.

One of the twelve disciples – the one named Judas Iscariot – went to the chief priests and asked, "What will you give me if I betray Jesus to you?" They counted out thirty silver coins and gave them to him. From then on Judas was looking for a good chance to hand Jesus over to them....

When it was evening, Jesus and the twelve disciples sat down to eat. During the meal Jesus said, "I tell you, one of you will betray me." The disciples were very upset and began to ask him, one after the other, "Surely, Lord, you don't mean me?" Jesus answered, "One who dips his bread in the dish with me will betray me...." Judas, the traitor, spoke up. "Surely, Teacher, you don't mean me?" he asked. Jesus answered, "So you say."

Matthew 26: 14-26

"...one of you will betray me."

Betrayal

The more Debbie talked, the more her sense of betrayal deepened: "How could he do this to me? And what about the kids?" She had just found out about the affair her husband was having with a close friend.

Deb continued: "How could she? She's been at our house so often that she's practically one of the family!" As Deb started dealing with the implications of the betrayal, her initial disbelief started to give way to anger and bitterness.

Judas went deliberately to the chief priests in order to betray his friend Jesus. Debbie's husband insists he hadn't been looking for an affair. "It just happened," he tried to explain. But, intentional or not, betrayal hurts. And its effect on a relationship is devastating.

Lord, help me to be a person whom my friends can trust.

Jesus rose from the table, took off his outer garment, and tied a towel around his waist. Then he poured some water into a washbasin and began to wash the disciples' feet and dry them with the towel around his waist. He came to Simon Peter, who said, "Never at any time will you wash my feet!"

"If I do not wash your feet," Jesus answered, "you will no longer be my disciple."

Simon Peter answered, "Lord, do not wash only my feet, then! Wash my hands and head, too...."

After Jesus had washed their feet... he said, "I, your Lord and Teacher, have just washed your feet. You, then, should wash one another's feet. I have set an example for you, so that you will do just what I have done for you."   *John 13: 1-15*

> "I have set an example for you..."

An example

With the miracles, the sermons and the teaching, it's only after this humble event that Jesus says, "I have set an example for you."

We had a pastor who was a great speaker; I remember loud exhortations, stiff-lipped faces. Me? I was scared. The sermons, I guess, had their desired effect.

A very different man followed. At gatherings, he was always in the background – Christmas baskets arranged by him, but always delivered by someone else. Events took place as the church became the centre of the community; someone else always spoke.

Not a great speaker. Not an eminent theologian... seemingly. He told me once, with characteristic humility, "I just try to find out what people need, and give it to them."

Lord, let me follow your example. Help me to serve others.

J udas went to the garden, taking with him a group of Roman soldiers, and some Temple guards sent by the chief priests and the Pharisees. Jesus knew everything that was going to happen to him, so he stepped forward and asked them, "Who is it you are looking for?" "Jesus of Nazareth," they answered. "I am he," he said....

Simon Peter, who had a sword, drew it and struck the High Priest's slave, cutting off his right ear. The name of the slave was Malchus. Jesus said to Peter, "Put your sword back in its place! Do you think that I will not drink the cup of suffering which my Father has given me?"
John 18: 1 – 19: 42

"...the cup of suffering which my Father has given me."

Reaching for the future

A devastating diagnosis, a rejection by my spouse, a notice of termination of my job, the death of that one person who is the mainstay of my life... how long does it take for hopes to unravel and dreams to die? How, in the confusion and powerlessness of those horrific moments, is it possible to believe in and reach for the future?

It must have seemed to those around Jesus that his arrest and condemnation were just a mistake soon to be corrected. Corrected, yes, but not as soon as hopes and dreams expected.

In his death, Jesus shows me how to believe in and reach for the future – to understand that I am not defined by death, but by my passionate experience of life.

**God of compassion, help me to remember
that I am never alone in moments of pain and loss.**

"Listen now, my people, and come to me;
come to me, and you will have life…."
Turn to the Lord and pray to him,
now that he is near.
Let the wicked leave their way of life
and change their way of thinking.
Let them turn to the Lord, our God;
he is merciful and quick to forgive.
"My thoughts" says the Lord,
"are not like yours,
and my ways are different from yours.
As high as the heavens are above the earth,
so high are my ways and thoughts
above yours."

Isaiah 55: 1-11

"…and my ways are different from yours."

God's will

As the only child (of parents who were both only children), I'm used to getting my way. So if I were in charge of the universe, my mother would never have had cancer. She'd struggled and suffered so much in life already, before this shocking blow. Watching her endure painful, humiliating procedures, I felt my certainty and faith float away.

As I write this, she's in remission, her white hair trying to sprout, and we can smile again. Today my faith is stronger, but not because my mother got a second chance.

Standing so close to the edge, I came to feel in my bones what I'd always known in my head: that I must accept God's will without always understanding it.

God, help me learn to live without answers.

Mary stood crying outside the tomb. While she was still crying, she bent over and looked in the tomb and saw two angels there dressed in white, sitting where the body of Jesus had been. "Woman, why are you crying?" they asked her. She answered, "They have taken my Lord away, and I do not know where they have put him!"

Then she turned around and saw Jesus standing there; but she did not know that it was Jesus.... She thought he was the gardener, so she said, "If you took him away, sir, tell me where you have put him, and I will go and get him." Jesus said to her, "Mary!" She turned toward him and said, "Rabboni!" (This means "Teacher.") ... Mary Magdalene went and told the disciples that she had seen the Lord.

John 20: 1-18

"Jesus said to her, 'Mary!'"

Clinging to hope

Mary loved Jesus so deeply that she went to the cemetery determined to do something. Love called for action. Early in the morning Mary left the other mourners, and followed her heart.

Mary probably didn't know exactly what she planned to do at Jesus' tomb. But when the "gardener" began asking questions, Mary knew how desperately she wanted to find Jesus.

Pain and anguish can blind me to reality just as they did Mary. Like her, often I can't see Jesus standing before me. I can only pray that he will call me by name and tell me the good news: God's love is stronger than death and, one day, I will experience that love in all its fullness, together with the ones I love.

**God, help me to recognize Jesus in "gardeners"
and hear when you call me by name.**

[T]he women] left the tomb and ran to tell his disciples....

While the women went on their way, some of the soldiers guarding the tomb went back to the city and told the chief priests everything that had happened. The chief priests met with the elders and made their plan; they gave a large sum of money to the soldiers and said, "You are to say that his disciples came during the night and stole his body while you were asleep. And if the Governor should hear of this, we will convince him that you are innocent, and you will have nothing to worry about." The guards took the money and did what they were told to do. And so that is the report spread around by the Jews to this very day.

Matthew 28: 8-15

> "...we will convince him that you are innocent...."

Blinded by fear?

How typical of human beings... of us. "Don't confuse me with facts; my mind is made up." Were the chief priests incapable of understanding the radical message, or did they fear it?

How often am I so committed to a belief that I cannot see the other side, even when it is shown to me? When my children challenge my prejudices and I refuse to see the validity in their arguments; when I do not see individuals because I'm blinded by racial stereotypes; when at work it has to be "my way or the highway."

The chief priests did not see because they did not want to see, or were afraid to see. How often do I blind myself to the truth?

Lord, let me be courageous enough to put aside my old ways when a new truth is shown to me.

The words of the Lord are true,
and all his works are dependable.
The Lord loves what is righteous and just;
his constant love fills the earth.
The Lord created the heavens by his command,
the sun, moon and stars by his spoken word....
When he spoke, the world was created;
at his command everything appeared....
The Lord watches over those who obey him,
those who trust in his constant love.

Psalm 33: 4-6, 9, 18-22

"The Lord created the heavens by his command..."

Mystery and miracles

My father realized early on that small children don't like "I don't know" as an answer. When we'd ask him, in our little house in the middle of nowhere, "How far is the moon, Daddy?" he'd give us a distance right down to the inch. It would invariably be a really big number, and we'd walk away mystified, but satisfied.

Now I'm a science teacher, of all things. I read and think about the origins of the universe, the vast reaches of space, the minute universe of the atom. And I still walk away mystified.

To paraphrase Einstein, there are only two ways to see things: as if nothing were a miracle; or as if everything were a miracle.

I like the latter.

**Dear God, wherever you are,
thank you for your wondrous creation.**

Wednesday | APRIL 15

Two of Jesus followers were going to a village named Emmaus, about seven miles from Jerusalem.... As they talked and discussed, Jesus himself drew near and walked along with them; they saw him, but somehow did not recognize him....

As they came near the village, Jesus acted as if he were going farther; but they held him back, saying, "Stay with us; the day is almost over and it is getting dark." So he went in to stay with them. He sat down to eat with them, took the bread, and said the blessing; then he broke the bread and gave it to them. Then their eyes were opened and they recognized him, but he disappeared from their sight. They said to each other, "Wasn't it like a fire burning in us when he talked to us on the road and explained the Scriptures to us?"   *Luke 24: 13-35*

"Wasn't it like a fire burning in us...?"

Joy needs to be shared

One day while walking in the woods, I happened upon a young deer grazing beside the trail. I stopped and looked with wonder at this magnificent creature. The deer, in turn, raised its head and looked directly at me. We stayed that way – caught up in something bigger than ourselves – for ages.

I could barely contain my excitement! How I wished to tell someone about it. As I continued my walk, I met another hiker coming down the mountain. Without hesitation, I blurted out what I'd just seen and experienced. In turn, he told me of a spectacular bird that he'd just seen higher up the trail.

Experiences of deep joy and insight need to be shared. Was this how the disciples felt on the road to Emmaus?

Open my eyes, Lord,
to the signs of new life that are all around me.

S uddenly the Lord himself stood among the disciples and said to them, "Peace be with you...." He said this and showed them his hands and his feet. They still could not believe, they were so full of joy and wonder....

Then he said to them, "These are the very things I told you about while I was still with you: everything written about me in the Law of Moses, the writings of the prophets, and the Psalms had to come true."

Then he opened their minds to understand the Scriptures, and said to them, "This is what is written: the Messiah must suffer and must rise from death three days later, and in his name the message about repentance and the forgiveness of sins must be preached to all nations."

Luke 24: 35-48

> "...they were so full of joy and wonder..."

Embracing all of life

"Say 'yes' to the best, and 'no' to the rest!" advised the retreat's motivational speaker. "Position yourself so that wonderful opportunities help to propel you forward." So why did I leave the presentation feeling unhappy and unmotivated?

I find myself wondering how Jesus managed to fill his disciples with "joy and wonder," while the speaker on that weekend retreat left me feeling empty and dissatisfied.

Jesus showed his disciples – through his words and his actions – that suffering and death are part of life, and that God promises to be with us through those hard times.

Do I believe that true happiness comes from living through *all* experiences – and not only the "wonderful" ones? That by embracing illness, loss, suffering and death, I will find peace?

Lord, when I want to turn away from the demands of life, help me turn back with open arms, as you did.

S imon Peter said, "I am going fishing...." So they went out in a boat, but all that night they did not catch a thing. As the sun was rising, Jesus stood at the water's edge, but the disciples did not know that it was Jesus. Then he asked them, "Young men, haven't you caught anything?"

"Not a thing," they answered. He said to them, "Throw your net out on the right side of the boat, and you will catch some." So they threw the net out and could not pull it back in, because they had caught so many fish.

The disciple whom Jesus loved said to Peter, "It is the Lord!"

John 21: 1-14

"...the disciples did not know that it was Jesus."

Another way

I have such a soft spot for Jesus' disciples – they're so weak and human, just like me. Here they display two of my favourite personal failings: blindness and stubbornness.

How often in my life have I followed their fishing technique: try something that doesn't work. Try it again. Repeat. Keep at it; maybe it will work this time. Don't give up now, you've only been at it all night. What's that? Try it another way? Well, what do you know? It works!

How often in my life have I, too, failed to see the Lord right before me – delivering mail, at the checkout counter, signing out my books at the library, asking for help with homework.

But the disciples learned. Maybe I will, too.

**Lord, open my eyes and my heart
so I can see what is right in front of me.**

The members of the Council were amazed to see how bold Peter and John were and to learn that they were ordinary men of no education.... "What shall we do with these men?" they asked. "Everyone in Jerusalem knows that this extraordinary miracle has been performed by them, and we cannot deny it. But to keep this matter from spreading any further among the people, let us warn these men never again to speak to anyone in the name of Jesus."

So they told them that under no condition were they to speak or to teach in the name of Jesus. But Peter and John answered them, "You yourselves judge which is right in God's sight – to obey you or to obey God. For we cannot stop speaking of what we ourselves have seen and heard."

Acts 4: 13-21

> "...they were ordinary men of no education..."

Speaking from experience

I used to think that I would have an easier time of "the faith thing" if only I could read the right books. Somehow, I developed this idea that belief could be buttressed by really difficult books. The more obscure tomes I read, especially if they were translated and hard to get, the more solid my own faith would become.

In today's reading, Peter and John amaze their educated interrogators. They talk from their hearts about the Jesus they know. This is what drives them and what confounds their critics. They reply with actual experience, not abstract theory.

I'm not dismissing serious research and study, but I am aware how much a one-sided approach can divert my attention from my actual experience of Jesus.

Dear Lord, let my faith and my understanding walk comfortably together on this lifelong journey towards you.

It was late that Sunday evening, and the disciples were gathered together behind locked doors, because they were afraid of the Jewish authorities. Then Jesus came and stood among them. "Peace be with you," he said. After saying this, he showed them his hands and his side. The disciples were filled with joy at seeing the Lord. Jesus said to them again, "Peace be with you. As the Father sent me, so I send you." Then he breathed on them and said, "Receive the Holy Spirit. If you forgive people's sins, they are forgiven; if you do not forgive them, they are not forgiven."

John 20: 19-31

"Peace be with you."

Pain transformed

The first time I visited Antonia in the hospital, I hesitated in the doorway of her room. A woman lay motionless in the other bed by the window, hooked up to an assortment of machines and feeding tubes. I'm nervous around illness, a little afraid.

Then a teenage boy in a motorized wheelchair zoomed by me and headed right to the bed by the window, cheerfully calling, "Hi, Mom!" Whatever could have happened to both mother and son? A car accident?

After the shock wore off, I noticed the flowers and balloons, the family photos everywhere. And taped to the wall by the window was a picture of the risen Lord, arms outstretched, surrounded by light. Pain and peace, fear and faith: tragedy transformed.

Risen Lord, come to wherever I am, and bring me peace.

J esus said, "I am telling you the truth: no one can see the kingdom of God without being born again."

"How can a grown man be born again?" Nicodemus asked. "He certainly cannot enter his mother's womb and be born a second time!"

"I am telling you the truth," replied Jesus, "that no one can enter the kingdom of God without being born of water and the Spirit. A person is born physically of human parents, but is born spiritually of the Spirit. Do not be surprised because I tell you that you must all be born again. The wind blows wherever it wishes; you hear the sound it makes, but you do not know where it comes from or where it is going. It is like that with everyone who is born of the Spirit."

John 3: 1-8

> "...without being born again."

Reborn each day

I remember when my friend Mary was "born again." It was a dramatic event for her and did bring about a dramatic change in her life. A couple of months later, however, the drama had died down, and she was back to "normal," with little mention of the event or its implications.

When I look at my own life, I feel like I've been born again… and again… and again. In fact, I feel like I'm reborn every morning as I get up and ask God to help me through this day.

Bob Dylan said, "Whoever is not in the process of being born is in the process of dying." For me, being born again is not a one-time event – it's a never-ending process.

**Lord, with each new day, let me be born again –
in faith, hope and love.**

The group of believers was one in mind and heart. None of them said that any of their belongings were their own, but they all shared with one another everything they had. With great power the apostles gave witness to the resurrection of the Lord Jesus, and God poured rich blessings on them all. There was no one in the group who was in need. Those who owned fields or houses would sell them, bring the money received from the sale, and turn it over to the apostles; and the money was distributed according to the needs of the people.

Acts 4: 32-37

> "...one in mind and heart."

United in love

Some years ago, a thirteen-year-old girl went missing in rural Newfoundland. Samantha Walsh was from Fleur-de-Lys on the island's northeast coast. Things like this weren't supposed to happen in our outports; our children were always considered safe.

With bated breath, the entire province waited – "one in mind and heart" – hoping for some sign of Samantha. She occupied our media, our conversations, our worries and our hearts.

After a month, Samantha's poor, battered body was found. Most Newfoundlanders had not known her but we loved her because she was one of our children. Like many, I carried a lump of grief around with me that week. We were all diminished by the horrible loss of Samantha. We still miss her.

God, may people everywhere be of one loving heart during difficult times.

For God loved the world so much that he gave his only Son, so that everyone who believes in him may not die but have eternal life....

Those who believe in the Son are not judged; but those who do not believe have already been judged, because they have not believed in God's only Son....

The light has come into the world, but people love the darkness rather than the light, because their deeds are evil. Those who do evil things hate the light and will not come to the light, because they do not want their evil deeds to be shown up. But those who do what is true come to the light in order that the light may show that what they did was in obedience to God.   *John 3: 16-21*

> "...those who do what is true come to the light..."

Moral choices

As an adult, I find morality to be more complex than it was when I was a child. Then, my mother told me that my guardian angel saw everything I did. So I guess I was "shamed" into good behaviour. At least it worked. Now it seems more complex... but is it?

I have a friend, an artist. I asked, "How do you know when to add another stroke to a painting?" Her answer: "If it makes it better, I put it in; if worse, I leave it out." Maybe morality is that simple: when I look at a choice in the light, will it make the world a better place, or worse?

Moral choices: so complex... or are they?

**Lord, may my words and actions today make life
a little gentler and kinder for those around me.**

will always thank the Lord;
I will never stop praising him....
Find out for yourself how good the Lord is.
Happy are those who find safety with him....
but he opposes those who do evil,
so that when they die, they are soon forgotten.
The righteous call to the Lord, and he listens;
he rescues them from all their troubles.
The Lord is near to those who are discouraged;
he saves those who have lost all hope.
Good people suffer many troubles,
but the Lord saves them from them all.

Psalm 34: 1, 8, 16-19

"The Lord is near to those who are discouraged…"

Hope amid despair

I am not easily discouraged: I tend to see the glass as half full, not half empty. I plough through rough spots on the road without losing hope.

A few years ago, however, I discovered that I can fall prey to the demons of self-doubt, low self-confidence and despair. Work deadlines were coming fast and furious; colleagues were counting on me to produce more in less time. Errors began to creep into my work, and I realized that I was losing control. I was conscious of my vulnerability; I prayed for strength, for hope.

I found that the Lord stayed near, encouraging me to complete each task in turn without looking back. That gave me the courage I needed to keep going.

Lord, sometimes I just can't do it all.
Hold my hand and lead me from despair to hope.

A Pharisee named Gamaliel, who was a teacher of the Law and was highly respected by all the people, stood up in the Council and said, "Fellow Israelites, be careful what you do to these men. You remember that Theudas appeared some time ago, claiming to be somebody great, and about four hundred men joined him. But he was killed, all his followers were scattered, and his movement died out. After that, Judas the Galilean appeared... but he also was killed, and all his followers were scattered. And so in this case, I tell you, do not take any action against these men. Leave them alone! If what they have planned and done is of human origin, it will disappear, but if it comes from God, you cannot possibly defeat them. You could find yourselves fighting against God!"   *Acts 5: 34-42*

> "...but if it comes from God..."

Living by God's will

When my parents died unexpectedly, I was shaken to my depths. My mother had been ill for a long time, but my father had always been a vigorous and energetic man. He certainly was not expecting to die, and his death especially taught me something about life.

What did I learn? Life is short and unpredictable. Don't waste energy on the unimportant. Time is finite and, once gone, does not return. Make every moment count. In religious language: find out what God put you here to do – then do it.

These were sobering lessons to learn, and the uncertain foundation they provide is sometimes frightening. But words like Gamaliel's give me added support: if my actions come from God, then I cannot be defeated.

Lord, you made me and I am yours.
Help me understand what you want me to do, and do it.

O Lord, I will always sing of your constant love;
I will proclaim your faithfulness forever.
I know that your love will last for all time,
that your faithfulness is as permanent as the sky....
The heavens sing of the wonderful things you do;
the holy ones sing of your faithfulness, Lord.
No one in heaven is like you, Lord;
none of the heavenly beings is your equal....
How happy are the people who worship you with songs,
who live in the light of your kindness!
Because of you they rejoice all day long,
and they praise you for your goodness.

Psalm 89: 1-2, 5-6, 15-16

"How happy are the people who worship you..."

Smelling the roses

I simply cannot be as busy as I think I am!
So often I feel pressed for time and do not fully experience whatever
I am doing. I am trying to change that mindset.

Last summer, while taking a morning walk, I smelled something
beautiful. Rather than pass by unthinkingly, I forced myself to stop
and find the source – a wild patch of rugosa roses. I made a promise
to myself: whenever I walked that way, I would stop, look and literally "smell the roses."

The first week or two, I would rush by them and have to go back.
By the end of the summer, though, I was looking forward to that
moment of prayer and praise – contemplating the last brave blooms
and the hardy hips.

Teach me to be attentive, Lord. Teach me to sing your praises.

T he two explained what had happened on the road, and how they had recognized the Lord when he broke the bread.... Suddenly the Lord himself stood among them and said, "Peace be with you." They were terrified, thinking that they were seeing a ghost. But he said to them, "Why are you alarmed? Why are these doubts coming up in your minds? Look at my hands and my feet, and see that it is I myself. Feel me, and you will know, for a ghost doesn't have flesh and bones, as you can see I have." He said this and showed them his hands and his feet. They still could not believe, they were so full of joy and wonder; so he asked them, "Do you have anything here to eat?" They gave him a piece of cooked fish, which he took and ate in their presence.

Luke 24: 35-48

> "...how they had recognized the Lord when he broke the bread..."

Being present

As a single parent with three active teenagers, I find myself hungry for meaningful "table talk." Suppers are often disrupted by the numerous and varied sports schedules (hockey and basketball seasons have just finished; soccer season will be starting soon), school meetings and commitments.

I often sit at the dinner table and watch in amazement as the food disappears. Conversation typically revolves around the latest game or how their favourite team is faring in the playoffs. It seems that we've hardly sat down before I'm asked, "May we be excused from the table?"

Rather than focusing on what is lacking, I need to remind myself that Jesus is present – even for that brief time – as we break bread together. And be filled with "joy and wonder" for the time we *do* share.

**Jesus, the disciples recognized you in the breaking of the bread.
Help me to see you in the meals I share with others.**

When the people found Jesus on the other side of the lake, they said to him, "Teacher, when did you get here?" Jesus answered, "I am telling you the truth: you are looking for me because you ate the bread and had all you wanted, not because you understood my miracles. Do not work for food that spoils; instead, work for the food that lasts for eternal life. This is the food which the Son of Man will give you, because God, the Father, has put his mark of approval on him."

So they asked him, "What can we do in order to do what God wants us to do?" Jesus answered, "What God wants you to do is to believe in the one he sent."

John 6: 22-29

"Do not work for food that spoils..."

Recipe for life

From time to time, my daughter asks me, "What was Gram's recipe for spaghetti sauce?" I tell her, but she is always disappointed with the results. She was nine years old when my mother died, and spaghetti sauce has never tasted the same.

I am not forgetting any secret ingredient, as my daughter suspects. It's just that the sauce my mother served was so thoroughly imbued with her own essence, her loving kindness, that it cannot be duplicated.

Likewise, Jesus pushes his followers to look beyond the surface of events for meaning. Discouraging them from quick fixes, he directs them to embrace the full mystery of who he is, and to believe in him. Otherwise they will miss the new life he offers.

Your words, O Lord, nourish and sustain me. Thank you.

"What miracle will you perform so that we may see it and believe you? What will you do? Our ancestors ate manna in the desert, just as the scripture says, 'He gave them bread from heaven to eat.'"

"I am telling you the truth," Jesus said. "What Moses gave you was not the bread from heaven; it is my Father who gives you the real bread from heaven. For the bread that God gives is he who comes down from heaven and gives life to the world."

"Sir," they asked him, "give us this bread always." "I am the bread of life," Jesus told them. "Those who come to me will never be hungry; those who believe in me will never be thirsty."   *John 6: 30-35*

"Those who come to me will never be hungry…"

Bread of life

Bread-making has always seemed like honest work to me. When I was at home with my young children, I used to enjoy plunging my fists into the dough, kneading it into our family's loaves. The smell of freshly baked bread was as welcome as the first warm days of spring.

When Jesus says that he is the "bread of life," he speaks not about bread that satisfies physical hunger, but about feeding us with God's own life. In a sense, my fresh bread fed both body and spirit. My children felt God's tender care for them in our warm Nova Scotia kitchen, and in the taste of homemade bread.

Yet Jesus is the true bread of life. Through him I know God's love, and can share it with others.

O God, show me how to be life-giving in my encounters with others today.

P raise God with shouts of joy, all people!
Sing to the glory of his name;
offer him glorious praise!
Say to God, "How wonderful are the things you do!
Your power is so great
that your enemies bow down in fear before you.
Everyone on earth worships you;
they sing praises to you,
they sing praises to your name."
Come and see what God has done,
his wonderful acts among people.
He changed the sea into dry land;
our ancestors crossed the river on foot.
There we rejoiced because of what he did.

Psalm 66: 1-7

"Praise God with shouts of joy!"

Joyful noise

Recently I set to work on my sadly neglected garden. It was a cool day and I felt the dampness of the ground beneath my feet. I gazed around at the weeds and at last year's seed pods, spilling in disarray around my little stone angel.

Despite the chaos in my garden, I was swept away by the bright sky, a cardinal's song from the cedar hedge, and the sheer joy of working in the fresh air. Surrounded by the wonder of God's creation, my heart filled with praise and thanksgiving!

So often I am overwhelmed by fear and anxiety about events that are beyond my control. That day, like the psalmist, I put aside my ever-present stress, and praised God with silent shouts of joy.

Thank you, dear God, for the many blessings in my world.

Now an Ethiopian eunuch, who was an important official in charge of the treasury of the queen of Ethiopia, was on his way home.... As he rode along, he was reading from the book of the prophet Isaiah. The Holy Spirit said to Philip, "Go over to that carriage and stay close to it." Philip ran over and heard him reading from the book of the prophet Isaiah.... The passage of scripture which he was reading was this: "He was like a sheep that is taken to be slaughtered, like a lamb that makes no sound when its wool is cut off. He did not say a word. He was humiliated, and justice was denied him. No one will be able to tell about his descendants, because his life on earth has come to an end."

The official asked Philip, "Tell me, of whom is the prophet saying this?" Then Philip began to speak; starting from this passage of scripture, he told him the Good News about Jesus.   *Acts 8: 26-40*

"No one will be able to tell about his descendants..."

The message lives on

My daughter, now 38, has desperately tried every means to have children, including in vitro fertilization. Nothing worked.

She is an only child. So are my wife and I. Thus the heritage of two formerly large families dwindles down to one person, who has no children. Our line is ending.

Both Isaiah and the Ethiopian taught by Philip assumed that the only way to pass on one's teaching and experience was through offspring. So if God's chosen one – whether the Suffering Servant or Jesus – died without leaving children, his message would die out with him.

Philip was the living evidence of a new way of continuing the heritage – through disciples, rather than descendants.

**When I get discouraged, God, remind me
that your ways never lead to a dead end.**

P raise the Lord, all nations!
Praise him, all peoples!
God's love for us is strong,
and his faithfulness is eternal.
Praise the Lord!

Psalm 117: 1-2

"God's love for us is strong..."

Praise the Lord!

At times, when God seems distant and un-
caring, the idea of giving praise seems so
strange. But then, when I see a magnificent sunset, praising God
suddenly makes all the sense in the world.

The idea of praising God is clearest to me when I see the most
precious of all creation: human beings. When a baby wraps her hand
around my finger, or when I visit someone in the hospital who is
calmly battling to stay alive, I know there is a God.

When a person faces their inevitable return to the Creator with
a deep sense of serenity, I know that God's love for us is strong. My
doubts are not gone forever – but for those few minutes, my faith is
strengthened.

**O God, at times you seem so distant.
Help me to look, and to see you in the people around me.**

J esus said, "I am telling you the truth: if you do not eat the flesh of the Son of Man and drink his blood, you will not have life in yourselves...."

Many of his followers heard this and said, "This teaching is too hard. Who can listen to it?"

Without being told, Jesus knew that they were grumbling about this, so he said to them, "Does this make you want to give up? Suppose, then, that you should see the Son of Man go back up to the place where he was before? What gives life is God's Spirit; human power is of no use at all. The words I have spoken to you bring God's life-giving Spirit. Yet some of you do not believe."

John 6: 53, 60-69

> "This teaching is too hard."

Leaven of love

It isn't immediately obvious why Jesus' listeners found this such a hard teaching. Scholars have a variety of theories, but I think Morrie (of Mitch Albom's book *Tuesdays with Morrie*) understood what Jesus was saying. Reflecting on what he'd learned about life while his body was dying from disease, Morrie said, "It's this simple: either we learn to love each other, or we die."

"Eating the flesh of the Son of Man" is about overcoming the divisions that keep us apart, not just from God but also from one another. It's about learning to love each other – despite our differences.

Morrie sensed, just as Jesus teaches, that we will not have life unless we leaven our lives with love.

God, open my heart to all those, near and far,
who are beside me on this journey.

See how much the Father has loved us! His love is so great that we are called God's children – and so, in fact, we are. This is why the world does not know us: it has not known God. My dear friends, we are now God's children, but it is not yet clear what we shall become. But we know that when Christ appears, we shall be like him, because we shall see him as he really is.

1 John 3: 1-2

> "...we are called God's children."

A child of God

I worked with a very sensitive and gifted student named Kyle. At a certain point, he came to acknowledge that he had received less than adequate parenting. He had been left on his own when his parents were going through a very messy separation – a time when he needed them most.

Kyle believes he got through this crisis because he was being cared for by another parent. He knew himself loved as a child of God.

Many of us have had less than perfect parenting – our human parents were often quite fragile creatures. To experience myself as a child of God is to live under a love and protection that will never fail me.

**God, I know you will love me even if all other loves should fail.
Thank you.**

J esus said, "I am telling you the truth: the man who does not enter the sheep pen by the gate, but climbs in some other way, is a thief and a robber. The man who goes in through the gate is the shepherd of the sheep. The gatekeeper opens the gate for him; the sheep hear his voice as he calls his own sheep by name, and he leads them out. When he has brought them out, he goes ahead of them, and the sheep follow him, because they know his voice. They will not follow someone else; instead, they will run away from such a person, because they do not know his voice.... The thief comes only in order to steal, kill and destroy. I have come in order that you might have life – life in all its fullness."

John 10: 1-10

> "...because they know his voice."

Hearing God's voice

From the top of the stairs, my young daughter calls for my husband, who is involved with the kitchen clean-up downstairs: "Daddy... Daaddy... Daaaaahdeeeeee!"

While she continues to call, I can't understand why we can hear him clearly, but he clearly can't hear us. Perhaps it's the sound of pots clattering, the hum of the dishwasher and the music on the radio that keep him from noticing that someone is calling him.

I think of all the practical distractions in my life that keep me from hearing people when they call to me. And I wonder about the many barriers that keep me from hearing God's voice. If I cut down on the unnecessary distractions in my life, then perhaps God's voice can lead me through the day.

God, help me hear your voice today. I am listening.

J esus was walking in Solomon's Porch in the Temple, when the people gathered around him and asked, "How long are you going to keep us in suspense? Tell us the plain truth: are you the Messiah?"

Jesus answered, "I have already told you, but you would not believe me. The deeds I do by my Father's authority speak on my behalf; but you will not believe, for you are not my sheep. My sheep listen to my voice; I know them, and they follow me. I give them eternal life, and they shall never die. No one can snatch them away from me. What my Father has given me is greater than everything, and no one can snatch them away from the Father's care. The Father and I are one."

John 10: 22-30

> "No one can snatch them away from me."

Loving protection

We were walking along a path by the river when suddenly a great, black cliff loomed up ahead, hung with ferns and full of caves. My seven-year-old daughter took one look at it and burst into tears. She wanted to turn back.

No amount of geological information could convince her that this was not a Bad Place. Finally, I simply promised to protect her and, holding my hand tightly, she bravely walked on past.

Being a parent teaches me how much God cares for me, if only I trust him. If I can walk my child past that cliff, how much more does God know and care for me, giving me what I need to confront my own looming fears, and helping me to move on.

**Loving God, give me a child's faith
in your loving guidance and protection.**

Jesus said in a loud voice, "Whoever believes in me believes not only in me but also in him who sent me. Whoever sees me sees also him who sent me. I have come into the world as light, so that everyone who believes in me should not remain in the darkness. If people hear my message and do not obey it, I will not judge them. I came, not to judge the world, but to save it…. The words I have spoken will be their judge on the last day! This is true, because I have not spoken on my own authority, but the Father who sent me has commanded me what I must say and speak. And I know that his command brings eternal life."

John 12: 44-50

"…his command brings eternal life."

Sad truths

Mary liked the three little kids who lived a few doors down. She talked to them and played a bit with them. Eventually she came to discover that there was violence in their home. In fact, she found out that other neighbours had called Children's Aid more than once. She didn't know why the kids hadn't been removed. "I wish I didn't know this," she told me.

"What are you going to do?" I asked.

"I'm going to spend more time with them and show more interest," she replied.

And she did. In fact, she became like a big sister to them. As today's reading says, once you know the truth, you are bound to it, and it must change the way you live.

Lord, give me the courage to face the truth and respond – even when the truth is uncomfortable.

Paul and his companions arrived in Antioch in Pisidia, and on the Sabbath they went into the synagogue and sat down. After the reading from the Law of Moses and from the writings of the prophets, the officials of the synagogue sent them a message: "Friends, we want you to speak to the people if you have a message of encouragement for them." Paul stood up, motioned with his hand, and began to speak:

"Fellow Israelites and all Gentiles here who worship God: hear me! The God of the people of Israel chose our ancestors and made the people a great nation during the time they lived as foreigners in Egypt. God brought them out of Egypt by his great power, and for forty years he endured them in the desert. He destroyed seven nations in the land of Canaan and made his people the owners of the land."

Acts 13: 13-25

> "…a message of encouragement for them."

Words of hope

As I listened to the young couple speaking their marriage vows, I couldn't help but wonder how they'd fare when things got a little bit rough and life was not quite so idyllic. Would their marriage promise remain strong "in sickness and in health, in good times and in bad, until death do us part…"?

Paul was asked to speak to the Israelite people in order to encourage them. So he told them their history: a story of hardship and of slavery in Egypt, of wandering in exile in the desert. Not a happy, carefree story, but one that *did* give the people hope. Why? Because it described God's promise to be faithful, to be with us "in good times and in bad…," and even beyond death.

**God, help me trust in your promise to remain faithful –
in good times and in bad.**

"**D**o not be worried and upset," Jesus told them. "Believe in God and believe also in me. There are many rooms in my Father's house, and I am going to prepare a place for you. I would not tell you this if it were not so. And after I go and prepare a place for you, I will come back and take you to myself, so that you will be where I am. You know the way that leads to the place where I am going."

Thomas said to him, "Lord, we do not know where you are going; so how can we know the way to get there?" Jesus answered him, "I am the way, the truth and the life; no one goes to the Father except by me."   *John 14: 1-6*

"...so how can we know the way to get there?"

Favourite apostle

Thomas gets my vote for favourite apostle. He never goes with the flow. He doesn't nod his head in agreement to fit in with the others. He doesn't mind looking like an idiot if he doesn't understand something. He voices the obvious question that everyone is thinking, but that no one wants to ask.

Jesus never seems exasperated by Thomas. He takes Thomas' question seriously and gives him a serious answer. I think he's secretly glad that at least one of the twelve isn't a sheep.

I wish I were more like Thomas. All too often I hang back, not wanting to appear foolish. But if I don't step forward and say, "Lord, which way should I go?" how will I ever find the room that is prepared for me?

Thomas, teach me your determination to find the truth.

"Now that you have known me, you will know my Father also, and from now on you do know him and you have seen him." Philip said to him, "Lord, show us the Father; that is all we need." Jesus answered, "For a long time I have been with you all; yet you do not know me, Philip? Whoever had seen me has seen the Father. Why, then, do you say 'Show us the Father'? Do you not believe, Philip, that I am in the Father and the Father is in me? The words that I have spoken to you do not come from me. The Father, who remains in me, does his own work. Believe me when I say that I am in the Father and the Father is in me."

John 14: 7-14

"Lord, show us the Father."

Signs of God's presence

The disciples just don't get it! They ask for proof but the proof they seek stands right in front of them.

I know how, when I feel alone and discouraged, I want a sign that God still cares. But so often I forget to look out my window or to glance up as I walk along – signs of God's presence surround me: a glimpse of sky, treetops waving in the wind, birds chirping. I forget to look in the faces of friends and family: eyes that sparkle with love, words that encourage, arms that reach out to hug.

Signs of God's tender love abound. These signs give me quiet joy and help to carry me through the tough times, if I but have eyes to see and ears to hear.

Loving God, give me eyes to see and ears to hear – and recognize – your presence today.

" I am the real vine, and my Father is the gardener. He breaks off every branch in me that does not bear fruit, and he prunes every branch that does bear fruit, so that it will be clean and bear more fruit....

"I am the vine, and you are the branches. Those who remain in me, and I in them, will bear much fruit; for you can do nothing without me. Those who do not remain in me are thrown out like a branch and dry up; such branches are gathered up and thrown into the fire. If you remain in me and my words remain in you, then you will ask for anything you wish, and you shall have it. My Father's glory is shown by your bearing much fruit; and in this way you become my disciples."

John 15: 1-8

"...he prunes every branch..."

Renewed life

We have an apple tree that hadn't been pruned in years. So last spring we cut the dead branches and suckers and burned them in a fire. It was a warm spring day and we stopped for a picnic, using the tree cuttings to cook our lunch.

There was a drought that summer, but the tree produced more apples than it did the year before. Before the apples ripened, deer came and ate them from the lower branches. But the upper branches were full and still ripening.

A week passed and I neglected to look at the tree. Returning to it, I found that all the apples had ripened and fallen, but there was no sign of them. The deer must have taken all the windfalls!

Take what I have, Lord, and distribute it as you see best.

When the crowds saw what Paul had done... they wanted to offer sacrifice to the apostles. When Barnabas and Paul heard what they were about to do, they tore their clothes and ran into the middle of the crowd, shouting, "Why are you doing this? We ourselves are only human beings like you! We are here to announce the Good News, to turn you away from these worthless things to the living God, who made heaven, earth, sea and all that is in them.... He has always given evidence of his existence by the good things he does: he gives you rain from heaven and crops at the right times; he gives you food and fills your hearts with happiness." Even with these words the apostles could hardly keep the crowd from offering a sacrifice to them.

Acts 14:5-18

> "...and fills your hearts with happiness."

Everyday miracles

The picture is vivid: people running around – filled with zeal but missing the point; the two disciples trying in vain to be heard. And what would happen when the miracles stopped? When life returned to normal – with sickness, hard work and those grey days?

On talk shows, people clamour for the latest weight-loss or pop-psychology guru. I've seen friends follow this or that trend that has "changed my life." It doesn't usually last very long.

What remains are the miracles of everyday life: the smile of a baby, the first crocuses, the world in a water droplet seen through a microscope. When I've seen people living Jesus' commandment to love their neighbour as themselves. I must look around and see that the kingdom of God is at hand.

Lord, let me hear your message, your real message, and live it.

"Peace is what I leave with you; it is my own peace that I give you. I do not give it as the world does. Do not be worried and upset; do not be afraid. You heard me say to you, 'I am leaving, but I will come back to you.' If you loved me, you would be glad that I am going to the Father; for he is greater than I. I have told you this now before it all happens, so that when it does happen, you will believe. I cannot talk with you much longer, because the ruler of this world is coming. He has no power over me, but the world must know that I love the Father; that is why I do everything as he commands me."

John 14: 27-31

"…it is my own peace that I give you."

"Pre-emptive" love

With so much talk of war in the news, who knows what state our world will be in by the time this reflection is published?

I am uneasy at how the word "peace" creeps into political speeches these days – often right next to "national security" and "pre-emptive strike" and "our way of life…." This is peace as the world seeks it. And my government seems to believe that peace is really possible on these terms.

In reality, such peace – today, as in Jesus' time – means protecting the prosperity of a few from the desires of the many. Jesus identifies peace with "pre-emptive" love, and security with a "way of life" marked by humble service. Not everyone who promises peace has Jesus' meaning in mind.

Dear Jesus, do not let me be deceived by worldly claims of peace. Keep me attuned to your peace instead.

S ome men came from Judea to Antioch and started teaching the believers, "You cannot be saved unless you are circumcised as the Law of Moses requires." Paul and Barnabas got into a fierce argument with them about this, so it was decided that Paul and Barnabas and some of the others in Antioch should go to Jerusalem and see the apostles and elders about this matter....

When they arrived in Jerusalem, they were welcomed by the church, the apostles and the elders, to whom they told all that God had done through them. But some of the believers who belonged to the party of the Pharisees stood up and said, "The Gentiles must be circumcised and told to obey the Law of Moses."

The apostles and the elders met together to consider this question.

Acts 15: 1-6

"The Gentiles must be circumcised..."

Rules and regulations

My friend Mark installs and maintains underground sprinkler irrigation systems. Last fall, the heavy cover on the industrial air compressor he was using slammed down, amputating the end of Mark's index finger.

His wife rushed him to the emergency department. For five hours, no one gave him any medication to ease his pain. Not even a Tylenol. By the time a doctor finally saw Mark, it was too late to re-attach the severed finger.

I don't blame the nurses, or the doctors. They have rules to follow. But those rules exist to protect the institution, not the patients.

Paul ran into the same problem. The rules protected the existing religion, not the converts.

**Forgive me, God, for times when I have thought
a rule mattered more than the person it affected.**

" I love you just as the Father loves me; remain in my love. If you obey my commands, you will remain in my love, just as I have obeyed my Father's commands and remain in his love."

John 15: 9-11

"I love you…"

Beyond words

Jesus says that to remain in his love, all we have to do is to love one another. Hey! That's easy! I love tons of people so I must be right in the middle of his love.

Jesus was talking to the disciples – who knew each other at their very best… and worst. I'm great at showing love to people outside our home, but fail on a daily basis within the orbit of my own family. At times my daughter doubts that she is important to me. "Of course you are!" I try to convince her. But my actions must give her a different message.

Once, at her bedtime, I was talking on the phone. After I hung up I nearly wept when I found her lying asleep clutching the book she'd wanted me to read to her.

**Lord, teach me to live love and not just speak about it –
especially with those closest to me.**

I have complete confidence, O God;
I will sing and praise you!
Wake up, my soul!
Wake up, my harp and lyre!
I will wake up the sun.
I will thank you, O Lord, among the nations.
I will praise you among the peoples.
Your constant love reaches the heavens;
your faithfulness touches the skies.
Show your greatness in the sky, O God,
and your glory over all the earth.

Psalm 57: 7-11

> "I have complete confidence, O God."

True confidence

When asked, "How are you?" I usually reply, "Fine!" – even when it's not entirely true.

I remember teaching a girl, a leader in our school: near the top of the honour roll and with lots of friends. She was, by all appearances, the "perfect" student. One day after class, she told me she felt worthless. "It's all an act," she said. "If people only knew what a phony I am." She lived in fear of people finding out the truth.

At times I feel the same way this young girl felt. I marvel at the confidence expressed in today's reading. How I'd like to believe in myself, and in God's love, so I could say with such enthusiasm, "I will wake up the sun!"

**Dear God, give me confidence in myself –
even when I feel I have very little to be confident about.**

The churches were made stronger in the faith and grew in numbers every day.

Paul and Timothy travelled through the region of Phrygia and Galatia because the Holy Spirit did not let them preach the message in the province of Asia. When they reached the border of Mysia, they tried to go into the province of Bithynia, but the Spirit of Jesus did not allow them. So they travelled right on through Mysia and went to Troas. That night Paul had a vision in which he saw a Macedonian standing and begging him, "Come over to Macedonia and help us!" As soon as Paul had this vision, we got ready to leave for Macedonia, because we decided that God had called us to preach the Good News to the people there.

Acts 16: 1-10

"Come over... and help us!"

Open to God

"Oh, come on!" I groaned as I slammed my fist against the dash and turned the ignition key yet another time. "Come on!!!" Sound familiar? When a car is flooded with fuel, you can turn the key till the cows come home, and it just won't start. It can't! Conditions in the engine aren't right.

Oddly enough, I've noticed my experience of God is much the same. Without the right conditions inside me, it's pointless for God to try to reach me. I'm not open. I won't respond.

But when I have taken the time to prepare my heart, and call, "Come over and help me!" the results can seem miraculous. God's love can heal even long-lingering hurts and sadness.

Loving God, give me the courage to examine my own life, in anticipation of your healing touch.

"I love you just as the Father loves me; remain in my love....

"I have told you this so that my joy may be in you and that your joy may be complete. My commandment is this: love one another, just as I love you. The greatest love you can have for your friends is to give your life for them. And you are my friends if you do what I command you. I do not call you servants any longer, because servants do not know what their master is doing. Instead, I call you friends, because I have told you everything I heard from my Father. You did not choose me; I chose you.... And so the Father will give you whatever you ask of him in my name. This, then, is what I command you: love one another."

John 15: 9-17

> "I call you friends..."

The gift of friendship

When I first met Michael I was terribly intimidated. He was my boss, and I was an intern. I knew very little, and he knew a lot. It took me a long time to stop worrying about my shortcomings and to get on with learning how to do the job. But, with his encouragement, I soon became competent and, more importantly, confident.

I don't remember when the shift from "boss" to "friend" happened. But for years now we have made it a priority to keep in touch. Though we have both moved on to different jobs we have remained close. His friendship is a great gift.

His trust in me – all those years ago – helped me to grow. It made all the difference, and it still does.

**Jesus, you teach me how to love.
May I come to call you "friend."**

We left by ship from Troas and sailed straight across to Samothrace, and the next day to Neapolis. From there we went inland to Philippi, a city of the first district of Macedonia.... On the Sabbath we went out of the city to the riverside, where we thought there would be a place where Jews gathered for prayer. We sat down and talked to the women who gathered there. One of those who heard us was Lydia from Thyatira, who was a dealer in purple cloth. She was a woman who worshipped God, and the Lord opened her mind to pay attention to what Paul was saying. After she and the people of her house had been baptized, she invited us, "Come and stay in my house if you have decided that I am a true believer in the Lord." And she persuaded us to go.

Acts 16: 11-15

> "Come and stay in my house…"

A woman's question

Paul and his companion Silas baptize Lydia, "a dealer in purple cloth," when they visit Macedonia. Following her baptism, Lydia's invitation to them seems more than a simple offer of hospitality. It sounds as if she is asking the two men to judge her: "Come and stay in my house if you have decided that I am a true believer." That is, if you find me worthy, Lydia seems to be saying.

Hers is a woman's question to the male leaders of the early church. Perhaps it is still a valid question for women to ask the men who lead the church today: "Stay in my house if you have decided that I am a true believer."

Lord, will it be our generation that witnesses the end of sexual discrimination in the church?

"Now I am going to him who sent me, yet none of you asks me where I am going. And now that I have told you, your hearts are full of sadness. But I am telling you the truth: it is better for you that I go away, because if I do not go, the Helper will not come to you. But if I do go away, then I will send him to you. And when he comes, he will prove to the people of the world that they are wrong about sin, because they do not believe in me; they are wrong about what is right, because I am going to the Father and you will not see me any more; and they are wrong about judgment, because the ruler of this world has already been judged."

John 16: 5-11

> "...they are wrong about what is right..."

Choosing what is right

Jesus promised to send the Helper to us. But why, in our day, does it seem so difficult to hear his voice? Can we really say that we know what's wrong and what's right?

I open the newspaper and read of regions in Africa where doctors don't even have Aspirin to relieve the pain of children suffering from cancer. I see pictures of the most affluent countries in the world where some people have no choice but to make the streets their home. I see articles that defame and expose our political leaders – and they, in turn, say, "I'll take the publicity."

And at times, my own moral choices are so complex, so unclear. How difficult to hear the Helper. How hard to listen.

God, help me to hear your voice telling me what's right.
Give me the strength to follow.

P raise the Lord!
Praise the Lord from heaven,
   you that live in the heights above....
Praise him, kings and all peoples,
princes and all other rulers;
young women and young men,
old people and children too.
Let them all praise the name of the Lord!
His name is greater than all others;
his glory is above earth and heaven.
He made his nation strong,
so that all his people praise him –
the people of Israel, so dear to him.
Praise the Lord!   *Psalm 148: 1-2, 11-14*

"Praise him…old people and children too."

Praise God

My infant daughter brought a lot of joy to the residents of the seniors'
home where my grandparents lived. As soon as we stepped off the
elevator, we were greeted with smiles and salutations in Ukrainian
that neither of us could decipher. Nonetheless, like celebrities, we
were beckoned to and fussed over.

During one visit, a neighbour down the hall held my daughter on
her lap. They seemed to be having quite the conversation and, based
on my daughter's gurgles and giggles, they understood each other
perfectly! The two shared something very special: they were simply
happy to be alive and in each other's presence.

I may not have understood their words, but I'm sure God did.

**Give me the confidence, God, to praise you
without worrying if I am completely understood.**

"In a little while you will not see me any more, and then a little while later you will see me." Some of his disciples asked among themselves, "What does this mean? He tells us that in a little while we will not see him, and then a little while later we will see him. What does this 'a little while' mean? We don't know what he is talking about!"

Jesus knew that they wanted to question him, so he said, "I said, 'In a little while you will not see me, and then a little while later you will see me.' I am telling you the truth: you will cry and weep, but the world will be glad; you will be sad, but your sadness will turn into gladness."

John 16: 16-20

"…a little while later you will see me."

Darkness and light

Sometimes I get discouraged, bogged down, frazzled. I begin to wonder if life has meaning. My sense of God's loving presence fades to grey. But I have a promise: Jesus says, "A little while later you will see me."

If I look back over the years, I see that periods of grey have alternated with periods of brightness: when life had meaning and direction. At other times, life looks very black: I lose a job, a home, a loved one.

But in the midst of my anguish I remember the promise: impossible as it may seem, these dark times will come to an end. "A little while later you will see me…. You will cry and weep; you will be sad, but your sadness will turn into gladness."

**Lord, help me to hang on through the darkest hours
until I see your light again.**

One night Paul had a vision in which the Lord said to him, "Do not be afraid, but keep on speaking and do not give up, for I am with you…." So Paul stayed there, teaching the people the word of God.

When Gallio was made the Roman governor of Achaia, Jews there got together, seized Paul, and took him into court. "This man," they said, "is trying to persuade people to worship God in a way that is against the law!"

Gallio said, "If this were a matter of some evil crime or wrong that has been committed, it would be reasonable for me to be patient with you. But since it is an argument about words and names and your own law, you yourselves must settle it. I will not be the judge of such things!"

Acts 18: 9-18

> "Do not be afraid, but keep on speaking…"

Speaking the truth

It had all started rather innocently. As was their habit, they'd gone out for a few beers after work. But then the guys began boasting about the materials they were swiping off the loading dock. Because the boxes were poorly labelled, they were able to sell them quickly.

He made a complaint to his shop steward, and now he is being asked to make his complaint public. But his wife has just been laid off, and his son wants to go to hockey camp. Will he hear the Lord say, "Do not be afraid, but keep on speaking and do not give up, for I am with you"?

Like Paul in today's reading, he discovered that there are consequences to speaking the truth in public.

**Lord, help me to speak your word of truth
in all that I say and do.**

C lap your hands for joy, all peoples!
Praise God with loud songs!
The Lord, the Most High, is to be feared;
he is a great king, ruling over all the world....
God is king over all the world;
praise him with songs!
God sits on his sacred throne;
he rules over the nations.
The rulers of the nations assemble
with the people of the God of Abraham.
More powerful than all armies is he;
he rules supreme.

Psalm 47: 1-2, 7-9

"...he rules supreme."

Hope for the hopeless

At times, I am overcome by the state of the world. I cringe when I hear the latest news of conflict, war, terrorist attacks and misguided judgment. How can we extricate ourselves from the mess we're in? How can we learn to love one another? We seem to be past the point of no return – with our zero tolerance, our prejudices and our inability to listen to one another.

When I feel this way, I remind myself that humans do not have the last word. God does: "More powerful than all armies is he; he rules supreme." These words give me hope. And although I can't see my way clear through the various wars and injustices, I take comfort in the knowledge that God can.

Lord, help me hold on to hope when conflict surrounds me.

urge you to live a life that measures up to the standard God set when he called you. Be always humble, gentle, and patient. Show your love by being tolerant with one another. Do your best to preserve the unity which the Spirit gives by means of the peace that binds you together....

Each one of us has received a special gift in proportion to what Christ has given.... It was he who "gave gifts to people"; he appointed some to be apostles, others to be prophets, others to be evangelists, others to be pastors and teachers. He did this to prepare all God's people for the work of Christian service, in order to build up the body of Christ. And so we shall all come together to that oneness in our faith and in our knowledge of the Son of God; we shall become mature people, reaching to the very height of Christ's full stature.

Ephesians 4: 1-13

> "It was he who 'gave gifts to people...'"

Hidden gifts

What a wonder it is – watching our children grow! My husband and I know this time of early childhood will pass quickly. Sometimes we are tempted to dream away the present by wondering about the future. What will our children be when they grow up? Will they be successful and happy?

One thing we know for sure: the source of their talents is a mystery. When we try to pin down what gifts we have passed on to our children, we are often surprised. They have gifts that are beyond our abilities and interests, that challenge us to grow in new directions.

God willing, they will develop into the people God intended them to be. May I have the wisdom to step out of the way.

**May all children be given the space to grow
into their God-given gifts.**

The disciples said to Jesus, "Now you are speaking plainly, without using figures of speech. We know now that you know everything; you do not need to have someone ask you questions. This makes us believe that you came from God."

Jesus answered them, "Do you believe now? The time is coming, and is already here, when all of you will be scattered, each of you to your own home, and I will be left all alone. But I am not really alone, because the Father is with me. I have told you this so that you will have peace by being united to me. The world will make you suffer. But be brave! I have defeated the world!"

John 16: 29-33

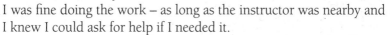

> "Do you believe now?"

Believing in myself

While studying lithography, a labour-intensive printmaking method, I took copious notes and asked questions ad nauseam.
I was fine doing the work – as long as the instructor was nearby and I knew I could ask for help if I needed it.

One day, as I arrived at the studio to do a major project, I found that I'd left my notes behind. Horrified and anxious, I pleaded for a deferral. But the instructor smiled knowingly and said, "This is probably the best thing that could happen." To my surprise, as I calmed down, I got involved in the work and discovered that I had internalized the process and didn't need my notes after all!

Like the disciples, I needed reassurance – and a little push.

**God, help me to trust all you have taught me
as I move into new experiences.**

J esus looked up to heaven and said, "Father, the hour has come. Give glory to your Son, so that the Son may give glory to you. For you gave him authority over all people, so that he might give eternal life to all those you gave him. And eternal life means to know you....

"I have made you known to those you gave me out of the world.... All I have is yours, and all you have is mine; and my glory is shown through them. And now I am coming to you; I am no longer in the world, but they are in the world. Holy Father! Keep them safe by the power of your name, the name you gave me, so that they may be one just as you and I are one." *John 17: 1-11*

> "For you gave him authority over all people..."

A parent's prayer

"You're not the boss of me!" When they were little, each of my three children shouted those words at one time or another. They sometimes hated being told what to do or having their will thwarted. And they resented parental authority as much as they misunderstood it. They thought it meant my wife or I could make them do whatever we wanted.

My authority is a responsibility, not a privilege. Being in charge means caring and worrying about my charges all the time, no matter what else is going on in my life.

Jesus understood this kind of authority. Here he is, at a critical moment in his life, praying not for himself but for those that he had been given authority over – "Father, keep them safe...." A true parent's prayer.

Lord, help me always to use my authority tenderly and hold those I love safe in your keeping.

" **A**nd now I am coming to you; I am no longer in the world, but they are in the world. Holy Father! Keep them safe by the power of your name, the name you gave me, so that they may be one just as you and I are one. While I was with them, I kept them safe by the power of your name…. I do not ask you to take them out of the world, but I do ask you to keep them safe from the Evil One. Just as I do not belong to the world, they do not belong to the world. Dedicate them to yourself by means of the truth; your word is truth. I sent them into the world, just as you sent me into the world. And for their sake I dedicate myself to you, in order that they, too, may be truly dedicated to you."

John 17: 11-19

> "Dedicate them to yourself…"

Watched over

What does it mean to be watched over the way God watches over us? I get an idea from the way I watch over my own child in the playground down the street, although I suspect I get bored long before God does!

I want to prevent my daughter from getting hurt. I want her to be happy. I want her to stretch to her full potential. Sometimes I stand back and watch as she takes risks; other times I actively encourage her, and delight with her in new discoveries. And I console her when she gets hurt.

When it's time to go, and she doesn't want to leave the playground, I often remind her of the wonderful meal we'll have together when we get home.

Help me to be aware of your deep care for me, O Lord, and to grow through the freedom you give me.

" I pray not only for them, but also for those who believe in me.... I pray that they may all be one. Father! May they be in us, just as you are in me and I am in you. May they be one, so that the world will believe that you sent me. I gave them the same glory you gave me, so that they may be one, just as you and I are one: I in them and you in me, so that they may be completely one, in order that the world may know that you sent me and that you love them as you love me.... I made you known to them, and I will continue to do so, in order that the love you have for me may be in them."

John 17: 20-26

"I pray that they may all be one."

Signs of love

I live in a group home with nine people, none of whom are related by blood. Our ages range from 20 to 76 years. Five have a mental handicap; several come from different cultural backgrounds; one speaks French and two speak German.

Our home life is not always harmonious. There are tensions and disagreements; we get on each other's nerves. However, what I see over and over is that those who have been labelled "handicapped" are the ones who bring us back together – who remind us to pray around the table after supper, who say "I'm sorry," who forgive so willingly, who tease and cajole and bring us back to laughter.

They are responsible for the overall harmony and laughter in our home – signs of Jesus' presence among us.

**Lord, keep me close to those who can teach me
about the unity you desire.**

After they had eaten, Jesus said to Simon Peter, "Simon son of John, do you love me more than these others do?" "Yes, Lord," he answered, "you know that I love you." Jesus said to him, "Take care of my lambs."

A second time Jesus said to him, "Simon son of John, do you love me?" "Yes, Lord," he answered, "you know that I love you." Jesus said to him, "Take care of my lambs."

A third time Jesus said, "Simon son of John, do you love me?" Peter became sad because Jesus asked him the third time, "Do you love me?" and so he said to him, "Lord, you know everything; you know that I love you!" Jesus said to him, "Take care of my sheep...." Then Jesus said to him, "Follow me!"   *John 21:15-19*

"Take care of my lambs."

Who will care for them?

I'm one of the lucky ones: A few years ago, I had a very serious health problem. I thought I was done for. I remember worrying about my children. Oh God, my children! Who will look after them? Luckily, that time I "dodged the bullet."

When I read today's passage, I get a picture of Jesus in my mind. I can see a look of care written on his face. Is there perhaps a tremor in his voice, as he thinks of those he loves, about to be left on their own?

And what does it mean for me, now? Perhaps the world will be a better place if, when I see someone in need, I feel what Jesus felt when he said, "Take care of my lambs."

**Lord, help me do my best
for those you have placed in my care.**

T he Lord is in his holy temple;
he has his throne in heaven.
He watches people everywhere
and knows what they are doing.
He examines the good
and the wicked alike;
the lawless he hates with all his heart.
He sends down flaming coals
and burning sulfur on the wicked;
he punishes them with scorching winds.

The Lord is righteous
and loves good deeds;
those who do them will live
in his presence.

Psalm 11:4-7

"The Lord is righteous and loves good deeds…"

Too quick to judge

I like to think that my list of "good guys" and "bad guys" matches God's list exactly. The "wicked" include all the usual suspects: murderers, thieves, rapists and anyone who happens to annoy me that day.

And it goes without saying that I'm one of the "righteous." It's reassuring to think of God, "up there," looking down angrily on all those evil folks.

When I lapse into this kind of self-righteous, simplistic thinking, it's usually because I feel threatened or uncertain. I'm looking for easy answers to baffling moral questions. My ego doesn't much like the truth: that only God is in the position to judge the good and the bad. Only God truly knows what is in another's heart.

Today, Lord, heal my hard, judgmental heart.

What I say is this: let the Spirit direct your lives, and you will not satisfy the desires of the human nature. For what our human nature wants is opposed to what the Spirit wants, and what the Spirit wants is opposed to what our human nature wants. These two are enemies, and this means that you cannot do what you want to do. If the Spirit leads you, then you are not subject to the Law....

The Spirit produces love, joy, peace, patience, kindness, goodness, faithfulness, humility and self-control. There is no law against such things as these. And those who belong to Christ Jesus have put to death their human nature with all its passions and desires. The Spirit has given us life; he must also control our lives.

Galatians 5: 16-25

> "...let the Spirit direct your lives..."

Room for the Spirit

One of my colleagues often uses the expression "Leave room for the Holy Spirit." At first this puzzled me, as she has the knack for covering all the bases. Everything she does seems brilliantly planned and executed.

Watching her work, I've come to recognize what makes her a remarkable mentor: she knows that she can't control everything. She listens to others with an intensity and respect that honours their input. I've seen her shift an agenda – with delight and enthusiasm – to incorporate the ideas of co-workers.

There have been times when I have been asked to take the helm and I've had my ego bruised when things didn't go my way. I must remember to leave room for the Holy Spirit to guide my words and actions.

Holy Spirit, lead me. I am willing to follow.

"Once there was a man who planted a vineyard, put a fence around it, dug a hole for the wine press, and built a watch-tower. Then he rented the vineyard to tenants and left home on a trip. When the time came to gather the grapes, he sent a slave to the tenants to receive from them his share of the harvest. The tenants grabbed the slave, beat him, and sent him back without a thing. Then the owner sent another slave; the tenants beat him over the head and treated him shamefully. The owner sent another slave, and they killed him; and they treated many others the same way, beating some and killing others. Last of all, then, he sent his son to the tenants.... But those tenants said to one another, 'This is the owner's son. Come on, let's kill him, and his property will be ours!'"

Mark 12: 1-12

> "...they treated many others the same way..."

Doing what's right

I get the point... I think. I could write about how many times I've been the tenants in today's reading: how many times I avoided "paying up." How many times I didn't do what's right.

But, to be honest, when I read and reread this story, I always think, "What would it be like to be one of this guy's slaves?" You know, you're slave number 19, thinking, "Oh no, I'm next." I mean, wouldn't you send the police, or go together for safety?

But life's like that, isn't it? Sometimes you have to go in, knowing you're going to get clobbered. Sometimes it's not easy to follow the master's orders. It's not easy to do your job, to do what's right.

Lord, let me go in and do what's right, even when it costs.

S ome Pharisees and some members of Herod's party were sent to Jesus to trap him with questions. They came to him and said, "Teacher, we know that you tell the truth, without worrying about what people think. You pay no attention to anyone's status, but teach the truth about God's will for people. Tell us, is it against our Law to pay taxes to the Roman emperor? Should we pay them or not?"

But Jesus saw through their trick and answered, "Why are you trying to trap me? Bring a silver coin, and let me see it." They brought him one, and he asked, "Whose face and name are these?" "The Emperor's," they answered. So Jesus said, "Well, then, pay to the Emperor what belongs to the Emperor, and pay to God what belongs to God."   *Mark 12: 13-17*

"But Jesus saw through their trick…"

The money trap

How familiar – and surprisingly contemporary – to see Jesus' enemies using honeyed words to trap him over money. After all, money-traps are set for us every day. Seductive voices flatter us endlessly. Buy this and you will be loved. Own that and you will be worthy. Put money in a retirement savings plan and your future will be secure. Vote for lower taxes and you will get what rightfully belongs to you.

Because I often do feel unworthy, unlovable and unsure about the future, I am tempted by these voices. I put my trust in money and start relying on what it can buy.

But then Jesus' response cuts through the seduction with a wakeup call to keep my priorities straight. Give to God what belongs to God.

**Lord, when I am weak and vulnerable,
help me hear the truth your quiet voice speaks.**

Some Sadducees said, "Teacher, Moses wrote this law for us: 'If a man dies and leaves a wife but no children, that man's brother must marry the widow....' Once there were seven brothers; the oldest got married and died without having children. Then the second one married the woman, and he also died without having children.... All seven brothers married the woman and died without having children. Last of all, the woman died. Now, when all the dead rise to life on the day of resurrection, whose wife will she be?"

Jesus answered them, "When the dead rise to life, they will be like the angels in heaven and will not marry. Now, as for the dead being raised:... it is written that God is the God of the living, not of the dead."

Mark 12: 18-27

> "...the God of the living, not of the dead."

A God who frees

I recently spent an afternoon with a notary, a lawyer and a property developer. It was a simple matter of positioning two parking spaces, but insults were flung, threats were uttered, and papers were thrown across the table. Our law binds us with words that seem cast in stone, and we use legal arguments to try to disable each other.

The Sadducees applied these same legal tools to the question of the resurrection. In the situation they described, there would be adultery, or polygamy, in heaven! Instead of answering their question, Jesus shifts the talk from death to life. Our legal tools, necessary for sorting out parking spaces, cannot pin God down, nor God's creatures. Instead, God liberates us from all that keeps us in the tomb.

**Lord, I cannot pin you down.
Help me embrace my life without calculation.**

A teacher of the Law came to [Jesus]: "Which commandment is the most important of all?"

Jesus replied, "The most important one is this: 'The Lord our God is the only Lord! Love the Lord your God with all your heart, with all your soul, with all your mind, and with all your strength.' The second most important commandment is this: 'Love your neighbour as you love yourself." There is no other commandment more important than these two."

The teacher of the Law said to Jesus, "Well done, Teacher! It is true, as you say... you must love God with all your strength; and you must love your neighbour as you love yourself. It is more important to obey these two commandments than to offer on the altar animals and other sacrifices to God."   *Mark 12: 28-34*

"Love your neighbour as you love yourself."

Love of neighbour

My Aunt Lillianne must be one of the most difficult people to love. Should you miss the darkest, most unpleasant aspect of any situation, Auntie will point it out. And she loses no time in broadcasting it to anyone who is willing to listen. She lies, cheats, gossips and seldom has a pleasant or sincere word to say to or about anyone else.

I am appalled that I am related to someone like this. And it distresses me that both instinct and etiquette urge me to associate with her during precious family moments.

It galls me even more to think that Auntie might be the "neighbour" whom I am called to love. But then, somebody else may be just as vexed at the call to love me.

Lord, help me to love that neighbour that I love least, and to be a more "lovable" neighbour to others.

H appy are those who depend
on the Lord their God,
   the Creator of heaven, earth and sea,
and all that is in them.
He always keeps his promises;
he judges in favour of the oppressed
and gives food to the hungry.
The Lord sets prisoners free
and gives sight to the blind.
He lifts those who have fallen…
He protects the strangers who live in our land;
he helps widows and orphans;
but takes the wicked to their ruin.

Psalm 146: 1-2, 5-10

"He protects the strangers who live in our land…"

Strangers in our land

Who are the "strangers" I encounter today? Perhaps they are the newly arrived Canadians in my child's class – struggling to learn and adapt to an unfamiliar language and culture.

Or perhaps they are the recently hired employees at work – feeling somewhat intimidated by the many skills and routines which they are expected to learn.

Could they be the "difficult" family members whose unconventional behaviour is often puzzling or even embarrassing to others?

And how do I respond to them? Do I turn away, choosing to ignore their needs? Or am I willing to risk ridicule and criticism from those around me by offering a welcoming smile and a friendly gesture to the strangers I meet?

**Lord, help me to accept and welcome
the strangers you send into my life.**

"Watch out for the teachers of the Law, who like to walk around in their long robes and be greeted with respect in the marketplace, who choose the reserved seats in the synagogues and the best places at feasts…"

As Jesus sat near the Temple treasury, he watched the people as they dropped in their money. Many rich men dropped in a lot of money; then a poor widow came along and dropped in two little copper coins, worth about a penny. He called his disciples together and said, "I tell you that this poor widow put more in the offering box than all the others. For the others put in what they had to spare of their riches; but she, poor as she is, put in all she had – she gave all she had to live on."

Mark 12: 38-44

"…she, poor as she is, put in all she had…"

Truly rich

How often I use my "poverty" as an excuse not to give. I don't have enough money, so I can't give to the person begging on the street; I don't have enough self-confidence, so I can't give a talk; I don't have enough time, so I can't visit a friend in hospital.

Yet the woman in today's reading, who had so very little, gave all she had.

She reminds me of my friend Jane, who is not able to read or write or drive a car or earn a big income, but who gives her friendship to me totally and without reserve. She helps me to forget about being preoccupied with all my inadequacies and to offer what I have, simply trusting it will be enough.

Lord, help me to find the freedom to give what I have, even when I feel poor.

The words of the Lord are true,
and all his works are dependable.
The Lord loves what is righteous and just;
his constant love fills the earth.
The Lord created the heavens by his command,
the sun, moon and stars by his spoken word....
When he spoke, the world was created;
at his command everything appeared....
The Lord watches over those who obey him,
those who trust in his constant love.
He saves them from death;
he keeps them alive in times of famine.
We put our hope in the Lord;
he is our protector and our help.

Psalm 33: 4-6, 9, 16-22

"When he spoke, the world was created..."

God's presence

Late last spring a storm brought our work to a halt. All we could do was take shelter and watch in amazement as the rains grew into streams that ran down from the hills through the hay fields.

The thunder boomed overhead, rattling everything that wasn't nailed down, and the lightning flashed repeatedly, sweetening the air. In one sharp crack that left our ears ringing, the lightning set fire to an old maple stump before our eyes!

Despite the soaking rain, that stump burned for three days after the storm. And this was only the voice of thunder and lightning! The living stone, the living waters that carve it – everything that lives speaks of God's presence among us and lifts us up.

**Lord, open my ears to hear your voice
at the heart of all things, calling them (and me) to life.**

"Happy are those who know they are spiritually poor; the kingdom of heaven belongs to them! Happy are those who mourn; God will comfort them! Happy are those who are humble; they will receive what God has promised! ... Happy are those who are merciful to others; God will be merciful to them! Happy are the pure in heart; they will see God! Happy are those who work for peace; God will call them his children! Happy are those who are persecuted because they do what God requires; the kingdom of heaven belongs to them! Happy are you when people insult you and persecute you and tell all kinds of evil lies against you because you are my followers. Be happy and glad, for a great reward is kept for you in heaven."

Matthew 5: 1-12

> "Happy are those who are humble..."

Sharing the kingdom

While I have a job, our family still can't make ends meet. Just this past Christmas, when the car broke down and an expensive plumbing accident occurred, it really came down to food *or* water. Christmas presents, groceries, the car and the plumbing couldn't all see the light of day.

Just as our patience reached the breaking point, God's gifts poured forth. Our new landlady delayed cashing the rent cheque; a neighbour paid in advance for an upcoming odd job; a $100 anonymous gift arrived by mail; a friend offered a loan to fix the car; and a bountiful hamper arrived at our door. With humility and tearful spirits, we received the kingdom of God.

How can I be the kingdom of God for someone else today?

**Loving God, let me be a living blessing
for those around me today.**

"You are like salt for the whole human race. But if salt loses its saltiness, there is no way to make it salty again. It has become worthless, so it is thrown out and people trample on it. You are like light for the whole world. A city built on a hill cannot be hid. No one lights a lamp and puts it under a bowl; instead it is put on the lamp stand, where it gives light for everyone in the house. In the same way your light must shine before people, so that they will see the good things you do and praise your Father in heaven."

Matthew 5: 13-16

"You are like light for the whole world."

Tending the lamp

A prolonged blackout some years back gave me a new appreciation for lamps. We were without electricity for many days and had to rely on candles and oil lamps for light. I learned very quickly that keeping an oil lamp shining brightly requires much care and attention to detail.

I had to be vigilant in replenishing the oil when it ran low. I needed to keep the wick trimmed and adjust the flame continually to keep the glass free of soot and grime. Even finding the right location for the lamp – where it could be of greatest benefit – was important.

Caring for that oil lamp reminded me that, in a similar way, I need to take care so that God's light can shine brightly through me.

**Lord, help me to be vigilant when caring for your light in me.
May it shine forth to help others see your love.**

There is nothing in us that allows us to claim that we are capable of doing this work. The capacity we have comes from God; it is he who made us capable of serving the new covenant, which consists not of a written law but of the Spirit. The written law brings death, but the Spirit gives life.

The Law was carved in letters on stone tablets, and God's glory appeared when it was given. Even though the brightness on Moses' face was fading, it was so strong that the people of Israel could not keep their eyes fixed on him. If the Law, which brings death when it is in force, came with such glory, how much greater is the glory that belongs to the activity of the Spirit!

2 Corinthians 3: 4-11

"…but the Spirit gives life."

Spirit-filled words

One day, a teacher who used to work with me dropped by the office. She had quit because she was tired of all the rules that kept her from "connecting" with her students. She was a real headache to her administrators: she didn't enforce the rules and she seldom followed them herself. But, in the short time she was with us, she touched the lives of many students.

And she was an inspiration to me, Mr. Play-by-the-rules. She showed me how important it is to let go and let the Spirit guide my life.

I was having a "dry" day when she popped her head in the door. We talked, and I felt my soul welling up with the Spirit, as water in the desert.

**Lord, send your life-giving Spirit
into my dry world of rules and laws.**

"**G**o and preach, 'The kingdom of heaven is near!' Heal the sick, bring the dead back to life, heal those who suffer from dreaded skin diseases, and drive out demons. You have received without paying, so give without being paid. Do not carry any gold, silver, or copper money in your pockets; do not carry a beggar's bag for the trip or an extra shirt or shoes or a walking stick. Workers should be given what they need.

"When you come to a town or village, go in and look for someone who is willing to welcome you.... When you go into a house, say, 'Peace be with you.' If the people in that house welcome you, let your greeting of peace remain; but if they do not welcome you, then take back your greeting."

Matthew 10:7-13

"...so give without being paid."

Small acts of kindness

My thirteen-year-old son and I watched the movie *Gandhi* the other night. I wondered to myself: Does my son have any role models who do good, for reasons other than money? He seems to be growing up in such a selfish, materialistic world.

A couple of days later, my son started French tutorials with a high school student named John. I knew John had already fulfilled his volunteer requirements for graduation, but when I insisted that he take money for the tutoring, he steadfastly refused. I pushed the money into his hand, but he wouldn't take it. "It's OK. I enjoy doing this," he said.

My son learned something important that day: acts of service and sacrifice can be most powerful when they're small.

**Lord, let me do some small kindness today,
expecting nothing in return.**

Yet we who have this spiritual treasure are like common clay pots, in order to show that the supreme power belongs to God, not to us. We are often troubled, but not crushed; sometimes in doubt, but never in despair; there are many enemies, but we are never without a friend; and though badly hurt at times, we are not destroyed. At all times we carry in our mortal bodies the death of Jesus, so that his life also may be seen in our bodies. Throughout our lives we are always in danger of death for Jesus' sake, in order that his life may be seen in this mortal body of ours. This means that death is at work in us, but life is at work in you.

2 Corinthians 4: 7-15

> "We are often troubled, but not crushed…"

Hope in the darkness

As I write this reflection, we live on a knife-edge between fear and hope. The daughter of good friends, a childhood friend of our oldest son, lies in a hospital, her future unknown.

She was rushed there after coming home from a party and collapsing in the doorway. The drugs found in her system have taken her far away. She doesn't know who she, or anyone else, is – and no one can say whether she will ever come back.

Her mother asks for prayers and her family and friends wait in anguish. And I hope that Paul is right, and that this good family, so deeply hurt, is not crushed and destroyed, and has a Friend to help them.

Lord, show your friendship to those in crisis. Give them the strength they need to make their way through this dark time.

P raise the Lord, my soul,
and do not forget how kind he is.
He forgives all my sins
and heals all my diseases.
He keeps me from the grave
and blesses me with love and mercy....
The Lord is merciful and loving,
slow to become angry and full of constant love.
He does not keep on rebuking;
he is not angry forever.
He does not punish us as we deserve
or repay us according to our sins and wrongs.
As high as the sky is above the earth,
so great is his love for those who honour him.   *Psalm 103: 1-4, 8-12*

> "...and blesses me with love and mercy."

Open to change

I like to think of myself as a kind and loving person. But recently I've had to acknowledge how unforgiving I can be, and how I tend to hold onto grudges. This realization has left me shaken, and somewhat at a loss as to how I can change.

Today's psalm offers me some hope. While I may want to make others pay for the hurt I've experienced, the psalm reminds me that God "does not keep on rebuking... and does not punish us as we deserve." God does not treat me as I have been treating others.

It's easy to be kind when things are running smoothly. When the going gets tough, if I can immerse myself in God's love, then I will remain open and loving towards others.

Lord, fill me with your love and mercy so that I can be more loving and merciful with those around me.

Moses built an altar at the foot of the mountain and set up twelve stones, one for each of the twelve tribes of Israel. Then he sent young men, and they burned sacrifices to the Lord and sacrificed some cattle as fellowship offerings. Moses took half of the blood of the animals and put it in bowls; and the other half he threw against the altar. Then he took the book of the covenant, in which the Lord's commands were written, and read it aloud to the people. They said, "We will obey the Lord and do everything that he has commanded."

Then Moses took the blood in the bowls and threw it on the people. He said, "This is the blood that seals the covenant which the Lord made with you when he gave all these commands."

Exodus 24: 3-8

> "This is the blood that seals the covenant…"

Sealed with blood

Moses sealed the covenant God made with the Israelites with blood collected from sacrificial animals. Jesus sealed the covenant God makes with us with his own flesh and blood.

This week my son, Matthew, celebrates his fifteenth birthday. As I think back to the day of his birth, I am reminded of the covenant I made with him – to love and protect, to nurture and cherish, all the days of my life. That promise was sealed with my own body and blood.

Perhaps the promise to love someone – through good times and difficult times – needs to be rooted in this very physical experience of flesh and blood. Somehow it makes it very real. It's not something to be taken lightly. It's not something easily forgotten.

**Loving God, help me to live from your promise
to love me always, and from my promise to love others.**

"You have heard that it was said, 'An eye for an eye, and a tooth for a tooth.' But now I tell you: do not take revenge on someone who wrongs you. If anyone slaps you on the right cheek, let him slap your left cheek too. And if someone takes you to court to sue you for your shirt, let him have your coat as well. And if one of the occupation troops forces you to carry his pack one mile, carry it two miles. When someone asks you for something, give it to him; when someone wants to borrow something, lend it to him."

Matthew 5: 38-42

"...do not take revenge on someone who wrongs you."

The law of love

Jesus' words are difficult to grasp, given the widespread call for revenge I hear almost daily. Following the terrorist attacks of September 11th, 2001, there was an outpouring of love and concern – even among strangers. People came from all over to help the victims of the attacks and their families. Volunteers shared food and clothing; they worked day and night, to the point of exhaustion, for the sake of their neighbour. It seemed like nations might learn something profound from this response.

But that hope appears to have been short-lived. The larger political response has been vengeful, based on a determination to find and destroy the perpetrators, as if this is the only course of action. Have we forgotten the words of Jesus? He allows no exceptions to his law of love.

Lord Jesus, help us find a way to make peace with those who have harmed us.

"You have heard that it was said, 'Love your friends, hate your enemies.' But now I tell you: love your enemies and pray for those who persecute you, so that you may become the children of your Father in heaven. For he makes his sun to shine on bad and good people alike, and gives rain to those who do good and to those who do evil. Why should God reward you if you love only the people who love you? Even the tax collectors do that! And if you speak only to your friends, have you done anything out of the ordinary? Even the pagans do that! You must be perfect – just as your Father in heaven is perfect."

Matthew 5: 43-48

> "You must be perfect…"

Being there

Who can possibly be perfect? In *Jonathan Livingston Seagull*, Richard Bach describes Jonathan, a seagull determined to fly faster than anyone. Finally Jonathan discovers that "perfect speed is being there." It isn't how fast you fly but how present you are. In Luke's version of this passage, Jesus says, "Be compassionate as God is compassionate." Jesus says, "Perfection is being there."

For the last three years of my brother's life, my parents delayed many of their retirement dreams and plans. Instead, they chose to welcome Don back into their home while he battled first (successfully) alcoholism and then (unsuccessfully) lung disease. But from his first faltering attempts at sobriety to his last faltering attempts to breathe, they were there for him.

Being perfect is being there.

Jesus, teach me to be there for others.

Remember that the person who plants few seeds will have a small crop; the one who plants many seeds will have a large crop. You should each give, then, as you have decided, not with regret or out of a sense of duty; for God loves the one who gives gladly. And God is able to give you more than you need, so that you will always have all you need for yourselves and more than enough for every good cause....

And God, who supplies seed for the sower and bread to eat, will also supply you with all the seed you need and will make it grow and produce a rich harvest from your generosity. He will always make you rich enough to be generous at all times, so that many will thank God for your gifts which they receive from us.

2 Corinthians 9: 6-11

> "...you will always have all you need..."

Giving gladly

I am tired. Tired of being a single parent for so long. Tired of being the only one responsible for the needs – physical, social and emotional – of my children. Tired of giving. I am so tired that at times I feel I can't give anymore.

Today's reading reminds me that God has promised to give me more than I need. So I'll always have all I need – for myself, and "more than enough for every good cause." I tend to forget that promise, and try to do it all on my own. No wonder I run out of steam!

Turning to God doesn't change the day-to-day reality of my life. But it does give me a sense of peace, knowing someone is there who cares.

**Lord, remind me that you are there
and have promised to supply my every need, and more.**

"When you pray, do not use a lot of meaningless words.... Your Father already knows what you need before you ask him.

"This, then, is how you should pray: 'Our Father in heaven: May your holy kingdom come; may your will be done on earth as it is in heaven. Give us today the food we need. Forgive us the wrongs we have done, as we forgive the wrongs that others have done to us. Do not bring us to hard testing, but keep us from the Evil One. If you forgive others the wrongs they have done to you, your Father in heaven will also forgive you. But if you do not forgive others then your Father will not forgive the wrongs you have done."   *Matthew 6: 7-15*

"...as we forgive the wrongs that others have done..."

The challenge to forgive

Forgive others! I nod in agreement when I read about some religious conflict in a far-off country. But when it comes to me? To really forgive others is the hardest test of all.

While playing hockey, my son was hit low. Feet up, he landed heavily on his head and neck. He lay still on the ice, unmoving. My first thought was, "No! He'll be a quadriplegic!" As I watched in fear, some nearby fans yelled, "That'll teach him to keep his head up! Get him off the ice and get the game going." What did I feel as I listened? What does a father feel?

Luckily, my son suffered only a minor concussion. Still, it's hard, so hard, to forgive as Jesus tells me to.

Lord, give me wisdom. Help me leave my rage behind before it becomes hatred. Help me forgive.

The Jewish authorities asked Pilate to allow them to break the legs of the men who had been crucified, and to take the bodies down from the crosses. They requested this because it was Friday, and they did not want the bodies to stay on the crosses on the Sabbath.... So the soldiers went and broke the legs of the first man and then of the other man who had been crucified with Jesus. But when they came to Jesus, they saw that he was already dead, so they did not break his legs. One of the soldiers, however, plunged his spear into Jesus' side, and at once blood and water poured out.... This was done to make the scripture come true: "Not one of his bones will be broken," and... "People will look at him whom they pierced."

John 19: 31-37

> "People will look at him whom they pierced."

The scars of violence

I can scarcely imagine or understand the brutality Jesus experienced in his final hours. I live in a world where this degree of brutality is experienced only vicariously – on TV or at the movies. I know that I can turn off the TV or walk out of the theatre, leaving such violence behind me.

Yet friends and colleagues who have experienced this type of horror first-hand remember it with each missed birthday and anniversary. They carry the mental and physical scars within their bodies. And the violence lives on in the stories that are retold within their families and communities.

In listening to their stories, I touch the story of the one who loved me so much that he was willing to suffer these extreme brutalities.

**Jesus, let me share your pain more deeply,
so I can better love you.**

E very year the parents of Jesus went to Jerusalem..... When the Festival was over, they started back home, but the boy Jesus stayed in Jerusalem. His parents did not know this; they thought that he was with the group, so they travelled a whole day and then started looking for him among their relatives and friends. They did not find him, so they went back to Jerusalem looking for him. On the third day they found him in the Temple, sitting with the Jewish teachers, listening to them and asking questions.... His mother said to him, "Son, why have you done this to us? Your father and I have been terribly worried trying to find you."

He answered them, "Why did you have to look for me? Didn't you know that I had to be in my Father's house?"

Luke 2: 41-51

> "...I had to be in my Father's house."

God's call

Hannah works for an international agency in countries that are devastated by war. It's her job to see that food, medicine and shelter get to thousands of refugees every day. It's a demanding job. And it's dangerous. A friend of hers was killed recently when his jeep hit a landmine.

Hannah doesn't see herself as heroic or even particularly adventuresome. She says she is simply doing the work she loves.

Hannah's parents, however, live from phone call to phone call, and their anxiety skyrockets when she misses her weekly contact with them. During their sleepless nights it's hard for them to see these countries and this work as a calling from God, hard to accept that she has to be in her Father's house.

**Lord, help me to trust you
when the people I love put themselves in danger.**

Then out of the storm the Lord spoke to Job.
Who are you to question my wisdom
with your ignorant, empty words?
Now stand up straight
and answer the questions I ask you.
Were you there when I made the world?
If you know so much, tell me about it....
Who closed the gates to hold back the sea
when it burst from the womb of the earth?
It was I who covered the sea with clouds
and wrapped it in darkness.
I marked a boundary for the sea
and kept it behind bolted gates.
I told it, "So far and no farther!
Here your powerful waves must stop."

Job 38: 1-4, 8-11

"Who are you to question my wisdom?"

Challenging words

Poor Job. Who among us could handle such a harsh accusation: "Who are you to question my wisdom with your ignorant, empty words?" Especially those of us who write and speak for a living!

God's knee-knocking challenge to Job – after no end of personal ruin – comes in the form of a beautiful poem that begins to settle the seeming wreck of a life that is Job's. It is as if God has thrown the pieces of Job's life up in the air and, with this powerful poetic statement, is allowing them to come back down into place – but cleansed by strong winds.

Yes, God has read the riot act to Job. In ways that may not seem so poetic, God reads it to us, too.

Lord, help me to sort the chaotic pieces of my life.

"Do not judge others, so that God will not judge you, for God will judge you in the same way you judge others, and he will apply to you the same rules you apply to others. Why, then, do you look at the speck in your brother's eye and pay no attention to the log in your own eye? How dare you say to your brother, 'Please, let me take that speck our of your eye,' when you have a log in your own eye? You hypocrite! First take the log out of your own eye, and then you will be able to see clearly to take the speck out of your brother's eye."

Matthew 7: 1-5

> "First take the log out of your own eye…"

Overlooking faults

"There is nothing we are more intolerant of," wrote Gertrude Stein, "than our own sins writ large in others."

I enjoy reminding people that the character traits they find annoying in others may be the same ones they dislike most about themselves. And do I hate it when others point out the same thing to me! Knowing all these clever insights from pop psychology is just fine. But they alone can't help me escape my "hall of mirrors" – of burning resentment of others and embarrassment at my own shortcomings.

I want so much to "fix" other people by bombarding them with advice, criticism, even angry sarcasm. But, if I recall my own imperfections, as difficult as it is, then other people's faults seem to shrink magically away.

**God, help me to mend my own shortcomings
and ignore those of others.**

"Do not give what is holy to dogs – they will only turn and attack you. Do not throw your pearls in front of pigs – they will only trample them underfoot.

"Do for others what you want them to do for you: this is the meaning of the Law of Moses and of the teachings of the prophets.

"Go in through the narrow gate, because the gate to hell is wide and the road that leads to it is easy, and there are many who travel it. But the gate to life is narrow and the way that leads to it is hard, and there are few people who find it."   *Matthew 7: 6, 12-14*

"But the gate to life is narrow…"

To go beyond

As a child, I loved to walk by the sea. My beloved seashore, though, was definitely not easy terrain. Breathtaking beauty, rugged cliffs and frightening drops were all connected by the narrowest of paths which clung precariously to the rocks. Many days I felt unsafe walking there, and would turn back at a point called "Devil's Gulch."

But one day I was possessed with a wild courage that drew me beyond that impasse. I was staggered by the most glorious vista I'd ever seen! I encountered a holy scene of beauty that was seared onto my heart forever.

Since then, I've longed many times for the return of that same wild courage. It's the courage I need to go beyond the wide, easy path today.

**May I step beyond my fears today, O God,
and trust you will see me through.**

Lord, you have examined me and you know me.
You know everything I do;
from far away you understand all my thoughts.
You see me, whether I am working or resting;
you know all my actions....
You created every part of me;
you put me together in my mother's womb.
I praise you because you are to be feared;
all you do is strange and wonderful.
I know it with all my heart.
When my bones were being formed,
carefully put together in my mother's womb,
when I was growing there in secret,
you knew that I was there.

Psalm 139: 1-3, 13-15

> "...you put me together in my mother's womb."

God's plan

I look at my almost-grown children and am filled with amazement as I watch them get ready to step into the unknown future that beckons to them. They are unique – down to the tiniest detail, more compli-cated and intricate than anything modern science can imagine.

Yet I remember placing my hand on my wife's swelling belly for each one, feeling the just-forming life growing and moving within, and wondering, "Who are you?"

I find it comforting to think that my knowledge of them is a mere suggestion of the knowledge God has of them. I'm reassured to think that the God who put together these marvellous creations surely has a purpose in mind for them. They are here for a reason.

**Lord, help all children learn their purpose on this earth,
and give them the strength to meet it.**

"Not everyone who calls me 'Lord, Lord' will enter the kingdom of heaven, but only those who do what my Father in heaven wants them to do....

"So then, anyone who hears these words of mine and obeys them is like a wise man who built his house on rock. The rain poured down, the rivers flooded over, and the wind blew hard against that house. But it did not fall, because it was built on rock.

"But anyone who hears these words of mine and does not obey them is like a foolish man who built his house on sand. The rain poured down, the rivers flooded over, the wind blew hard against that house, and it fell. And what a terrible fall that was!"

Matthew 7: 21-29

"...it did not fall, because it was built on rock."

A supporting love

My mother was a woman of deep faith. Widowed at 29, with two small children, and living in a strange country, she kept our family together and in our own home.

At times Mother did not know where the money would come from, but she always prayed and worked hard to make ends meet. Through the years, her hard work and faith in God were rewarded. She retired comfortably and gave generously to others in need.

As the older child, I shared my mother's fears about paying the bills, and about an uncertain future. Over the years, I've struggled with anxiety. Now I turn to my mother's source of consolation, confident that God will support me with loving care.

**O God, when I am lonely and afraid,
help me to recognize your presence in my life.**

Happy are those who obey the Lord,
who live by his commands.
Your work will provide for your needs;
you will be happy and prosperous.
Your wife will be like a fruitful vine in your home,
and your children will be like young olive trees around your table.
A man who obeys the Lord
will surely be blessed like this.
May the Lord bless you from Zion!
May you see Jerusalem prosper
all the days of your life!

Psalm 128: 1-5

"…will surely be blessed like this."

One generation

I treasure the image of my father cradling his first grandchild in his worn and stubby hands. Retirement had not been easy for him. Then suddenly his world began to glow with light and hope and new meaning.

The baby was my young brother's; neither my sister nor I have children in our marriages. I think our parents had resigned themselves to seeing only one, rather than two generations follow them.

At times I look back and ponder what might have been, what could have been, if children had been part of my story. And I find it hard to relate to the multi-generational focus of today's reading when I look to a future that is, genealogically speaking, the end of a line.

Dear God, may I never feel alone, even when I am alone.

A Roman officer met Jesus and begged for help: "Sir, my servant is sick in bed at home, unable to move and suffering terribly."

"I will go and make him well," Jesus said.

"Oh no, sir," answered the officer. "I do not deserve to have you come into my house. Just give the order, and my servant will get well...."

When Jesus heard this, he was surprised and said to the people following him, "I tell you, I have never found anyone in Israel with faith like this...." Then Jesus said to the officer, "Go home, and what you believe will be done for you."

And the officer's servant was healed that very moment.

Matthew 8: 5-17

"When Jesus heard this, he was surprised..."

A surprise gift

A number of years ago, I taught religious education in a Catholic high school. I had a good sense of young people and knew how they labelled one another: the preps, the head bangers, the jocks, and so on. I tried to keep an open mind and not fall into the labelling game myself.

One day I was reading through the students' papers about their notion of God. I can't remember the details of his paper but I can remember being surprised at one student's insights. The main reason I was so surprised was that this student was a classic "head banger" – heavy metal t-shirt, long hair, studs. My experience had been that many of this "kind" of student had no use for religion or God.

What a gift he gave me!

Lord, keep my mind and heart open to the faith in others!

There was a woman who had suffered terribly from severe bleeding for twelve years, even though she had been treated by many doctors. She had spent all her money, but instead of getting better she got worse all the time. She had heard about Jesus, so she came behind him, saying to herself, "If I just touch his clothes, I will get well."

She touched his cloak, and her bleeding stopped at once; and she had the feeling inside herself that she was healed of her trouble. At once Jesus knew that power had gone out of him, so he turned around in the crowd and asked, "Who touched my clothes...?"

The woman realized what had happened to her, so she came, trembling with fear, knelt at his feet, and told him the whole truth. Jesus said, "My daughter, your faith has made you well. Go in peace, and be healed of your trouble."   *Mark 5: 21-43*

"She touched his cloak..."

True healing

My friend Janet lives with lupus, a chronic, debilitating disease. Someday, medical science may cure her; in the meantime, her only hope is the hem of Jesus' cloak.

Janet isn't waiting for a medical miracle, though I'm certain she'd welcome one. Instead, she embraces a miracle of a different sort – the grace of living each day to its fullest. Being as present as possible to her husband, her children, her friends and herself. She isn't "known" by her disease, but instead by her wry wit, her warm love and her good cheer.

Not every day, of course, but on most days, Janet does manage to touch the hem of Jesus' cloak simply by living well in this moment – and then in the next, and in the next.

God, let me make the most of life, one moment at a time.

J esus asked his disciples, "Who do people say the Son of Man is?" "Some say John the Baptist," they answered. "Others say Elijah, while others say Jeremiah or some other prophet."

"What about you?" he asked them. "Who do you say I am?" Simon Peter answered, "You are the Messiah, the Son of the living God."

"Good for you, Simon son of John!" answered Jesus. "For this truth did not come to you from any human being, but it was given to you directly by my Father in heaven. And so I tell you, Peter: you are a rock, and on this rock foundation I will build my church, and not even death will ever be able to overcome it. I will give you the keys of the kingdom of heaven."

Matthew 16: 13-19

"Who do you say I am?"

Living into the mystery

I'm not Peter. I'm one of the silent eleven, the ones who don't answer when Jesus asks them who they think he is. Sure, like them, I can repeat what others say: he's the Son of God, a prophet, a Jewish reformer, a social revolutionary, an ordinary man whose followers made him out to be something preposterous. And that's just for starters.

But if you ask me who I think he is… well, I just don't know. Sometimes I think I do, but always, at that moment, Jesus slips away into something I can't quite grasp.

Peter was lucky, for Jesus revealed the truth directly to him. For me, getting to know Jesus has become a journey into mystery, with not one but many possible answers.

Lord, you are an ever-mysterious presence in my life that I can't fully grasp. Help me to know you better.

" The kingdom of heaven is like this. Once there was a king who decided to check on his servants' accounts. He had just begun to do so when one of them was brought in who owed him millions of dollars. The servant did not have enough to pay his debt, so the king ordered him to be sold as a slave, with his wife and his children and all that he had, in order to pay the debt. The servant fell on his knees before the king. 'Be patient with me,' he begged, 'and I will pay you everything!' The king felt sorry for him, so he forgave him the debt and let him go."

Matthew 18: 23-27

"The king felt sorry for him, so he forgave him…"

Show no mercy

I teach in an inner-city school with a lot of challenging students. Their job is to try to bend the rules; my job is to enforce them. Sometimes it's tough to know when to bend and when to stick to the law. Why is it that we feel to show mercy is a sign of weakness?

No doubt the king in today's reading felt the need to assert his authority in the beginning. It was only when he really listened to how his decision would affect the life of the slave that he changed his mind.

I will remember this the next time one of my students pleads for a little mercy from me. May I have the same wisdom to know when to bend a little.

Loving God, help me to temper my judgment with mercy.

Whehn Jesus came to Gadara, he was met by two men who came out of the burial caves there. These men had demons in them and were so fierce that no one dared travel on that road. At once they screamed, "What do you want with us, you Son of God?"

Not far away there was a large herd of pigs feeding. So the demons begged Jesus, "If you are going to drive us out, send us into that herd of pigs."

"Go," Jesus told them; so they left and went off into the pigs. The whole herd rushed down the side of the cliff into the lake and was drowned. The men who had been taking care of the pigs ran away and went into the town, where they told the whole story.

Matthew 8: 28-34

> "...no one dared travel on that road."

Beyond my fears

As the last security gate clicked behind me I could feel my panic rising. It was my first time inside the Mental Health Centre, and images of "crazy people" filled my head. I was the newest member of a community outreach team, and I wasn't sure what or whom I might meet at the centre. I was afraid.

In the days that followed that visit and through subsequent debriefings, I learned to examine my fear and to replace it with compassion.

So often it's my own ignorance and fear that keep me from travelling the road with those who are most marginalized. Today's reading reminds me that Jesus was not afraid of that road. I know I will find him there when I travel it again.

Jesus, give me courage to follow you beyond my doubts, beyond my fears.

Thursday | JULY 2

The people brought Jesus a paralyzed man, lying on a bed. When Jesus saw how much faith they had, he said to the paralyzed man, "Courage, my son! Your sins are forgiven." Then some teachers of the Law said to themselves, "This man is speaking blasphemy!"

Jesus perceived what they were thinking, and so he said, "Why are you thinking such evil things? Is it easier to say, 'Your sins are forgiven,' or to say, 'Get up and walk'? I will prove to you, then, that the Son of Man has authority on earth to forgive sins." So he said to the paralyzed man, "Get up, pick up your bed, and go home!" The man got up and went home. *Matthew 9: 1-8*

"The people brought Jesus a paralyzed man…"

Get up and walk

Stories of biblical healings bother me. I don't doubt that they happened, but I can't help wondering why they don't still happen. Despite fervent and frequent prayer, a friend's cancer is not getting better. Nor is another friend's heart failure. My daughter could not get pregnant. My wife's glaucoma did not disappear.

Then I read this passage again. And I see that the man Jesus healed was paralyzed.

I remember the paralysis I feel when I need to phone someone I have wronged, to apologize. The paralysis I feel confronting hostility or opposition. The paralysis most editors suffer when they first attempt to improve a manuscript. Yet somehow we find the strength to continue.

Maybe healings are still going on, after all.

**When I can't motivate myself to act, Lord, I turn to you.
Tell me to get up and walk.**

One of the disciples, Thomas, was not with them when Jesus came. So the other disciples told him, "We have seen the Lord!" Thomas said, "Unless I see the scars of the nails in his hands and put my finger on those scars and my hand in his side, I will not believe."

A week later the disciples were together again indoors. The doors were locked, but Jesus came and stood among them and said, "Peace be with you." Then he said to Thomas, "Put your finger here, and look at my hands; then reach out your hand and put it in my side. Stop your doubting, and believe!" Thomas answered him, "My Lord and my God!"

Jesus said, "Do you believe because you see me? How happy are those who believe without seeing me!"   *John 20: 24-29*

"Stop your doubting, and believe!"

Doubting Thomas

When I was young, the hard-headed Thomas shocked me slightly. How could he have spent so much time with Jesus and still be so skeptical? How could he doubt his friends?

Gradually I came to like Thomas and, as my own uncertainty and questions grew, I even saw him as something of a role model. I felt envious that his doubts had been so easily put to rest. Who wouldn't say, "My Lord and my God" with the resurrected Jesus standing right there in front of them? But where does that leave those of us who weren't there?

Today I still like Thomas – although from a slightly different perspective. Life has taught me that struggling with doubt is good for the soul.

Lord, there are no scars for me to see nor wounds to touch. Help me with my doubts, my questions.

saac sent for his older son Esau and said, "Go out into the country, and kill an animal for me. Cook me some of that tasty food that I like, and bring it to me. After I have eaten it, I will give you my final blessing before I die."

Rebecca said to Jacob, "Go to the flock and pick out two fat young goats, so that I can cook them…. You can take it to Isaac to eat, and he will give you his blessing before he dies…." Then she took Esau's best clothes and put them on Jacob. She put the skins of the goats on his arms and on the hairless part of his neck:… Then Jacob went to his father and said, "Father!"

"Yes," he answered. "Which of my sons are you?" Jacob answered, "I am your older son Esau. Please sit up and eat some of the meat that I have brought you, so that you can give me your blessing."

Genesis 27: 1-5, 9-10, 15-29

> "Jacob answered, 'I am your older son Esau.'"

Lies and deception

When our son was about ten years old, he came home one day with a handful of valve caps he had stolen off cars parked on the street. Their value was minimal. Their loss didn't affect the tires. But I made him return them. I went with him, door-to-door, as he confessed to his theft and replaced the caps.

"Honesty is the best policy," my mother taught me.

And yet today's story tells me that a whole nation was based on a deception. Jacob and his mother conspired to steal the blessing, the birthright, that belonged to his older brother, so that his descendants could become God's chosen people.

Is it okay to lie to achieve God's purposes?

Life is complicated, God.
I need your wisdom to help me find my way.

J esus went back to his hometown, and on the Sabbath he began to teach in the synagogue. Many people were there; and when they heard him, they were all amazed. "Where did he get all this?" they asked. "What wisdom is this that has been given him? How does he perform miracles? Isn't he the carpenter, the son of Mary, and the brother of James, Joseph, Judas, and Simon? Aren't his sisters living here?" And so they rejected him.

Jesus said, "Prophets are respected everywhere except in their own hometown and by their relatives and their family."

He was not able to perform any miracles there, except that he placed his hands on a few sick people and healed them. He was greatly surprised, because the people did not have faith.

Mark 6: 1-6

"…except in their own hometown…"

Those with whom I live

So I'm not the only one who takes the people closest to me for granted! Yesterday, for example, a small but delightful thing happened that I barely noticed. My daughter was chattering away, telling me a charming story she'd made up about a mouse that lived in a suitcase with holes at the bottom for his legs to stick out. Busy with work, I hardly listened to her.

As a self-employed mother, I face the daily challenge of switching from work to family, and back again. I often fail, and when I stop to make supper or read a story, I'm not always truly present.

Today's reading inspires me to be more appreciative of the people with whom I live; that's where the miracles are going to happen.

Lord, give me eyes to see the signs of your presence all around me, each and every day.

A Jewish official came to Jesus and said, "My daughter has just died; but come and place your hands on her, and she will live." So Jesus got up and followed him....

A woman who had suffered from severe bleeding for twelve years came up behind Jesus and touched the edge of his cloak. She said to herself, "If only I touch his cloak, I will get well." Jesus turned around and saw her, and said, "Courage, my daughter! Your faith has made you well." At that very moment the woman became well.

Then Jesus went into the official's house. When he saw the musicians for the funeral and the people all stirred up, he said, "Get out, everybody! The little girl is not dead – she is only sleeping!" ... Jesus went into the girl's room and took hold of her hand, and she got up.

Matthew 9: 18-26

> "So Jesus got up and followed him..."

Trust that heals

I am astonished at this Jewish leader whose daughter has just died, and the woman who has been bleeding (and was therefore untouchable) for twelve years. They trust that just a touch from Jesus will bring healing.

I can't even conceive of such trust. When I am overwhelmed by my problems, I either blame someone else, resign myself to my miserable fate, or pester Jesus with long speeches without really hoping for much response.

Even the people around these two had accepted their fate as already sealed. Both were at the end of their own resources. The instant they turned to Jesus in simplicity of heart, and with trust, he walked into their lives, touched them at the centre of their pain, and healed them.

**Lord, you care about the dead or shameful areas of my life.
Touch me and heal me.**

Some people brought to Jesus a man who could not talk because he had a demon. But as soon as the demon was driven out, the man started talking, and everyone was amazed. "We have never seen anything like this in Israel!" they exclaimed. But the Pharisees said, "It is the chief of the demons who gives Jesus the power to drive out demons."

Jesus went around visiting all the towns and villages. He taught in the synagogues, preached the Good News about the kingdom, and healed people with every kind of disease and sickness. As he saw the crowds, his heart was filled with pity for them, because they were worried and helpless, like sheep without a shepherd.

Matthew 9: 32-38

"...they were worried and helpless..."

Like sheep

If there's one animal that my behaviour resembles when I am harassed, it's a sheep. The first thing that goes is my focus, and I run in every direction at once, and achieve nothing.

My behaviour has a snowball effect: the less I achieve, the more I panic. It is my family who suffers most from this sheep-like state. Qualities such as patience, listening and attentiveness disappear into the hills with a wag of their woolly tails.

I know that the only way to recover is to stop everything and bleat pitifully for my shepherd. Only God can cast out the demon of the pervasive messages of modern life that are so destructive of family and relationships.

Lord, at times I feel as if I have a demon within me.
Have pity on me and heal me.

J esus called his twelve disciples together and gave them authority to drive out evil spirits and to heal every disease and every sickness. These are the names of the twelve apostles: first, Simon (called Peter) and his brother Andrew; James and his brother John, the sons of Zebedee; Philip and Bartholomew; Thomas and Matthew, the tax collector; James son of Alphaeus, and Thaddaeus; Simon the Patriot, and Judas Iscariot, who betrayed Jesus.

These twelve men were sent out by Jesus with the following instructions: "Do not go to any Gentile territory or any Samaritan towns. Instead, you are to go to the lost sheep of the people of Israel. Go and preach, 'The kingdom of heaven is near!'"

Matthew 10: 1-7

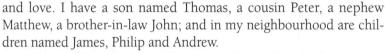

"These are the names of the twelve apostles..."

Called by name

I have a hard time connecting scripture with the reality of my life here and now. But the list of names in today's reading links me directly: these are the names of people I know and love. I have a son named Thomas, a cousin Peter, a nephew Matthew, a brother-in-law John; and in my neighbourhood are children named James, Philip and Andrew.

The connection between the names, then and now, allows me to imagine the disciples as regular people who have simply taken on a more challenging role in the community.

And, since there's nothing extraordinary about them, they encourage me to do today what they did 2000 years ago: "Go and preach, 'The kingdom of heaven is near!'"

**Lord, open my ears so I may hear you calling me
to proclaim the kingdom.**

"Go and preach, 'The kingdom of heaven is near!' Heal the sick, bring the dead back to life, heal those who suffer from dreaded skin diseases, and drive out demons. You have received without paying, so give without being paid. Do not carry any gold, silver or copper money in your pockets; do not carry a beggar's bag for the trip or an extra shirt or shoes or a walking stick. Workers should be given what they need.

"When you come to a town or village, go in and look for someone who is willing to welcome you, and stay with him until you leave that place.... And if some home or town will not welcome you or listen to you, then leave that place and shake the dust off your feet."

Matthew 10: 7-15

"...do not carry a beggar's bag for the trip..."

An unseen love

Memories flash before me as I think of Jesus walking among the disciples, straightening a robe, brushing off a shoulder, worried as he watches them go off to a future they cannot see.

Thirty years ago, my mother brushed me off and sent me away to college. I remember her watching from the window, receding in the distance as I ventured off into the world. Twenty years later, I watched my son go off alone, to his friend's fourth birthday party.

As God watches us go to find our joys and sorrows, struggling and stumbling on our way, does he worry? Does God, like me and my mother before me, like Jesus with his disciples, send his love along – unseen but always there to help me through?

God, as I go out into the world,
let me always be aware of your presence.

"Listen! I am sending you out just like sheep to a pack of wolves. You must be as cautious as snakes and as gentle as doves. Watch out, for there will be those who will arrest you and take you to court, and they will whip you in the synagogues. For my sake you will be brought to trial before rulers and kings, to tell the Good News to them and to the Gentiles. When they bring you to trial, do not worry about what you are going to say or how you will say it; when the time comes, you will be given what you will say. For the words you will speak will not be yours; they will come from the Spirit of your Father speaking through you."

Matthew 10: 16-23

"...you will be given what you will say."

Open to the Spirit

The other day a telemarketer called my cousin Tim, offering a year's subscription to the local newspaper. "I won't be able to use a year's subscription," Tim said "I'm dying of cancer."

"Well, then," said the voice, "how about a six-week trial subscription of the new national newspaper?" Concentrating on a prepared speech made the telemarketer deaf to what Tim was saying.

Jesus tells me not to worry about what I am going to say. Then I can pay attention to the real-life problems of the people I meet – with all their complexity. If I have kept myself open to the Spirit in prayer and reflection, I can trust in the Spirit to give me the right words to use at the right moment.

Lord, help me to see and hear what's around me, rather than blindly trying to impose my ready-made answers.

"Whatever is now covered up will be uncovered, and every secret will be made known. What I am telling you in the dark you must repeat in broad daylight, and what you have heard in private you must announce from the housetops. Do not be afraid of those who kill the body but cannot kill the soul; rather be afraid of God, who can destroy both body and soul in hell. For only a penny you can buy two sparrows, yet not one sparrow falls to the ground without your Father's consent. As for you, even the hairs of your head have all been counted. So do not be afraid; you are worth much more than many sparrows!

"Those who declare publicly that they belong to me, I will do the same for them before my Father in heaven."   *Matthew 10: 24-33*

"So do not be afraid…"

Precious in God's eyes

A few years after the event, some friends and family of those killed in the World Trade Center on September 11, 2001, travelled to Iraq to meet and pray with Iraqi people who also had lost loved ones through violence. This gesture put a human face on a people and a country on whom public fear had been projected. They discovered their common humanity and compassion for one another.

This action – of moving towards that which we fear – reminds me of how I used to be afraid of people with disabilities. But when I came to know several disabled individuals personally, in fact I discovered a treasure.

In today's reading, Jesus tells us, "Do not be afraid." He invites us to discover that each human life, like the sparrow, is precious in God's eyes.

**Lord, help me to move beyond my fears
to discover the worth of each person.**

H e called the twelve disciples together and sent them out two by two. He gave them authority over the evil spirits and ordered them, "Don't take anything with you on the trip except a walking stick – no bread, no beggar's bag, no money in your pockets. Wear sandals, but don't carry an extra shirt." He also told them, "Wherever you are welcomed, stay in the same house until you leave that place. If you come to a town where people do not welcome you or will not listen to you, leave it and shake the dust off your feet. That will be a warning to them!"

So they went out and preached that people should turn away from their sins. They drove out many demons, and rubbed olive oil on many sick people and healed them.

Mark 6: 7-13

> "...stay in the same house..."

Stay awhile

Many years ago, two of my friends set out to find where they could be of service to people. They travelled for a year and eventually came back to their native city where, in one of the poorest neighbourhoods, they established a "community of presence."

In the ordinariness of their daily lives, their homes have become places of refuge for men and women who have no other place to turn, places of safety for children whose homes are not safe havens.

Now, nearly 30 years later, the neighbourhood has changed: people are taking pride in their property, there is less violence and there is a strong sense of hope – because two people were willing to "stay in the same house" and serve the Lord.

Thank you, Lord, for people who witness to your love with their lives.

What if the Lord had not been on our side?
Answer, O Israel!
"If the Lord had not been on our side
when our enemies attacked us,
then they would have swallowed us alive
in their furious anger against us;
then the flood would have carried us away,
the water would have covered us,
the raging torrent would have drowned us."
Let us thank the Lord,
who has not let our enemies destroy us....
Our help comes from the Lord,
who made heaven and earth.

Psalm 124: 1-8

"What if the Lord had not been on our side?"

On our side?

This is where David, the psalmist, and I part company. The idea that God takes sides gives me shivers. I must stop myself from concluding there are God-sanctioned losers.

Was God taking sides when the tsunami rolled over Southeast Asia? I remember that the newspapers were filled with commentary from non-believers and believers alike: God is cruel, God is kind, God is mystery, God is fiction. It was all quite chilling – in the face of the international outpouring of compassion and assistance.

But I'm with David when he says, "our help comes from the Lord," because that help is never what I expect – or even recognize. It will take me a lifetime to recognize the actions of God in this world.

Dear God, give me the courage to trust in your presence, even amid contradiction and confusion.

T he people in the towns where Jesus had performed most of his miracles did not turn from their sins, so he reproached those towns. "How terrible it will be for you, Chorazin... [and] Bethsaida! If the miracles which were performed in you had been performed in Tyre and Sidon, the people there would have long ago put on sackcloth and sprinkled ashes on themselves, to show that they had turned from their sins! I assure you that on Judgment Day God will show more mercy to the people of Tyre and Sidon than to you! And as for you, Capernaum... if the miracles which were performed in you had been performed in Sodom, it would still be in existence today! You can be sure that on Judgment Day God will show more mercy to Sodom than to you!"

Matthew 11: 20-24

> "If the miracles which were performed in you..."

A call to change

I cringe when Jesus sounds so angry. I'd rather he pray serenely, bless the children, teach the crowds, work a miracle – do the sorts of things he does in popular pictures. I imagine the people of Chorazin and Bethsaida felt the same way.

Jesus is angry because, even after he went about doing good, the people still refused to repent – just as I hesitate to make any radical changes in my life. I still measure out my commitment to him on a day-to-day basis.

It's easy to say I just don't like the image of an angry Jesus. It's a lot more honest to say that my discomfort is with his anger and what it implies about me. I could, this very moment, repent. Will I?

**Jesus, help me to take my focus off your anger
and to put it on my repentance.**

One day while Moses was taking care of the sheep and goats of his father-in-law Jethro, the priest of Midian, he led the flock across the desert and came to Sinai, the holy mountain. There the angel of the Lord appeared to him as a flame coming from the middle of a bush. Moses saw that the bush was on fire but that it was not burning up. "This is strange," he thought. "Why isn't the bush burning up? I will go closer and see."

When the Lord saw that Moses was coming closer, he called to him from the middle of the bush and said, "Moses! Moses!" He answered, "Yes, here I am." God said, "Do not come any closer. Take off your sandals, because you are standing on holy ground."
Exodus 3: 1-6, 9-12

"...you are standing on holy ground."

Glimpses of God

Jane has an amazing capacity to give love, even in the face of difficulties. Born with Down's syndrome, she spent much of her childhood in a large institution where she experienced many difficult and oppressive situations. Yet her irrepressible buoyancy helps her to keep smiling. She walks with a determined stride and a mischievous sense of play.

I marvel at Jane. Her resilient spirit reminds me of the burning bush that Moses saw, which was "on fire but... was not burning up."

Moses was tending his sheep – making his daily rounds – when he came upon the amazing bush. At times, my daily life can seem monotonous. But then, unexpectedly, in the people I meet, I catch sudden glimpses of God's ardent, irrepressible love.

Lord, may I be attentive to the signs of your love today.

"Come to me, all of you who are tired from carrying heavy loads, and I will give you rest. Take my yoke and put it on you, and learn from me, because I am gentle and humble in spirit; and you will find rest. For the yoke I will give you is easy, and the load I will put on you is light."

Matthew 11:28-30

"...the load I will put on you is light."

A lighter load

I try to imagine the people listening to Jesus: bodies aching from work, or eyes weary from studying the law. Has the load of living ever been light – for anyone?

Are they listening to Jesus at the end of their day, the sun beating down on them? Or is it late, and they're bathed in the light of the moon?

I remember a night, and the moon in my window. My wife and one child sick; I'm wearily pacing the floor with the other child. Feeling the load. Then, looking up at the moon, thinking, "In 30 years, what would I pay to be here, holding this child, having this moment again?" And my load became lighter: duty became joy, obligation became a gift.

It's funny how love changes things.

**Lord, let me accept what is sent to me as gift.
Help me realize that my load is light.**

Jesus was walking through some wheat fields on a Sabbath. His disciples were hungry, so they began to pick heads of wheat and eat the grain. When the Pharisees saw this, they said to Jesus, "Look, it is against our Law for your disciples to do this on the Sabbath!"

Jesus answered, "Have you never read what David did that time when he and his men were hungry? He went into the house of God, and he and his men ate the bread offered to God, even though it was against the Law for them to eat it.... I tell you that there is something here greater than the Temple. The scripture says, 'It is kindness that I want, not animal sacrifices.' If you really knew what this means, you would not condemn people who are not guilty."   *Matthew 12: 1-8*

> "It is kindness that I want, not animal sacrifices."

Breaking the rules

As a teacher, I struggle every day with the issue of *rules*. Rules provide structure and order – essential things when there are 1500 teenagers in the same building!

On the other hand, I am dealing with human beings – and the rules can get in the way of compassion and understanding.

The Pharisees wanted to adopt a "zero tolerance" approach. As parenting guru Barbara Coloroso has said, "Zero tolerance means zero thinking." And zero compassion.

How many times have I been the exception to the rule? I must allow others the same dignity. The spirit of the law is, indeed, more important than the letter. When faced with a choice between a person's needs and the rules, I'll go with the person.

Lord, give me the wisdom to put people first,
and to show compassion in applying rules of any kind.

The Israelites set out on foot from Rameses for Sukkoth. There were about 600,000 men, not counting women and children. A large number of other people and many sheep, goats and cattle also went with them. They baked unleavened bread from the dough that they had brought out of Egypt, for they had been driven out of Egypt so suddenly that they did not have time to get their food ready or to prepare leavened dough.

The Israelites had lived in Egypt for 430 years. On the day the 430 years ended, all the tribes of the Lord's people left Egypt. It was a night when the Lord kept watch to bring them out of Egypt; this same night is dedicated to the Lord for all time to come as a night when the Israelites must keep watch

Exodus 12: 37-42

"...they did not have time to get their food ready..."

Stepping out

The Israelites didn't follow their own time-table. When God invited them to freedom, they didn't even wait for the bread to rise; they carried the dough on their backs. They walked alongside people who weren't of their own crowd, driving herds of animals before them across the desert. As they set out, how free did they feel?

What stops me from casting off my shackles? I don't feel ready to set out on the journey to which God invites me: there's unfinished business, baggage I'd have to take with me. Reluctance to be with people I might not have chosen as friends. Freedom? That desert looks pretty bleak from here. I'll have to take that first step blind, ready or not.

Lord, there isn't a better moment. I'll go now.

The Lord is my shepherd;
I have everything I need.
He lets me rest in fields of green grass
and leads me to quiet pools of fresh water.
He gives me new strength.
He guides me in the right paths,
as he has promised.
Even if I go through the deepest darkness,
I will not be afraid, Lord,
for you are with me.
Your shepherd's rod and staff protect me....
I know that your goodness and love
will be with me all my life;
and your house will be my home
as long as I live.

Psalm 23: 1-6

"I will not be afraid, for you are with me."

In dark times

My daughter and her husband have long wanted a baby. Several months ago, my daughter got pregnant. When she lost the baby shortly afterward, we took comfort in the fact that she had at least conceived.

When she got pregnant again, we were thrilled. We felt that God had heard our prayers and had turned his merciful face towards her.

A few weeks later, she lost the second baby.

What is there to say to my daughter and her husband? They want to know why this has happened, even though they realize that no answer will take away their pain. I only pray they continue to trust that God is with them, no matter how dark life seems.

**Lord, guide all those who struggle to know you
in their deepest darkness.**

When the king of Egypt was told that the people had escaped, he and his officials changed their minds... and [the king] pursued the Israelites, who were leaving triumphantly. The Egyptian army, with all the horses, chariots and drivers, pursued them and caught up with them where they were camped by the Red Sea.

When the Israelites saw the king and his army marching against them, they were terrified and cried out to the Lord for help. They said to Moses, "Weren't there any graves in Egypt? Did you have to bring us out here in the desert to die? Look what you have done by bringing us out of Egypt...." Moses answered, "Don't be afraid! Stand your ground, and you will see what the Lord will do to save you today...."

The Lord said to Moses, "Why are you crying out for help? Tell the people to move forward. Lift up your walking stick and hold it out over the sea. The water will divide, and the Israelites will be able to walk through the sea on dry ground."   *Exodus 14: 5-18*

"Don't be afraid!"

Passing to new life

Today's passage makes me think of my eldest son, who is on the verge of leaving home. For the most part, he feels confident about his choices, and wants to be treated as an adult. Other days, things look a little scary, and he wants me to reassure, even solve his problems.

Like Moses, I encourage my son not to be afraid. To trust the process. To trust himself. To know that God is with him – even when he is frightened and unsure.

I am reminded that I too need to turn to God for guidance. And to respond with patience to my son's anxiety. I need to believe that God is with us, and will see us safely through to the other side.

God, when I face new challenges,
help me to know that you are with me.

M oses held out his hand over the sea, and the Lord drove the sea back with a strong east wind. It blew all night and turned the sea into dry land. The water was divided, and the Israelites went through the sea on dry ground, with walls of water on both sides. The Egyptians pursued them and went after them into the sea with all their horses, chariots, and drivers. Just before dawn the Lord looked down from the pillar of fire and cloud at the Egyptian army and threw them into a panic. He made the wheels of their chariots get stuck, so that they moved with great difficulty. The Egyptians said, "The Lord is fighting for the Israelites against us. Let's get out of here…!"

On that day the Lord saved the people of Israel from the Egyptians.

Exodus 14: 21 – 15: 1, 20-21

> "…the Israelites went through the sea on dry ground…"

The journey to freedom

The Israelites walked to freedom with "walls of water on both sides" of them. What a dramatic story! But does God still lead people from the dark confines of slavery to the bright light of freedom today?

Karyn yearned to be free from the slavery of an eating disorder. It had remained a secret for so long, and it was ruining her life. Then, one day, driven by the desire to break free, she found the courage to tell her secret to a trusted counsellor.

Her journey back to freedom has begun. Not to say that it will be quick or easy. The "enemy" lurks at every twist and turn of the road. But with God at her side, Karyn believes she can walk this path with confidence.

Lord, give me the insight to recognize where I am not free, and the courage to seek the freedom you promise.

Mary Magdalene went to the tomb and saw that the stone had been taken away from the entrance.... She turned around and saw Jesus standing there; but she did not know that it was Jesus. She thought he was the gardener, so she said to him, "If you took him away, sir, tell me where you have put him, and I will go and get him."

Jesus said to her, "Mary!" She turned toward him and said in Hebrew, "Rabboni!" (This means "Teacher.")

Jesus told her, "Go to my brothers and tell them that I am returning to him who is my Father and their Father." So Mary Magdalene went and told the disciples that she had seen the Lord.

John 20: 1, 11-18

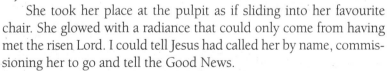

"So Mary Magdalene went and told…"

Words that heal

I met Mary Magdalene recently. She was nineteen years old, and I heard her preach at her grandpa's funeral. I couldn't believe my ears.

She took her place at the pulpit as if sliding into her favourite chair. She glowed with a radiance that could only come from having met the risen Lord. I could tell Jesus had called her by name, commissioning her to go and tell the Good News.

And she did: she spoke of God's love, the rifts in her grandpa's family, and God's promise of consolation. Her words aimed straight for hurting hearts. There was no place to hide from their healing power.

Mary Magdalene, help me to proclaim the Good News with courage and with boldness.

The disciples asked Jesus, "Why do you use parables when you talk to the people?"

Jesus answered, "The reason I use parables in talking to them is that they look, but do not see, and they listen, but do not hear or understand. So the prophecy of Isaiah applies to them: 'This people will listen and listen, but not understand; they will look and look, but not see, because their minds are dull, and they have stopped up their ears and have closed their eyes.'

"As for you, how fortunate you are! Your eyes see and your ears hear. I assure you that many prophets and many of God's people wanted very much to see what you see, but they could not, and to hear what you hear, but they did not."   *Matthew 13: 10-17*

"Your eyes see and your ears hear."

Seeing God

Recently I saw the work of Marion Tuu'luq, an Inuit artist from Nunavut. For more than 80 years she captured vivid images of her life in the Arctic through the media of fabric and thread. As I walked through room after room of large, hand-stitched wall hangings, I was spellbound by the beautiful patterns of animals, human faces, hearts, fish, leaves and flowers.

Marion Tuu'luq's life on the land had been hard – only four of her sixteen children survived. Yet her fabric paintings showed her faith in God, her joy in the seasons, and her unique creative vision that celebrated the interconnectedness of all living things.

How fortunate she was: her eyes could see and her ears could hear the signs of God's creation.

Thank you, bountiful God, for the gift of life.

"Those who hear the message about the kingdom but do not understand it are like the seeds that fell along the path. The Evil One comes and snatches away what was sown in them. The seeds that fell on rocky ground stand for those who receive the message gladly as soon as they hear it. But it does not sink deep into them, and they don't last long. So when trouble or persecution comes because of the message, they give up at once. The seeds that fell among thorn bushes stand for those who hear the message; but the worries about this life and the love for riches choke the message, and they don't bear fruit. And the seeds sown in the good soil stand for those who hear the message and understand it: they bear fruit."

Matthew 13: 18-23

> "Those who hear the message about the kingdom…"

Life's thorn bushes

In a way, I'm like all those soil conditions – my struggles taking different forms at different times. *Hearing but not understanding* – how often am I in a situation, just not knowing what to do? *Seeds on rocky ground that don't sink deep* – while I may agree with this passage, when parents start to dissect my son's soccer coach, do I say, "Let the one who is without sin…"?

But it's *the thorn bushes* most of all – in the rough and tumble of everyday life, it's hard to keep focused on what is true and important. Concerns about school closures, layoffs and how to pay for the repairs to the bathroom close in, choking me. They are like the thorn bushes, and every day I must hack them down to keep them at bay.

Lord, may I be fertile ground for your love.

T he wife of Zebedee asked Jesus a favour.... "Promise me that these two sons of mine will sit at your right and your left when you are king."

"You don't know what you are asking for," Jesus answered the sons. "Can you drink the cup of suffering that I am about to drink?" "We can," they answered.

"You will indeed drink from my cup," Jesus told them, "but I do not have the right to choose who will sit at my right and my left. These places belong to those for whom my Father has prepared them."

Jesus called the disciples together and said, "If one of you wants to be great, you must be the servant of the rest; and if one of you wants to be first, you must be the slave of the other."

Matthew 20: 20-28

> "...you must be the servant of the rest."

Leading by example

I think that I'm a lot like Zebedee's wife. I want my young daughter to be brilliant and am eager for others to recognize her brilliance.

But today's reading reminds me that I shouldn't try to teach her how to impress others. Rather, I need to teach her how to recognize the hopes and the needs of others, and to respond to them. And the best way to teach my daughter is through example.

I am challenged to examine my own life and ask: In my relationships, do I try to get the upper hand? Do I look for recognition for myself? Or do I try to love others the way Jesus loved – humbly, willing to give of my time, my energy, my material goods, even my life?

Lord, in my relationships, teach me to seek the other's good instead of recognition for myself.

A ll your creatures, Lord, will praise you,
and all your people will give you thanks.
They will speak of the glory of your royal power
and tell of your might….
All living things look hopefully to you,
and you give them food when they need it.
You give them enough
and satisfy the needs of all.
The Lord is righteous in all he does,
merciful in all his acts.
He is near to those who call to him,
who call to him with sincerity.

Psalm 145: 10-11, 15-18

"All living things look hopefully to you…"

Following God

Sometimes I find the sunflowers preaching to me. They grow – nearly two metres tall – in my backyard garden. When I glance their way in the morning, I see their huge blooms bending eastward. Later, near midday, they stretch themselves straight up towards the sky. And by afternoon they have twirled themselves to reach towards the setting sun in the west.

I never actually see them move, but they "look hopefully" towards the sun all day long, knowing that its light offers them the nourishment they need.

These flowers make me ask myself whether I follow God as well as they follow the sun. I seldom do, but their silent swoop across the day reminds me to bring myself back to the One who nourishes me.

God, draw me to your goodness all day long,
as the sun draws the sunflower.

"The kingdom of heaven is like this. A man takes a mustard seed and sows it in his field. It is the smallest of all seeds, but when it grows up, it is the biggest of all plants. It becomes a tree, so that birds come and make their nests in its branches."

Jesus told another parable: "The kingdom of heaven is like this. A woman takes some yeast and mixes it with a bushel of flour until the whole batch of dough rises."

Jesus used parables to tell these things to the crowds; he would not say a thing to them without using a parable. He did this to make come true what the prophet had said, "I will use parables when I speak to them; I will tell them things unknown since the creation of the world."

Matthew 13: 31-35

"It is the smallest of all seeds…"

The small things

A friend of mine is getting old. I think of him often these days. He was the pastor of our parish and he accomplished many things. He was an innovator. He took a musty old parish and brought it to life. Within a few short years it had become the most vibrant parish in the area, with many people involved.

When I think of him, however, it is not those great things I remember. I always think of the small things: a laugh in difficult, trying times. A compliment to someone who had helped out. Now and then, a pizza for the youth.

Those who knew him then remember all those small things. He would say he did nothing. But he'd be wrong.

Lord, let me start by being kind,
by paying attention to the small things.

"The man who sowed the good seed is the Son of Man; the field is the world; the good seed is the people who belong to the kingdom; the weeds are the people who belong to the Evil One; and the enemy who sowed the weeds is the Devil. The harvest is the end of the age, and the harvest workers are angels. Just as the weeds are gathered up and burned in the fire, so the same thing will happen at the end of the age; the Son of Man will send out his angels to gather up out of his kingdom all those who cause people to sin and all others who do evil things, and they will throw them into the fiery furnace…. Then God's people will shine like the sun in their Father's kingdom."

Matthew 13: 36-43

> "The harvest is the end of the age…"

Leave the weeds

Community life is often messy. There are always "weeds" in it: people who I feel don't quite belong. They think differently than I do or take up too much space. I'm tempted to think, "If only that person wasn't here, the community would be perfect."

The problem is that my judgments are not always reliable. Often that irritating person has something vital to contribute: something that I can't or am not willing to see at the time.

Jesus tells me it is dangerous to judge. I might be damaging some of the wheat in trying to pull out what I consider to be weeds. I am a much better community member if I can refrain from judging, and instead encourage the wheat to grow, even when it seems to be weedy.

**Lord, help me to be non-judgmental
of those with whom I live and work.**

"**A**s Jesus and his disciples went on their way, he came to a village where a woman named Martha welcomed him in her home. She had a sister named Mary, who sat down at the feet of the Lord and listened to his teaching. Martha was upset over all the work she had to do, so she came and said, "Lord, don't you care that my sister has left me to do all the work by myself ? Tell her to come and help me!"

The Lord answered her, "Martha, Martha! You are worried and troubled over so many things, but just one is needed. Mary has chosen the right thing, and it will not be taken away from her."

Luke 10: 38-42

"...troubled over so many things..."

A fine balance

Recently I helped organize a conference that required a lot of backroom work. Some of the participants commented, "We didn't see and interact with the team enough; they always seemed so busy!"

I'm often faced with this dilemma: do I get the job done or do I take time to listen to God speaking to me – through others?

Every now and again, God calls me to set aside time to be still. But spending a day or two on retreat doesn't seem to be an efficient use of my time.

I know that spending time listening to God is what gives me life. Getting the things done in my home and work is important, also. Knowing – and living – the balance is the key.

Lord, help me as I search for balance in my life.

Thursday | JULY 30

" The kingdom of heaven is like this. Some fishermen throw their net out in the lake and catch all kinds of fish. When the net is full, they pull it to shore and sit down to divide the fish: the good ones go into the buckets, the worthless ones are thrown away. It will be like this at the end of the age: the angels will go out and gather up the evil people from among the good and will throw them into the fiery furnace....

"Do you understand these things?" Jesus asked them. "Yes," they answered. So he replied, "This means, then, that every teacher of the Law who becomes a disciple in the kingdom of heaven is like a home-owner who takes new and old things out of his storage room."   *Matthew 13: 47-52*

"...and sit down to divide the fish..."

Letting God judge

Sylvia had worked her heart out providing leadership to a local environmental project. Then, just as all her efforts were beginning to bear fruit, the president of the association managed to squeeze her out and garner all the credit for himself.

The people who'd worked with Sylvia began organizing a petition to have the president removed. But Sylvia asked them to drop the idea. An attempted coup would drain everyone's energy away from the important job of making their town a healthier place to live.

We are all caught up in the net of life: the selfish with the generous, the phony with the genuine. Like Sylvia, I find peace of mind leaving it to God to sort out who gets the credit in the end.

**Lord, keep my eyes fixed on the important goals in life.
Don't let resentment distract me.**

Friday | JULY 31

When Jesus finished telling these parables, he left that place and went back to his hometown. He taught in the synagogue, and those who heard him were amazed. "Where did he get such wisdom?" they asked. "And what about his miracles? Isn't he the carpenter's son? Isn't Mary his mother, and aren't James, Joseph, Simon, and Judas his brothers? Aren't all his sisters living here? Where did he get all this?" And so they rejected him.

Jesus said to them, "A prophet is respected everywhere except in his hometown and by his own family." Because they did not have faith, he did not perform many miracles there.

Matthew 13: 54-58

"Where did he get such wisdom?"

Seeing the truth

Not so long ago, a dear friend of mine died. The services at both the funeral home and the church were filled to overflowing. Friends, neighbours and colleagues came to express their deep sorrow at his passing and to share with one another stories of his life among them. To my surprise, my friend's family was unprepared for this response and exclaimed, "We're overwhelmed! We thought no one would be here."

How sad that they did not know their son and brother as the trusted confidant, respected colleague, committed parent, caring friend and neighbour that so many had come to know and love.

How sad that, holding onto old familiar views of them, I miss discovering who my own family members and friends have become.

**Lord, help me to love others –
not as they were, but as they are.**

The Lord commanded Moses to give the following regulations to the people of Israel…. "Count seven times seven years, a total of forty-nine years. Then, on the tenth day of the seventh month, the Day of Atonement, send someone to blow a trumpet throughout the whole land. In this way you shall set the fiftieth year apart and proclaim freedom to all the inhabitants of the land. During this year all property that has been sold shall be restored to the original owner or the descendants, and any who have been sold as slaves shall return to their families. You shall not plant your fields or harvest the grain that grows by itself or gather the grapes in your unpruned vineyards. The whole year shall be sacred for you."

Leviticus 25: 1, 8-17

"Count seven times seven years…"

Necessary rest

Late one evening, after several hours of conversation around the dinner table, I asked our host about the importance of being Jewish. Clearly, he was not rigorous about his religion. He had served us steak garnished with Stilton cheese, a mix of meat and dairy products – definitely *not* kosher.

"It starts with the Sabbath," he said, thoughtfully. "On the seventh day, God rested. On the seventh day, we are to follow God's example. That's the foundation of all Judaism."

The seventh day, the seventh year, the seventh group of seven years. At the seventh of anything, they rested. They rested their relationships, setting slaves free. They rested the land that produced their crops. They rested from their travels, so that they could begin anew the next day.

**If taking time off was good enough for you,
God, can I afford not to?**

The whole Israelite community set out from Elim, and on the fifteenth day of the second month after they had left Egypt, they came to the desert of Sin. They complained to Moses and Aaron: "We wish that the Lord had killed us in Egypt. There we could at least sit down and eat meat and as much other food as we wanted. But you have brought us out into this desert to starve us all to death."

The Lord said to Moses, "Now I am going to cause food to rain down from the sky for all of you. The people must go out every day and gather enough for that day. In this way I can test them to find out if they will follow my instructions. On the sixth day they are to bring in twice as much as usual."

Exodus 16: 1-5, 9-15

"They complained to Moses and Aaron…"

Blaming the leader

It's almost a rule: when things go wrong, people blame their leaders. So when the desert turned out to be less like paradise than the fertile banks of the Nile, the Hebrew people blamed Moses and Aaron.

Last summer, my friend Dave and I hiked up the Geraldine Lakes in Jasper National Park. I thought we were just going to the base of a waterfall. But Dave was ahead. And Dave kept going – up a viciously slippery gully clogged with scree, right to the top of the falls. When I finally caught up with him, I protested, "Why did you lead us all the way up here?"

"Don't blame me," he shrugged. "Every time I looked back, you were right behind me!"

**God, remind me that I share responsibility
for whatever happens – to me, to my nation, to my world.**

There were foreigners travelling with the Israelites. They had a strong craving for meat, and even the Israelites themselves began to complain: "If only we could have some meat! In Egypt we used to eat all the fish we wanted, and it cost us nothing.... But now our strength is gone. There is nothing at all to eat – nothing but this manna day after day!"

Moses heard all the people complaining as they stood around in groups at the entrances of their tents. He was distressed because the Lord had become angry with them, and he said to the Lord, "Where could I get enough meat for all these people? They keep whining and asking for meat. I can't be responsible for all these people by myself; it's too much for me!"
Numbers 11: 4-15

"They keep whining..."

Complaints! Complaints!

When I read Scripture, I usually look for something elevated, wise or out of the ordinary. It is, after all, the word of God. But today, I could only laugh!

Poor Moses. Obviously he hadn't had to deal with children before leading his people through the desert. Otherwise, he would have been familiar with the complaints that were driving him crazy: "Yuck. Not this again!" Or "My friend's food is way better than this." And "Why can't I have...?" What parent hasn't secretly thought, "I can't put up with this anymore"?

Moses, here's a tip: enjoy the day. The 40 years in the desert will be over before you know it. And you'll look back to those complaining years and say, "You know what? It was a lot of fun."

Lord, thank you for the many challenges you have given me – especially my children.

Be merciful to me, O God,
because of your constant love.
Because of your great mercy
wipe away my sins!
Wash away all my evil
and make me clean from my sin!
I recognize my faults;
I am always conscious of my sins....
Create a pure heart in me, O God,
and put a new and loyal spirit in me.
Do not banish me from your presence;
do not take your holy spirit away from me

Psalm 51: 1-4, 10-11

"I recognize my faults..."

The gift of forgiveness

Thunder and lightning on a sticky August day. Thunderstorms raging on the home front, too. His drinking was getting out of hand. Again. Harsh words, tempers flaring, hurt feelings. Maybe this time she really would throw him out. When they both left for work, the silence between them was deafening.

He came home first, carrying an armful of summer flowers. Frantically seaching the cupboards, he muttered to himself, "Must find a vase. Make that two. Or even three!" The flowers had to be waiting when she came home from the office. He was desperate to make peace, to start over. Again.

It takes courage to say, "You were right. It's my fault. I'm sorry. Forgive me." Courage, humility, plain speaking... helped along by three vases of summer flowers.

**Thank you, Lord, for your gift of forgiveness
that awaits me every day of my life.**

A Canaanite woman came to Jesus. "Son of David! Have mercy on me, sir! My daughter has a demon and is in a terrible condition." But Jesus did not say a word to her. His disciples begged him, "Send her away! She is following us and making all this noise!"

Jesus replied, "I have been sent only to the lost sheep of the people of Israel." At this the woman came and fell at his feet. "Help me, sir!" she said. Jesus answered, "It isn't right to take the children's food and throw it to the dogs."

"That's true, sir," she answered, "but even the dogs eat the leftovers that fall from their masters' table." So Jesus answered her, "You are a woman of great faith! What you want will be done for you." And at that very moment her daughter was healed.   *Matthew 15: 21-28*

> "...but even the dogs eat the leftovers that fall..."

A human response

We're taught that Jesus was both human and divine. So many biblical stories illustrate the divine side, but, in today's passage, he appears very human – I mean, "leftovers and dogs"? It's hard for me to see the divine side of Jesus here.

But there *are* two admirable human qualities in the story: the persistence of the woman, and Jesus' willingness to change. Maybe he was tired: one more person, and an outsider to boot! But she keeps on asking for help.

Did Jesus shake his head when he realized his "No" was a knee-jerk reaction? Sometimes, when I'm tired, I just say "No," too. That's when I need to stop, give my head a shake and rethink my position. And listen. And keep listening.

**Dear God, when everything in me wants to say "No,"
help me to stop and consider before answering.**

Thursday | AUGUST 6

We have not depended on made-up stories in making known to you the mighty coming of our Lord Jesus Christ. With our own eyes we saw his greatness. We were there when he was given honour and glory by God the Father, when the voice came to him from the Supreme Glory, saying, "This is my own dear Son, with whom I am pleased!" We ourselves heard this voice coming from heaven, when we were with him on the holy mountain.

So we are even more confident of the message proclaimed by the prophets. You will do well to pay attention to it, because it is like a lamp shining in a dark place until the Day dawns and the light of the morning star shines in your hearts.

2 Peter 1: 16-20

"...it is like a lamp shining in a dark place..."

In dark times

Helen's daughter committed suicide last week. Again and again Helen asks herself, "Where did I go wrong? Why wasn't my love enough for her? What if I'd called her that evening – would she still be alive?" And then the waves of crushing sorrow roll over her.

What can I say to Helen? Any well-intentioned phrases I might offer won't ease her terrible distress. If I were in her place, words of comfort would only seem to mock the depth of my pain.

Then I remember how devastated the disciples were when Jesus died. But God triumphed over death: God's love shines like a lamp in a dark place. In this time of anguish, I cling to the hope that eventually Helen will experience that light.

**Lord, give me the faith and hope to hang on –
even in the darkest nights of sorrow.**

Jesus said to his disciples, "If any of you want to come with me, you must forget yourself, carry your cross, and follow me. For if you want to save your own life, you will lose it; but if you lose your life for my sake, you will find it. Will you gain anything if you win the whole world but lose your life? Of course not! There is nothing you can give to regain your life. For the Son of Man is about to come in the glory of his Father with his angels, and then he will reward each one according to his deeds. I assure you that there are some here who will not die until they have seen the Son of Man come as King."

Matthew 16: 24-28

"…you must forget yourself…"

Letting go

There's a story about a man who is in a ferocious struggle with a wildcat. When someone offers to help subdue it, he gasps: "Actually, I'm trying to let him go!"

In today's reading, Jesus says that I have to stop trying to save my own life. To let go of that wildcat. I try, Jesus. I try.

I try to get past the mortgage payment, and the car that needs fixing, and the money I don't have to fix it. I try to get past the kids' university tuition, and the deadlines, and the meetings, and the world's problems. Try as I might, I can't seem to let go of that wildcat.

Now and then, I do let go, and I experience the peace you offer. But then that wildcat snarls again.

Lord, let me not be trapped by my own struggles.
Free me from myself.

A man knelt before Jesus and said, "Sir, have mercy on my son! He is an epileptic and has such terrible attacks that he often falls in the fire or into water. I brought him to your disciples, but they could not heal him."

Jesus answered, "How unbelieving and wrong you people are! How long do I have to put up with you?" Jesus gave a command to the demon, and it went out of the boy, and he was healed. The disciples asked Jesus, "Why couldn't we drive the demon out?" "It was because you do not have enough faith," answered Jesus. "I assure you that if you have faith as big as a mustard seed, you can say to this hill, 'Go from here to there!' and it will go. You could do anything!"

Matthew 17: 14-20

"You could do anything!"

Moving mountains

Jesus says that faith can move mountains… but it's so much easier *not* to believe. I know that the obstacles that block my ability to give love freely are only as big as I allow them to be. But insecurity, the fear of rejection and my stubborn pride rise within me and loom like mountains.

Deep down, if I believe that good can triumph over evil, any obstacle can be turned into an opportunity. I think of the reconciliation that has taken place in South Africa. What a model for other troubled spots around the world and, closer at home, for my own relationships!

Believing in God's love, I am energized to seek new ways to relate with others. I might even move a few mountains!

Dear God, help me believe that the power of love
can move mountains, especially when I am most afraid.

The people started grumbling about him, because he said, "I am the bread that came down from heaven." So they said, "This man is Jesus, son of Joseph, isn't he? We know his father and mother. How, then, does he now say he came down from heaven?"

Jesus answered, "Stop grumbling among yourselves…. The prophets wrote, 'Everyone will be taught by God.' Anyone who hears the Father and learns from him comes to me…. I am telling you the truth… I am the bread of life. Your ancestors ate manna in the desert, but they died. But the bread that comes down from heaven is of such a kind that whoever eats it will not die. I am the living bread that came down from heaven. If you eat this bread, you will live forever."

John 6: 41-51

> "Stop grumbling among yourselves."

Stop grumbling

As a teenager, I thought that being critical, whenever I had the opportunity to express my opinion, was a sign of wisdom. Then a high school teacher gently reminded me that "grumble and stumble" go together.

She was right. My grumbling became a habit, one that robbed me of my inner peace. And, because I usually grumbled to others, it also spread division. Yet, beneath my critical attitude, I always longed for that peace of heart which seemed so hard to achieve.

I have difficulty accepting that the world does not run according to my wishes. My challenge is to trust that the Spirit is active in our world, bringing about God's will… even when it's not the way I'd do things.

Lord, make me a channel of your peace
in all that I say and do today.

" **I** am telling you the truth: a grain of wheat remains no more than a single grain unless it is dropped into the ground and dies. If it does die, then it produces many grains. Those who love their own life will lose it; those who hate their own life in this world will keep it for life eternal. Whoever wants to serve me must follow me, so that my servant will be with me where I am. And my Father will honour anyone who serves me."

John 12: 24-26

"...unless it is dropped into the ground and dies."

Certified seed

Often I sow winter rye as a cover crop over my garden. I plant "certified" seed so I don't have to worry about the quality of the seeds. Still, even in the best of circumstances, not all the seeds will produce.

God lavishly plants "certified" seeds within me: generosity, understanding and kindness. Faced with the frosts, droughts and storms of life, however, some of these seeds fail to germinate or thrive. During times of adversity, I often place limits on how I respond to others' needs.

At other times, the harvest in my heart is abundant: one seed can produce many grains. When I let God's gifts grow and develop within me, integrity, compassion and a spirit of giving become the lush cover crop of my soul.

Creator God, help me respond generously to your many calls to accept abundant life.

The disciples came to Jesus, asking, "Who is the greatest in the kingdom of heaven?" So Jesus called a child to come and stand in front of them, and said, "I assure you that unless you change and become like children, you will never enter the kingdom of heaven. The greatest in the kingdom of heaven is the one who humbles himself and becomes like this child. And whoever welcomes in my name one such child as this, welcomes me....

"See that you don't despise any of these little ones. Their angels in heaven, I tell you, are always in the presence of my Father in heaven."
Matthew 18: 1-5, 10-14

"Who is the greatest...?"

The wrong question

The wrong question will hardly ever get you to the right answer. My daughter once asked me, "Daddy, how many miles are there until Christmas?" It was a sincere question; she really wanted to know something. But I couldn't answer the question she asked: you can't measure time in miles.

Jesus uses a child – the epitome of humility – to make a similar point: you can't use greatness to measure *value* in the kingdom of God. Then he goes even further, telling his disciples the right word, the right category to measure the distance between here and the kingdom: welcome.

So, how many "welcomes" until the kingdom? As many as it takes until everyone is welcome. And with each one, we get a little closer.

**Jesus, teach me to welcome others
as freely as you welcome them.**

" If your brother sins against you, go to him and show him his fault. But do it privately, just between yourselves. If he listens to you, you have won your brother back. But if he will not listen to you, take one or two other persons with you. And if he will not listen to them, then tell the whole thing to the church....

"I tell all of you: what you prohibit on earth will be prohibited in heaven, and what you permit on earth will be permitted in heaven.

"And I tell you more: whenever two of you on earth agree about anything you pray for, it will be done for you by my Father in heaven. For where two of three come together in my name, I am there with them."

Matthew 18: 15-20

"Where two of three come together in my name, I am there..."

From conflict to peace

I hate conflict. I would rather avoid it than confront it. This is especially true if I am the one who has been wronged. How can I tell a person who has hurt me about my pain, my anger, and the impact of his or her words or actions? The bible verse about picking the splinter out of the other's eye versus the log in my own eye plagues my mind.

I like the ancient words of advice: Speak to an opponent with words that are first of all, true; second, necessary; and third, kind. Dealing with a difficult situation is not easy; it's easier to walk away! But, I know, when I have stayed to talk through a misunderstanding, I have found God's healing presence there.

Dear God, give me courage to speak when I have been wronged. Help me trust that you will be with me, with us.

Peter asked, "Lord, if my brother keeps on sinning against me, how many times do I have to forgive him? Seven times?" "No, not seven times," answered Jesus, "but seventy times seven, because the kingdom of heaven is like this. Once there was a king who decided to check on his servants' accounts. He had just begun to do so when one of them was brought in who owed him millions of dollars. The servant did not have enough to pay his debt…. The servant fell on his knees before the king. 'Be patient with me,' he begged…. The king felt sorry for him, so he forgave him the debt.

"Then the man went out and met one of his fellow servants who owed him a few dollars. He grabbed him and started choking him. 'Pay back what you owe me!' he said. His fellow servant begged him, 'Be patient with me, and I will pay you back!' But he refused; instead, he had him thrown into jail until he should pay the debt.
Matthew 18: 21 – 19: 1

"How many times do I have to forgive him?"

Forgiving others

Almost 20 years ago, I admitted to addiction and my life changed forever. Shortly thereafter, I began working with fellow recovering addicts. The sheer relevance of today's reading sets my teeth on edge.

There have been times when I've worked with someone for six months or a year – believing that I had really helped him or her to overcome the addiction – only to have that person return to the treatment centre in full-blown relapse.

I know at some level that the person has a disease, just as I do, but playing the role of the unjust servant comes easily to me. I forget the mercy shown me and begin to abuse my fellow servants. Forgiving 70 times seven is a difficult standard.

**God, the thought of forgiving anyone is overwhelming.
Help me realize that forgiveness comes from you.**

Some Pharisees tried to trap Jesus by asking, "Does our Law allow a man to divorce his wife for whatever reason he wishes?" Jesus answered, "Haven't you read the scripture that says that in the beginning the Creator made people male and female? And God said, 'For this reason a man will leave his father and mother and unite with his wife, and the two will become one.' So they are no longer two, but one. No human being must separate, then, what God has joined together."

The Pharisees asked him, "Why, then, did Moses give the law for a man to hand his wife a divorce notice and send her away?" Jesus answered, "Moses gave you permission to divorce your wives because you are so hard to teach. But it was not like that at the time of creation. I tell you, then, that any man who divorces his wife for any cause other than her unfaithfulness, commits adultery if he marries some other woman."

Matthew 19: 3-12

"...in the beginning the Creator made people male and female..."

Back to basics

In today's passage, I like the way Jesus answers the Pharisees. He doesn't get caught up with their legal wrangling about marriage and the Law. Instead, Jesus goes back to when God created men and women – out of love and delight – to complete the work of creation.

So often, in my relationships, I complicate matters by splitting hairs over who is right or wrong. How I need to be reminded of the love and delight that brought us together in the first place.

Similarly, my children and I become sidetracked when we get caught up in who said what. The need to be right pales when we get back to the basics – of love, respect and consideration for one another, and delight in one another's company.

God of love, give me the wisdom to focus my energy on the goodness of my relationships.

When Elizabeth heard Mary's greeting, the baby moved within her. Elizabeth was filled with the Holy Spirit and said, "You are the most blessed of all women, and blessed is the child you will bear…."

Mary said, "My heart praises the Lord; my soul is glad because of God my Saviour, for he has remembered me, his lowly servant! From now on all people will call me happy, because of the great things the Mighty God has done for me. His name is holy; from one generation to another he shows mercy to those who honour him. He has stretched out his mighty arm and scattered the proud with all their plans. He has brought down mighty kings from their thrones, and lifted up the lowly. He has filled the hungry with good things, and sent the rich away with empty hands."

Luke 1: 39-56

> "…and lifted up the lowly."

An open heart

Marie called with wonderful news: she was leaving for China to bring her new daughter home! When the question of names came up, I suggested Hannah, for Mary's Magnificat echoed the Song of Hannah found in the book of Samuel. Both these prayers of praise tell how God turns oppression upside down and thwarts the evil plans of the mighty and the powerful.

Here we have a tiny girl – classified as a burden by some in her society because of her sex – being lifted up into a loving embrace. And we have this woman, opening her heart and life to cherish and nourish all the promise the tiny girl carries. Each one playing her part in the great things God is doing in our midst. Magnificent!

**God, let my soul praise you,
and help me to turn the world right-side up.**

will always thank the Lord;
I will never stop praising him.
I will praise him for what he has done;
may all who are oppressed listen and be glad!
Proclaim with me the Lord's greatness;
let us praise his name together!
Honour the Lord, all his people;
those who obey him have all they need....
Would you like to enjoy life?
Do you want long life and happiness?
Then keep from speaking evil
and from telling lies.
Turn away from evil and do good;
strive for peace with all your heart.   *Psalm 34: 1-2, 9-14*

> "I will always thank the Lord."

Simple gratitude

After graduating from university, I decided to live and work in Peru for a year. Before leaving, I embarked on the adventure of learning Spanish, and I was pleased with my early success with simple words and phrases.

As the class moved into more complicated grammatical territory, I began to worry. "How," I asked, "am I ever going to remember all of this?" I have never forgotten my teacher's reply: "When you are learning a language, the phrase 'thank you' is the only one you really need to know!"

He was right. There were times when I was overwhelmed by the generosity shown me by those who had so little. A heartfelt "gracias" went farther than any fancy phrase ever could.

**Generous God, as I go through this day,
let "thank you" often be on my lips.**

"Teacher," a man asked, "what good thing must I do to receive eternal life?" "Why do you ask me concerning what is good?" answered Jesus. "Keep the commandments if you want to enter life."

"What commandments?" he asked. Jesus answered, "Do not commit murder; do not commit adultery; do not steal; do not accuse anyone falsely; respect your father and your mother; and love your neighbour as you love yourself."

"I have obeyed all these commandments," the young man replied. "What else do I need to do?" Jesus said to him, "If you want to be perfect, go and sell all you have and give the money to the poor, and you will have riches in heaven; then come and follow me." When the young man heard this, he went away sad, because he was very rich.

Matthew 19: 16-22

> "...go and sell all you have..."

Lighten up!

I like following commandments that I can grasp. Sure, I've been tempted, but I've avoided murder and adultery... so far! I try to be truthful about others, respect elders and love my neighbour (okay, and her barking dog, too).

But I am troubled when Jesus says "go and sell all you have...." All of it? My piano? My favourite teapot? Everything? Even my garden gnomes? What is Jesus really saying?

In a word or two, I suppose he's saying, "Lighten up." What load of things occupies my hands? There are rooms in my house that are full of "things" I seldom use. My hands are often busy with servicing the things in my life instead of serving others. How might I change this today?

Jesus, I hear your words. What do they mean for me today?

"I assure you: it is much harder for a rich person to enter the kingdom of God than for a camel to go through the eye of a needle." When the disciples heard this, they were completely amazed. "Who, then, can be saved?" they asked. Jesus answered, "This is impossible for human beings, but for God everything is possible." Then Peter spoke up. "Look, we have left everything and followed you. What will we have?" Jesus said to them, "You can be sure... everyone who has left houses or brothers or sisters or father or mother or children or fields for my sake, will receive a hundred times more and will be given eternal life. But many who now are first will be last, and many who now are last will be first."

Matthew 19: 23-30

"Who, then, can be saved?"

False security

The last thing I am is rich, so I'd never think to buy my way into heaven! Yet the disciples' response won't let me dismiss this passage as easily as I'd like to. Like me, these guys have neither huge incomes nor hefty bank accounts. So who then, if not the rich, can be saved: the poor, the politically correct, doers of good deeds, those holding the right beliefs?

But here's the catch: each alternative simply places my trust in another type of wealth – and places me before God thinking I am secure. Then I hear Jesus say, wealth can't save you – period.

Now, worse than amazed, I am lost. Now the disciples' question becomes mine. And Jesus' answer becomes good news to me: God alone can – and will – save me.

Jesus, move me beyond efforts to earn your love.
Let me instead trust the love you offer me freely.

"The kingdom of heaven is like this. Once there was a man who [hired] some men to work in his vineyard. He agreed to pay them the regular wage, a silver coin a day.... When evening came, the owner told his foreman, 'Call the workers and pay them their wages.' The men who had begun to work at five o'clock were paid a silver coin each. So when the men who were the first to be hired came to be paid, they thought they would get more; but they too were given a silver coin each. They took their money and started grumbling against the employer.... 'Listen, friend,' the owner answered, 'I have not cheated you. After all, you agreed to do a day's work for one silver coin.... Are you jealous because I am generous?'" And Jesus concluded, "So those who are last will be first, and those who are first will be last."   *Matthew 20: 1-16*

"Are you jealous because I am generous?"

Not fair?

I think of myself as someone who's worked all day in the vineyard, struggling (with varying degrees of success) to be a "good person" my whole life. So why do so many end-of-the-day slackers not only get picked to work for God, but also land some of the best assignments?

A less-than-perfect king called David writes the psalms. God hands the ten commandments to a stuttering murderer named Moses, and the "Twelve Steps" to a bankrupt alcoholic stockbroker. And what about that unlikely hero, Oskar Schindler?

Sometimes I feel like the composer Salieri in *Amadeus*, listening to that crazy, undeserving Mozart play another of his glorious concerti. The kingdom operates on God's grace, not on my limited ideas about "fairness."

**God, help me appreciate everyone's contribution:
big or small, early or just-in-time.**

Thursday | AUGUST 20

"The kingdom of heaven is like this. Once there was a king who prepared a wedding feast for his son. He sent his servants to tell the invited guests to come to the feast, but they did not want to come.... The king was very angry...; then he called his servants and said to them, 'My wedding feast is ready, but the people I invited did not deserve it. Now go to the main streets and invite to the feast as many people as you find.' So the servants went out into the streets and gathered all the people they could find, good and bad alike....

"The king went in to look at the guests and saw a man who was not wearing wedding clothes. 'Friend, how did you get in here without wedding clothes?'"

Matthew 22: 1-14

> "...but they did not want to come..."

Ready to party

The greatest party invitation they'd ever received – and they were all too busy to come.

Throughout the day I am pulled in a hundred directions, and they're all worthwhile: work, volunteer commitments, a friend in trouble. So when my gentle two-year-old invited me to play yesterday, I said, "I just have to..." and carried on with what I was doing. After several tries she became angry, and I realized I was turning down the most precious request of the day.

I sat down to play with her, but she sensed my mind was elsewhere – I wasn't "wearing wedding clothes." It was only when I let go of everything and gave her my full attention that she was satisfied... and we started to party.

Give me the grace to recognize your invitation, Lord, and to accept it with a joyful and undivided heart.

When the Pharisees heard that Jesus had silenced the Sadducees, they came together, and one of them, a teacher of the Law, tried to trap him with a question. "Teacher," he asked, "which is the greatest commandment in the Law?"

Jesus answered, "'Love the Lord your God with all your heart, with all your soul, and with all your mind.' This is the greatest and the most important commandment. The second most important commandment is like it: 'Love your neighbour as you love yourself.' The whole Law of Moses and the teachings of the prophets depend on these two commandments."

Matthew 22: 34-40

"Love the Lord…"

Back to basics

Traditional fishing communities have the most rickety structures imaginable: the fishing stages. Fragile-looking weaves of saplings lashed together provide a working shelter for the catch of the day, where it is landed and dried.

But the foundations are utterly incredible! Tiny, knurled spindles extend down to the ocean rocks below. The entire structure rests on these few stark points of contact. I've been baffled to understand why they haven't been swept away long ago. But they persevere. Decades pass and they weather the sea's many attempts to claim them. It's astounding.

Nothing to look at by the world's standards, but they possess a tenacious grip on the solid rock that rests just below them. "Love the Lord your God…." Seems solid enough!

God of all ages, bring me back to the basics today.

Boaz said to Ruth, "Let me give you some advice. Don't gather grain anywhere except in this field. Work with the women here…. I have ordered my men not to molest you. And whenever you are thirsty, go and drink from the water jars that they have filled."

Ruth bowed down with her face touching the ground, and said to Boaz, "Why should you be so concerned about me? Why should you be so kind to a foreigner?"

Boaz answered, "I have heard about everything that you have done for your mother-in-law since your husband died. I know how you left your father and mother and your own country and how you came to live among a people you had never known before. May the Lord reward you for what you have done." *Ruth 2: 1-3, 8-11; 4: 13-17*

"…everything that you have done for your mother-in-law…"

Women who care

The biblical Ruth sounds like many of the women I know: having raised one family, they now find themselves taking care of their in-laws. I know women who are caring for the needs of their parents, their in-laws, and their own children, often simultaneously, and often commuting great distances.

But I find that the one who is concerned about caring for the elderly isn't always the one who actually carries out the practical tasks of that care.

As much as I, and the men that I know, want to become involved, the burden seems to fall to our wives, sisters or sisters-in-law. As in Ruth's time, for women, after a day's work, there's still more to do.

**Dear God, when it comes to caring, there's often a gap
between what I should do and what I end up doing.
Help me narrow this gap.**

J esus said to them, "I am telling you the truth: if you do not eat the flesh of the Son of Man and drink his blood, you will not have life in yourselves...."

Many of his followers heard this and said, "This teaching is too hard. Who can listen to it?"

Without being told, Jesus knew that they were grumbling about this, so he said to them, "Does this make you want to give up? Suppose, then, that you should see the Son of Man go back up to the place where he was before? What gives life is God's Spirit; human power is of no use at all. The words I have spoken to you bring God's life-giving Spirit. Yet some of you do not believe."

John 6: 53, 60-69

"What gives life is God's Spirit..."

Turning to God

On a good day I can easily fall into the trap of believing that I am in control of my life. Everyone wakes up healthy and gets out the door on time. I complete a work assignment ahead of schedule, tackle a list of calls and correspondence, do the laundry, even bake some cookies before the kids arrive home. How well organized I am!

Inevitably, though, it's not long before I'm forced to face my limitations – again. An illness in the family, a devastating phone call, a strained relationship: all of a sudden I feel so powerless!

At such times, I can either give in to despair, or turn with trust to the God who is the true source and centre of my life.

Spirit of God, deepen my trust in your life-giving power, both in good times and in bad.

P hilip found Nathanael and told him, "We have found the one whom Moses wrote about in the book of the Law and whom the prophets also wrote about. He is Jesus son of Joseph, from Nazareth." "Can anything good come from Nazareth?" Nathanael asked. "Come and see," answered Philip. When Jesus saw Nathanael coming to him, he said about him, "Here is a real Israelite; there is nothing false in him!" Nathanael asked him, "How do you know me?" Jesus answered, "I saw you when you were under the fig tree before Philip called you." "Teacher," answered Nathanael, "you are the Son of God! You are the King of Israel!" Jesus said, "Do you believe just because I told you I saw you when you were under the fig tree? You will see much greater things than this!"

John 1:45-51

> "You will see much greater things than this!"

The bigger picture

So often I see events only in terms of how they affect me. When my child's school had to close, I worried about how I'd manage. When a bus strike loomed, I wondered how I'd get to work. When bad weather hit, I wondered how long I would have my mother-in-law in the house. The bigger issues – the needs of the school community, justice for bus workers, the trials others faced during the storm – were secondary.

I often respond to situations as Nathanael responded to Jesus. I'm interested when I'm part of the story, indifferent when I'm not. How many of the greater things do I miss when I respond to life in this way: when I fail to look beyond my own immediate interests.

**Jesus, help me look beyond my own concerns
to see the bigger picture each day.**

"How terrible for you, teachers of the Law and Pharisees! You hypocrites! You give to God one tenth even of the seasoning herbs, such as mint, dill and cumin, but you neglect to obey the really important teachings of the Law, such as justice and mercy and honesty. These you should practise, without neglecting the others. Blind guides! You strain a fly out of your drink, but swallow a camel!

"How terrible for you, teachers of the Law and Pharisees! You hypocrites! You clean the outside of your cup and plate, while the inside is full of what you have gotten by violence and selfishness. Blind Pharisee! Clean what is inside the cup first, and then the outside will be clean too!"

Matthew 23: 23-26

"Clean what is inside the cup first..."

Wanted: justice

A girl with a bag of beans met me in the grocery store and asked if I could buy them for her. She followed me as I picked up bread, rice, beans, and a treat – peanut butter. When I chose a one kilo bag of beans, she exchanged the two-kilo bag she held for a one-kilo bag like mine.

As we left the store, I noticed her four siblings and mother huddled with cardboard and rags surrounding them. I wanted to take the girl back into the store to buy bread, rice and peanut butter. Instead, I grabbed a cab, threw her 20 centavos, and met her eyes. Hungry, calm eyes met my worried, anxious eyes.

I never saw the family again.

**Forgive me, God. I so often fail to practise justice,
mercy and faith.**

S urely you remember, our friends, how we worked so that we would not be any trouble to you as we preached to you the Good News from God. You are our witnesses, and so is God, that our conduct toward you who believe was pure, right, and without fault. You know that we treated each one of you just as parents treat their own children. We encouraged you, we comforted you, and we kept urging you to live the kind of life that pleases God....

And there is another reason why we always give thanks to God. When we brought you God's message, you heard it and accepted it, not as a message from human beings but as God's message. For God is at work in you who believe. *I Thessalonians 2: 9-13*

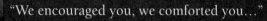

"We encouraged you, we comforted you..."

Words of encouragement

Some of my happiest childhood memories are of my Aunt Lillian, or "Lila." After my father's death when I was four years old, she was someone to whom I could turn, someone who had time to listen to me. In a very dark time, she was always patient, always kind. Her home was a welcoming place.

Paul brings strength to the Thessalonians after they have suffered persecution for their faith in Christ, and he reminds them that they are not alone in their suffering: "We encouraged you, we comforted you, and we kept urging you to live the kind of life that pleases God."

Just as Paul supported these early Christians in their faltering faith, Lila encouraged and comforted me so that I could trust God in an uncertain world.

Thank you, O God, for being with me when I need you.

I n all our trouble and suffering we have been encouraged about you, friends. It was your faith that encouraged us…. Now we can give thanks to our God for you. We thank him for the joy we have in his presence because of you. Day and night we ask him with all our heart to let us see you personally and supply what is needed in your faith.

May our God and Father himself and our Lord Jesus prepare the way for us to come to you! May the Lord make your love for one another and for all people grow more and more and become as great as our love for you. In this way he will strengthen you, and you will be perfect and holy in the presence of our God.   *I Thessalonians 3: 7-13*

> "It was your faith that encouraged us…"

Love in practice

Not long ago, a young man died. Faced with the death of this much-loved man, friends asked me, "Where was your God?" I replied that God was indeed present – in the actions of those who knew and cared for him.

No one could control the course of this man's illness; no one could banish the struggle or sorrow of his family. Feeling powerless, everyone wanted to help, to pray, to bake – to perform all the domestic rituals of love. In response to the unravelling of one young life, the hearts of friends, acquaintances and strangers were knit together in loving concern.

To those who doubt the existence of a compassionate God, I can only say that I saw, mirrored in a hundred hearts, the reflection of God's enduring love.

**Lord, in the midst of trouble and suffering,
help me to look around me for the signs of your loving presence.**

"Once there were ten young women who took their oil lamps and went out to meet the bridegroom. Five of them were foolish, and the other five were wise. The foolish ones took their lamps but did not take any extra oil with them, while the wise ones took containers full of oil for their lamps. The bridegroom was late in coming, so they began to nod and fall asleep. It was already midnight when the cry rang out, 'Here is the bridegroom! Come and meet him!' The ten young women woke up and trimmed their lamps. Then the foolish ones said to the wise ones, 'Let us have some of your oil, because our lamps are going out....'"

Jesus concluded, "Watch out, then, because you do not know the day or the hour."
Matthew 25: 1-13

"...did not take any extra oil with them..."

Packing the essentials

Packing my daughter's diaper bag for an outing is always a challenge. Let's see: diapers, a bib, extra clothing, a snack, water, a suitable toy that will distract her but not others. No matter how hard I try, it always seems that I forget something essential. Like the foolish women, I think I am prepared, only to find that I've overlooked something really important.

How many times have I forgotten to put humour and understanding in the bag? How often have I found myself with enough wipes but not enough patience? Sometimes I am like the women who have lamps without enough oil.

Today I will try not to be distracted by unimportant details. I will remember to carry the essentials.

**Lord, help me to prepare for today's journey
with the things that are truly necessary.**

Saturday | **AUGUST 29**

On Herod's birthday…the daughter of Herodias came in and danced, and pleased Herod and his guests. So the king said to the girl, "What would you like to have? I will give you anything you want." With many vows he said to her, "I swear that I will give you anything you ask for, even as much as half my kingdom!" So the girl went out and asked her mother, "What shall I ask for?"

"The head of John the Baptist," she answered.

The girl hurried back at once to the king and demanded, "I want you to give me here and now the head of John the Baptist on a plate!"

This made the king very sad, but he could not refuse her because of the vows he had made in front of all his guests. So he sent off a guard at once with orders to bring John's head.   *Mark 6: 17-29*

> "I swear that I will give you anything you ask for…"

Unwise promises

I might have been twelve, visiting the fabled Crystal Gardens indoor swimming pool in Victoria, BC. A group of us stood safely below, mocking a boy who was having second thoughts about jumping off the high board.

"Go on, chicken," I taunted. "It's easy!"

"Oh yeah?" he retorted. "Then let's see you do it, big mouth!"

I could not disgrace myself before my peers. Somehow, I did it. I don't remember how.

But I remember that episode now, and feel an uncomfortable kinship with Herod. He, too, bragged before his peers. "Oh yeah?" said his step-daughter, in effect. "Then let's see you do it, big mouth!"

Like me, Herod lacked the courage to admit that he had spoken rashly.

Keep me from making promises I should not keep.
Stop me from keeping promises I should not have made.

Lord, who may enter your Temple?
Who may worship on Zion, your sacred hill?
Those who obey God in everything
and always do what is right,
whose words are true and sincere,
and who do not slander others.
They do no wrong to their friends
nor spread rumours about their neighbours....
They always do what they promise,
no matter how much it may cost.
They make loans without charging interest
and cannot be bribed to testify against the innocent.
Whoever does these things will always be secure. *Psalm 15: 1-5*

"Those who obey God in everything..."

Everyday saints

The psalmist's portrait of a person of unswerving integrity reminds me of my mother, who died 20 years ago. A post-war British immigrant, she was an unassuming person who never sought the limelight. Yet everything she did reflected her strength of character and her sheer, ordinary goodness. Widowed in her 40s, she rose to the challenges of raising two children on her own. Her professional life as a nurse was marked by a compassion that extended far beyond duty. Her family and her many friends knew she could always be counted on for love, support, forgiveness and encouragement. She was, I think (though she would laugh at the notion), a holy person.

My mother's example offers me hope when I am faced with my daily responsibilities – that I, too, may share in God's holiness.

**Lord, thank you for the everyday saints and heroes
you send into my life.**

Jesus went to Nazareth, where he had been brought up, and on the Sabbath he went as usual to the synagogue. He stood up to read the Scriptures and was handed the book of the prophet Isaiah.... The people in the synagogue were all well impressed with him and marvelled at the eloquent words that he spoke. They said, "Isn't he the son of Joseph?"

He said, "I am sure that you will quote this proverb to me, 'Doctor, heal yourself....' I tell you this," Jesus added, "prophets are never welcomed in their hometown...."

When the people in the synagogue heard this, they were filled with anger. They rose up, dragged Jesus out of town, and took him to the top of the hill [where] they meant to throw him over the cliff. *Luke 4: 16-30*

"Isn't he the son of Joseph?"

More than the role

From what little we know of his childhood, Jesus was a pretty normal kid. So why did the people who lived alongside Jesus suddenly became so hostile towards him? Why did his old friends and neighbours mock his claim of being the messiah?

One of the hardest things I've found growing up is overcoming the roles that were assigned to me in childhood. Whenever I've tried to change or grow, the voices of the past – and some times even *people* from the past – are there to say, "Who do you think you are?" People are afraid of change – whatever form it takes.

Jesus did not let his old neighbours hold him back. He went forward. I try to draw strength from his example.

Jesus, you lived out your true calling.
Give me the courage to live out mine.

Jesus went to Capernaum, a town in Galilee, where he taught the people…. In the synagogue was a man who had the spirit of an evil demon in him; he screamed out in a loud voice, "Ah! What do you want with us, Jesus of Nazareth? Are you here to destroy us? I know who you are: you are God's holy messenger!" Jesus ordered the spirit, "Be quiet and come out of the man!" The demon threw the man down in front of them and went out of him without doing him any harm. The people were all amazed and said to one another, "What kind of words are these? With authority and power this man gives orders to the evil spirits, and they come out!" And the report about Jesus spread everywhere in that region. *Luke 4: 31-37*

"…you are God's holy messenger!"

In the face of evil

What a life of torment and misery the man with the evil demon must have led! And yet Jesus had the power to drive out that evil force and make the man well.

Every day I see people on the streets tormented by their own demons: addictions, or mental illness, or crushing bad luck. I know that some of these street people also suffer from the effects of childhood abuse. Still, it's so difficult for me to face their pain – and their demands – that, to my shame, I sometimes cross the street hoping to avoid them.

I wonder how I could make a difference in the life of at least one of these abandoned people. How can I be "God's holy messenger" as Jesus was?

Lord, give me some of your wisdom, your strength, your power to drive out evil and heal its effects.

J esus left the synagogue and went to Simon's home. Simon's mother-in-law was sick with a high fever and they spoke to Jesus about her. He went and stood at her bedside and ordered the fever to leave her. The fever left her, and she got up at once and began to wait on them.

After sunset all who had friends who were sick with various diseases brought them to Jesus; he placed his hands on every one of them and healed them all.   *Luke 4: 38-44*

> "...she got up at once
> and began to wait on them."

A mother's love

Simon Peter's mother-in-law had a lot to put up with. First her daughter marries this none-too-bright fisherman. Then he quits his job to follow a mysterious, possibly dangerous, teacher. Then he brings home a bunch of the man's followers for dinner – while she is lying sick in bed!

But the mysterious teacher cures her. And she does what so many other mothers I know would do: she gets out of bed to pitch in and help with the meal.

I am amazed by people like that – people like my own mother. A little fatigue or a few aches and pains can't stop her. She'll arrive at my home for a visit carrying a suitcase full of groceries to cook my favourite meal.

God, humble me and make me grateful for generous men and women. Help me learn from them.

One day Jesus was standing on the shore while the people pushed their way up to him to listen to the word of God. He saw two boats pulled up on the beach; the fishermen had left them and were washing the nets. Jesus got into one of the boats – it belonged to Simon – and asked him to push off a little from the shore. Jesus sat in the boat and taught the crowd.

When he finished speaking, he said to Simon, "Push the boat out further and you and your partners let down your nets...." "Master," Simon answered, "we worked hard all night long and caught nothing. But if you say so, I will let down the nets." They let them down and caught such a large number of fish that the nets were about to break.
Luke 5: 1-11

> "Jesus asked him to push off a little..."

Beyond the expected

The TV cameraman spent his first day in the refugee camp peering through the eyepiece of his camera, framing pictures that would tell "the story" back home. Then Nick's batteries ran out and he had to put away his camera. He began walking around, talking to people. "Only then was I able to see the refugees as human beings," he exclaimed, "not as pictures to record!"

When Jesus interrupted Peter's work and asked him to push away from shore, Peter was able to hear Jesus and answer a life-changing call.

When my daily tasks are interrupted by a computer crash, or a co-worker's negligence, or a sick child who needs to stay home, it may be an opportunity for me to step back and listen for God's call.

Lord, help me use the setbacks and interruptions in my life as a time to discover your plan for me.

Some people said to Jesus, "The disciples of John fast frequently and offer prayers, and the disciples of the Pharisees do the same; but your disciples eat and drink."

Jesus answered, "Do you think you can make the guests at a wedding party go without food as long as the bridegroom is with them? Of course not! But the day will come when the bridegroom will be taken away from them, and then they will fast."

Jesus also told them this parable: "You don't… pour new wine into used wineskins, because the new wine will burst the skins, the wine will pour out, and the skins will be ruined. Instead, new wine must be poured into fresh wineskins! And you don't want new wine after drinking old wine." *Luke 5: 33-39*

"…the new wine will burst the skins…"

Room for the Spirit

In the Middle Ages, some churches in Europe were built with "Holy Spirit holes" – openings that were left in the roof to remind people that God's Spirit could move freely about, both within and beyond the church building. It was an architectural attempt to reflect the theological truth that God is like new wine: always in ferment, always expanding. God is free to move within – and beyond – our buildings, our worship, and our best ideas.

Sometimes, when I look at the church today, I think it's time to put some Holy Spirit holes in our buildings again – and see whether that opens up a little breathing space in our imaginations, as well.

> **Dear God, give me a faith with enough holes
> for you to move around a bit.**

At one time you were far away from God and were his enemies because of the evil things you did and thought. But now, by means of the physical death of his Son, God has made you his friends, in order to bring you, holy, pure and faultless, into his presence. You must, of course, continue faithful on a firm and sure foundation, and must not allow yourselves to be shaken from the hope you gained when you heard the gospel. It is of this gospel that I, Paul, became a servant – this gospel which has been preached to everybody in the world. *Colossians 1: 21-23*

"...on a firm and sure foundation..."

A firm foundation

Most days I walk to work. Whatever the season, I love to observe the gardens, trees and birds along my route. One day, a house I had always walked by was no longer standing! Well, part of it – the foundation – was still there, but the walls and roof were gone.

Within a few weeks, new walls had gone up. A couple of months later, the whole building was finished. It isn't the same house, but it will stand strong on the foundation that was laid decades ago.

When my life takes unexpected turns, I think about that house. As long as it rests on a firm foundation, it will stand tall. And as long as I trust in God and do not allow myself to be shaken, I will walk in the light of faith.

**Lord, sometimes the walls around me come tumbling down.
Help me to remember that if my foundation is firm, all will be well.**

S ome people brought him a man who was deaf and could hardly speak, and they begged Jesus to place his hands on him. So Jesus took him off alone, away from the crowd, put his fingers in the man's ears, spat, and touched the man's tongue. Then Jesus looked up to heaven, gave a deep groan, and said to the man, "Ephphatha," which means, "Open up!"

At once the man was able to hear, his speech impediment was removed, and he began to talk without any trouble. Then Jesus ordered the people not to speak of it to anyone; but the more he ordered them not to, the more they told it. And all who heard were completely amazed. "How well he does everything!" they exclaimed. "He even causes the deaf to hear and the dumb to speak!"   *Mark 7: 31-37*

> "At once the man was able to hear…"

Open to newness

My friend's grandson Stefan was born totally deaf. Two years ago, he got a cochlear ear implant. Cochlear implants don't amplify sounds, like a hearing aid. They feed electrical impulses directly to the brain.

The first time the technicians turned the volume control up, Stefan's eyes "just popped wide open," said his proud grandfather. "It was a totally new experience for him."

Some people oppose implants. A deaf person is not diminished by not being able to hear, they insist.

Those of us blessed with hearing can imagine what a loss it would be to do without. It occurs to me that many people apply the same logic to their faith. We resist new ideas because we want to believe that we're just fine as we are.

Pop my ears and eyes open, God.
Let me welcome your new experiences, whatever they are.

Monday | SEPTEMBER 7

J esus went into a synagogue…. A man was there whose right hand was paralyzed. Some teachers of the Law and some Pharisees wanted a reason to accuse Jesus of doing wrong, so they watched him closely to see if he would heal on the Sabbath…. Jesus said to the man, "Stand up and come here to the front." The man got up and stood there. Then Jesus said to them, "I ask you: What does our Law allow us to do on the Sabbath? To help or to harm? To save someone's life or destroy it?" He looked around at them all; then he said to the man, "Stretch out your hand." He did so, and his hand became well again. They were filled with rage and began to discuss… what they could do to Jesus.

Luke 6: 6-11

> "To help or to harm?"

Pharisee mode

Some days I wake up to discover I'm in "Pharisee mode." The announcer on the radio is annoying, the editorials in the newspapers are stupid, the dumb cat invariably trips me on the stairs, and the toast ends up burnt. These are the days I find it painfully easy to see the things that are wrong with everything and everyone around me. Of course, I have done nothing to cause any of this!

Deep down I know I feel this way because I'm overtired, or worried about money, work or my parents'. health. But falling headlong into this uncomfortable darkness can be paralyzing. That's when I need to stop, take a deep breath, and stretch out my withered hands and heart to God for healing.

Lord, before I criticize someone today, help me to stop and look at the fear or the hurt that lies within me.

T his is the list of the ancestors of Jesus Christ…. From Abraham to King David: Abraham, Isaac, Jacob, Judah and his brothers; then Perez and Zerah (their mother was Tamar), Hezron, Ram, Amminadab, Nahshon, Salmon, Boaz (his mother was Rahab), Obed (his mother was Ruth), Jesse, and King David.

From David to the time when the people of Israel were taken into exile: David, Solomon (his mother was the woman who had been Uriah's wife), Rehoboam, Abijah, Asa, Jehoshaphat, Jehoram, Uzziah, Jotham, Ahaz, Hezekiah, Manasseh, Amon, Josiah, and Jehoiachin and his brothers.

From the time after the exile to the birth of Jesus: Jehoiachin, Shealtiel, Zerubbabel, Abiud, Eliakim, Azor, Zadok, Achim, Eliud, Eleazar, Matthan, Jacob and Joseph, who married Mary, the mother of Jesus, who was called the Messiah.   *Matthew 1: 1-24*

> "This is the list of the ancestors of Jesus Christ…"

An example

These days I am often nameless, known only as my children's "Dad." Most times I sit and watch them play, work, struggle, fall down and get up. I'd like to jump in, but I know my contribution must remain one of guidance and, at times, offering some advice. I hope I'm a good example.

And here is Joseph, just one more name – squeezed between his illustrious ancestors and his son, the Messiah. A quiet man, maybe one of our great examples of acceptance, humility and faith. What did Jesus learn from him?

What can Joseph teach me? To accept that I must let go of my children – so that they can become themselves – trusting they will go on to fulfill their destinies.

**Lord, give me faith enough to let my children go,
trusting that they will go where they must.**

Y ou have been raised to life with Christ, so set your hearts on the things that are in heaven…. When he appears, then you too will appear with him and share his glory!

But now you must get rid of all these things: anger, passion and hateful feelings. No insults or obscene talk must ever come from your lips. Do not lie to one another, for you have put off the old self with its habits and have put on the new self. This is the new being which God, its Creator, is constantly renewing in his own image, in order to bring you to a full knowledge of himself. As a result, there is no longer any distinction between Gentiles and Jews, circumcised and uncircumcised, barbarians, savages, slaves and free, but Christ is all, Christ is in all.

Colossians 3: 1-11

> "…there is no longer any distinction…"

Beyond colour

The other day at swimming lessons my toddler talked about the "brown boy" in the pool. My heart sank. Suddenly we had crossed a new threshold – one that is often fraught with fear, racism, shame and suspicion. What should I say to my daughter?

We live in a world of racial profiling. Since September 11th we have learned more about what divides us than what brings us together. It has led us to war, and has put years of peacekeeping in jeopardy.

My daughter had no idea about the impact her comments had on me. She continued on about the boy: "He's funny. He has red pants and a nice smile." She laughed. I was relieved. I wondered how I can teach her to recognize his smile first, and not the colour of his skin.

Loving God, help me to recognize your divine presence in everyone I meet today.

You are the people of God; he loved you and chose you for his own. So then, you must clothe yourselves with compassion, kindness, humility, gentleness and patience. Be tolerant with one another and forgive one another whenever any of you has a complaint against someone else.... And to all these qualities add love, which binds all things together in perfect unity. The peace that Christ gives is to guide you in the decisions you make; for it is to this peace that God has called you together in the one body. And be thankful. Christ's message in all its richness must live in your hearts. Teach and instruct one another with all wisdom.... Everything you do or say, then, should be done in the name of the Lord Jesus, as you give thanks through him to God the Father. *Colossians 3:12-17*

> "And be thankful."

Gratitude

Miriam knows she should count her blessings and be grateful. "I have food to eat and a roof over my head. I live in a free country, and have friends and family." But, at nearly 80 years of age, Miriam is struggling with the losses of old age: a decline in her energy and mobility, the death of her oldest friends.

"I think that gratitude is a gift," I say to Miriam. "We don't control our feelings. But we can shape our thoughts, and they affect what we feel."

Our conversation reminds me to pay attention to my own blessings. An unexpected kindness. A flash of beauty. The knowledge that I'm loved. And that I can say, "Thank you, God," even when I'm feeling overwhelmed by the darker side of life.

**Lord, help me to pay attention to the love
and beauty around me. Remind me to thank you.**

Friday | **SEPTEMBER 11**

Jesus told them this parable: "One blind man cannot lead another one; if he does, both will fall into a ditch. No pupils are greater than their teacher; but all pupils, when they have completed their training, will be like their teacher.

"Why do you look at the speck in your brother's eye, but pay no attention to the log in your own eye? How can you say to your brother, 'Please, brother, let me take that speck out of your eye,' yet cannot even see the log in your own eye? You hypocrite! First take the log out of your own eye, and then you will be able to see clearly to take the speck out of your brother's eye."

Luke 6: 39-42

"First take the log out of your own eye..."

Self-examination

"I can't get my life under control," Susan whined. "My house is a mess, I'm way behind at work, and the neighbours are complaining about my yard." I wanted to shake her. Instead of moaning, why didn't she just pitch in and get on with the jobs that needed doing?

Then I looked around at my own life. The laundry was piling up, a stack of unanswered letters spilled over on my desk, and the mess in my garden called out for attention. I realized how much I'd been procrastinating. A little effort could lift a big weight of undone jobs off my shoulders.

Time to get the log out of my own eye, I realized, and to stop worrying about the speck in Susan's.

Lord, help me to recognize and change those failings in my life that blind me to the goodness in others.

" Every tree is known by the fruit it bears....

Why do you call me, 'Lord, Lord,' and yet don't do what I tell you? Anyone who comes to me and listens to my words and obeys them – I will show you what he is like. He is like a man who, in building his house, dug deep and laid the foundation on rock. The river flooded over and hit that house but could not shake it, because it was well built. But anyone who hears my words and does not obey them is like a man who built his house without laying a foundation; when the flood hit that house it fell at once – and what a terrible crash that was!"

Luke 6: 43-49

"...and laid the foundation on rock."

Rock solid

They've started to build a skyscraper near my parents' home. From my parents' perspective, watching day-by-day, not much appears to be happening in that big hole in the ground. But for anyone who looks in every few weeks, as I do, the progress with the foundation is obvious.

Many of my relationships – with family and with friends – are built on solid foundations. Over the years, we've worked at developing mutual trust, understanding and respect. These help us survive the tough times when words cannot make things right and the way ahead seems uncertain.

Other relationships are more fragile. When hard times hit, the relationship collapses. Later I am usually able to see that I had neglected to build a foundation at all.

**Lord, help me to build relationships on foundations
that are firm enough to withstand the storms of life.**

The danger of death was all around me;
the horrors of the grave closed in on me;
I was filled with fear and anxiety.
Then I called to the Lord,
"I beg you, Lord, save me...."
The Lord saved me from death;
he stopped my tears
and kept me from defeat.
And so I walk in the presence of the Lord
in the world of the living.
I kept on believing, even when I said,
"I am completely crushed,"
even when I was afraid and said,
"No one can be trusted."

Psalm 116: 1-11

"...the horrors of the grave closed in on me..."

Lifted up

Depression can be as life-threatening as death itself. Today's psalm reminds me of a time when "death was all around me" and I felt more dead than alive. Coping with my husband's illness and death, then with the responsibility of raising three young children alone, I wondered if I would survive. Did I even care?

Deep-seated fears and anxieties held me in their grip, paralyzing me. I sank lower and lower into hopelessness and, like the psalmist writes, felt "completely crushed." Where to turn? Whom to trust?

Looking back, I now recognize that I was carried – gently held – in the thoughts and prayers of concerned friends and relatives. And I thank the living God who sent such love and support in my time of need.

God, when life seems so empty, may I recognize your hand at work – carrying me and giving me a reason to believe.

He always had the nature of God, but he did not think that by force he should try to remain equal with God. Instead of this, of his own free will he gave up all he had, and took the nature of a servant. He became like a human being and appeared in human likeness. He was humble and walked the path of obedience all the way to death – his death on the cross. For this reason God raised him to the highest place above and gave him the name that is greater than any other name.

Philippians 2: 6-11

> "…and walked the path of obedience…"

True obedience

Robert was diagnosed with multiple sclerosis some 15 years ago. He probably wanted to cling to his identity as a fully abled person. He could have stood resolute in anger at how this disease has humbled him. And I'm sure he has had (and maybe still has) such moments.

But, having been "humbled" into early retirement, Robert chose instead a path of "obedience." "Obedience" comes from the Latin word for "to hear." Since finding himself out of work and in a wheelchair, Robert has chosen *to hear* the voices of the less fortunate – from his wheelchair! He has become a full-time volunteer, investing his energy, wit and wisdom in a multitude of local community projects.

Robert is, for me, a tiny window into the mystery of God-with-us.

**God, help me see reflections of your presence
in those around me.**

The child's father and mother were amazed at the things Simeon said about him. Simeon blessed them and said to Mary, his mother, "This child is chosen by God for the destruction and the salvation of many in Israel. He will be a sign from God which many people will speak against and so reveal their secret thoughts. And sorrow, like a sharp sword, will break your own heart."
Luke 2: 33-35

"This child is chosen by God..."

Jesus in our arms

Every baby deserves to be greeted the way Simeon greeted Jesus.

When I was pregnant, my partner and I separated. I didn't know what to do or where to go. I started smoking again. I felt guilty that the anguish I felt and my smoking would damage my baby, yet I couldn't seem to stop either. Friends and family rallied around, and the baby was born.

There's a photo that I often show my daughter. It's of the first moment that I held her in my arms, and my face is radiant with happiness.

Beyond all the hurt and the guilt, here was new life, promise, hope – God's unlimited mercy incarnate. Many women give birth in more difficult circumstances than I did, yet they take their new babies in their arms, and fall in love, and praise God.

Jesus, you were once a newborn baby.
Let us hold you in every baby born, and praise God.

J esus continued, "Now to what can I compare the people of this day? What are they like? They are like children sitting in the marketplace. One group shouts to the other, 'We played wedding music for you, but you wouldn't dance! We sang funeral songs, but you wouldn't cry!' John the Baptist came, and he fasted and drank no wine, and you said, 'He has a demon in him!' The Son of Man came, and he ate and drank, and you said, 'Look at this man! He is a glutton and wine drinker, a friend of tax collectors and other outcasts!' God's wisdom, however, is shown to be true by all who accept it."
Luke 7: 31-35

"God's wisdom…"

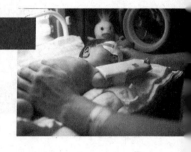

Open to joy and pain

My friends Jane and Frank conceived a child whom the doctors said would have a severe disability and would not live longer than a few days. Despite advice to the contrary, they chose to bring their child to birth. It was a journey of trust and of hope.

When their son was born, Jane and Frank were filled with joy, delighting in this new life and in parenthood. Jason lived longer than anyone expected – 17 days – sustained by the intensity of his parents' love. When he died, their grief was immense.

At Jason's funeral, I was moved by Jane and Frank's openness to love, and to both the joy and the pain involved in their decision. I sensed God was profoundly present in their lives.

**Lord, may I be open to receive you in ways
that might be different than I imagine.**

A Pharisee invited Jesus to have dinner with him…. A woman who lived a sinful life… brought an alabaster jar full of perfume and stood behind Jesus, by his feet, crying and wetting his feet with her tears. Then she dried his feet with her hair, kissed them, and poured the perfume on them. When the Pharisee saw this, he said to himself, "If this man really were a prophet, he would know who this woman is who is touching him; he would know what kind of sinful life she lives!"

Jesus said, "Simon, do you see this woman? I came into your home, and you gave me no water for my feet, but she has washed my feet with her tears and dried them with her hair…. I tell you, then, the great love she has shown proves that her many sins have been forgiven. But whoever has been forgiven little shows only a little love."

Luke 7: 36-50

> "…the great love she has shown…"

Don't judge

It was raining like mad and I was driving back to my office. She was standing on the corner, hitchhiking. I stopped, and she got in.

I pulled out into the traffic, looked over at her and asked, "Where are you headed?" She reached over and touched my knee. "Wherever you want." "What do you mean?" "I'll give you a good time for forty bucks." I was shocked. "What is a woman like you doing mixed up with this kind of stuff?" "I have four kids in school, and there is never enough money. But listen, if we are just going to talk, I want to get out at this corner. OK?"

Compassion struggled with judgment as the Pharisee drove back to the office.

God, it is so easy to judge someone by what I see on the outside. Help me not to judge, but to understand.

Friday | SEPTEMBER 18

Some time later Jesus travelled through towns and villages, preaching the Good News about the kingdom of God. The twelve disciples went with him, and so did some women who had been healed of evil spirits and diseases: Mary (who was called Magdalene), from whom seven demons had been driven out; Joanna, whose husband Chuza was an officer in Herod's court; and Susanna, and many other women who used their own resources to help Jesus and his disciples.

Luke 8: 1-3

"...and many other women..."

A role model

Our neighbour Mrs. Wall didn't travel through towns and villages preaching the Good News. In fact, most days she travelled the distance between the sink, the stove and her kitchen table. But those short steps more than revealed the face of God to anyone who was fortunate enough to spend time in her presence.

"Midda Wall," as we called her, would look out her kitchen window and see us walking up her driveway. By the time we were at her door, she'd have filled the kettle and set it to boil. Over a very milky cup of tea and homemade cookies, she'd listen – to whatever was on our minds. And she'd always have an encouraging word or comforting hug to offer.

Like Jesus, Mrs. Wall's loving presence brought healing and peace to the lives of those she touched.

Lord, help me to recognize your loving presence in all who seek to follow you.

269

"Once there was a man who went out to sow grain. As he scattered the seed in the field, some of it fell along the path, where it was stepped on, and the birds ate it up. Some of it fell on rocky ground, and when the plants sprouted, they dried up because the soil had no moisture. Some of the seed fell among thorn bushes, which grew up with the plants and choked them. And some seeds fell in good soil; the plants grew and bore grain, one hundred grains each." His disciples asked Jesus what this parable meant, and he answered, "The knowledge of the secrets of the kingdom of God has been given to you, but to the rest it comes by means of parables."

Luke 8: 4-15

"Once there was a man who went out to sow grain."

Seeds of grace

Recently a neighbour asked to borrow a power tool. I lent it to him, but all the time he had it I kept worrying about how soon he would return it and what condition it would be in.

There is a stingy, fearful side to me. I tend to parcel out my goods and kindnesses a little at a time. I fear I might need them later. I fear someone might take advantage of me if I'm too generous.

How different God is from me. Neither fearful nor stingy. Holding nothing back. Not concerned about looking foolish. God sows seeds of grace everywhere – without worrying where they will land or how worthy the soil is. I hope that I may do the same.

**Lord, help me be open to your words,
so that I may grow to be more like you.**

Where there is jealousy and selfishness, there is also disorder and every kind of evil. But the wisdom from above is pure first of all; it is also peaceful, gentle and friendly; it is full of compassion and produces a harvest of good deeds; it is free from prejudice and hypocrisy....

Where do all the fights and quarrels among you come from? They come from your desires for pleasure, which are constantly fighting within you. You want things, but you cannot have them, so you are ready to kill; you strongly desire things, but you cannot get them, so you quarrel and fight. You do not have what you want because you do not ask God for it. And when you ask, you do not receive it, because your motives are bad; you ask for things to use for your own pleasures. *James 3: 16 – 4: 3*

> "You want things... so you quarrel and fight."

True freedom

I know that hunger for wanting to possess "things." The feeling can be so strong that it takes over my entire body and mind. It's as if I am starving: I must satisfy that craving or all will be lost.

When I focus on acquiring things, my world becomes very small, very limited. I look at what others have and want it for myself. I find myself forgetting to consider the big picture.

These days I'm learning to let go of these old thought patterns and behaviours. And I'm trying to make more space in my life for "wisdom from above."

Today, I just got back from an hour of garage-saling. I bought nothing, and lived.

God, satisfy me with your wisdom. May I possess the knowledge of your love... and know that it will be enough.

J esus left that place, and as he walked along, he saw a tax collector, named Matthew, sitting in his office. He said to him, "Follow me." Matthew got up and followed him.

While Jesus was having a meal in Matthew's house, many tax collectors and other outcasts came and joined Jesus and his disciples at the table. Some Pharisees saw this and asked his disciples, "Why does your teacher eat with such people?"

Jesus heard them and answered, "People who are well do not need a doctor, but only those who are sick. Go and find out what

is meant by the scripture that says: 'It is kindness that I want, not animal sacrifices.' I have not come to call respectable people, but outcasts."   *Matthew 9:9-13*

"It is kindness that I want…"

Wanted: kindness

I feel that Jesus is talking to me directly. While I may not offer dead birds or animals on an altar, I am aware of the times when my words and actions, while socially acceptable, are empty. They lack kindness.

I think of how I routinely speak to my children in an angry and frustrated way. I may be "right" in insisting that their chores be done, that they don't use "bad" language, that they learn "good" manners. But all of that is empty, meaningless, if my words lack kindness.

In my striving to do what is "right," I need to be reminded that I stand in need of Jesus' loving acceptance. In that love I find the strength to be kind to others, especially those who are vulnerable.

**Dear God, help me when I do what is "right,"
but with the "wrong" spirit in my heart.**

J esus' mother and brothers came to him, but were unable to join him because of the crowd. Someone said to Jesus, "Your mother and brothers are standing outside and want to see you."

Jesus said to them all, "My mother and brothers are those who hear the word of God and obey it."

Luke 8: 19-21

"...those who hear the word of God..."

Family

My family tends to be clannish. We describe each other in terms of relationship by marriage, by degree, and so forth. The intent is certainly not to exclude other people, but maybe to add something special when we are related. Or so we tell ourselves.

This past Christmas I received an unexpected gift from a person whom I admire greatly. We don't socialize, but we share deeply held values. My six-year-old grandson was with me when I opened her gift. He seemed puzzled, as if he couldn't understand something. He said, "Is Jeanne family?

Not sure how best to answer, I finally said, "Yes, in a way." Later, telling Jeanne the story and seeing her reaction, I realized that she was family, in a most profound way.

Lord, help me hear your word and follow your commands, for only then will I find my true home.

Jesus called the twelve disciples together and gave them power and authority to drive out all demons and to cure diseases. Then he sent them out to preach the kingdom of God and to heal the sick, after saying to them, "Take nothing with you for the trip: no walking stick, no beggar's bag, no food, no money, not even an extra shirt. Wherever you are welcomed, stay in the same house until you leave that town; wherever people don't welcome you, leave that town and shake the dust off your feet as a warning to them."

The disciples left and travelled through all the villages, preaching the Good News and healing people everywhere. *Luke 9: 1-6*

"Take nothing with you for the trip..."

Real security

On a recent business trip, my husband arrived at his destination only to find that the airline had lost his luggage. He was upset at the prospect of three days of meetings without his own clothing and personal effects. In his situation I would have been frantic.

Reading today's scripture, I am tempted to wonder why Jesus told his disciples to travel without their usual supports. How would an extra shirt get in the way?

But maybe it is not only the possessions, but also our dependence on them, that is the problem. For the kingdom of God to flourish, we must get rid of our material entanglements. Then God can give us gifts greater than any security we can provide ourselves.

**Jesus, when I am tempted to justify my needs,
help me trust in your loving care.**

When Herod, the ruler of Galilee, heard about all the things that were happening, he was very confused, because some people were saying that John the Baptist had come back to life. Others were saying that Elijah had appeared, and still others that one of the prophets of long ago had come back to life. Herod said, "I had John's head cut off; but who is this man I hear these things about?" And he kept trying to see Jesus.

Luke 9: 7-9

> "...who is this man
> I hear these things about?"

Letting go of control

Herod didn't like the talk going around about Jesus. Something was happening that was beyond his control.

Like Herod, I am threatened by a loss of control in my life – especially when it comes to relationships. Will this person start asking too much of me, or contradict my way of seeing things? I must admit that Jesus threatens my control, too. If I let him into my life, will he ask me to give up something I cherish: a possession, my status or an attitude?

Herod reacted by killing what he feared. I react by keeping Jesus at a safe distance, reading endless books about spirituality instead of actually spending time with him. What would happen if I were willing to yield control and let Jesus into my life?

**Lord, give me the grace to recognize the source of my fears.
Help me risk my life for you.**

One day when Jesus was praying alone, the disciples came to him. "Who do the crowds say I am?" he asked them. "Some say that you are John the Baptist," they answered. "Others say that you are Elijah, while others say that one of the prophets of long ago has come back to life." "What about you?" he asked them. "Who do you say I am?" Peter answered, "You are God's Messiah." Then Jesus gave them strict orders not to tell this to anyone. He also told them, "The Son of Man must suffer much and be rejected by the elders, the chief priests, and the teachers of the Law. He will be put to death, but three days later he will be raised to life."

Luke 9: 18-22

> "Jesus gave them strict orders not to tell this to anyone."

Living the questions

Why did Jesus give the disciples strict orders not to tell anyone? This secrecy has always puzzled me – in today's reading as well as in my life today.

Why does this young mother have MS? Why do children die? Why floods, tornadoes or hurricanes? Why, Lord, why? Why the suffering, the wailing mothers, the widows with broken hearts? Why? Even Jesus felt this way on the cross: "Why have you abandoned me?"

The answer comes in brief glimmers. I've glimpsed it in the father of a murdered high school boy as he forgives his son's killer. I see it in the love I experience with my family and friends. And I stumble on, feeling my way through the questions, on my voyage back to God.

**God, let me hear some answers to my questions.
Give me the strength to carry on until I do.**

Yet we who have this spiritual treasure are like common clay pots, in order to show that the supreme power belongs to God, not to us. We are often troubled, but not crushed; sometimes in doubt, but never in despair; there are many enemies, but we are never without a friend; and though badly hurt at times, we are not destroyed. At all times we carry in our mortal bodies the death of Jesus, so that his life also may be seen in our bodies. Throughout our lives we are always in danger of death for Jesus' sake, in order that his life may be seen in this mortal body of ours. This means that death is at work in us, but life is at work in you.

2 Corinthians 4: 7-15

"We are often troubled, but not crushed..."

Within real life

Wouldn't it be great to rise above all of life's worries and concerns? To never be weighed down by illness, financial woes or discord? How I long for such a time.

And I'm still foolish enough to believe that it's possible – *if* I could just find the key: the money, the time or the right way of solving my problems. I spend so much energy trying to escape my human condition and its frustrating limitations.

Today's reading reminds me that true contentment lies in soulful living, and not in magical solutions. Living well *in* (and not above) the tensions of life is where God meets me, and comforts me.

It may not be glamorous, but real life is where God is found.

Lord, give me courage to face the reality of my life, so that I can reveal your light to others.

J ohn said to Jesus, "Teacher, we saw a man who was driving out demons in your name, and we told him to stop, because he doesn't belong to our group."

"Do not try to stop him," Jesus told them, "because no one who performs a miracle in my name will be able soon afterward to say evil things about me. For whoever is not against us is for us. I assure you that anyone who gives you a drink of water because you belong to me will certainly receive a reward.

"If anyone should cause one of these little ones to lose faith in me, it would be better for that person to have a large millstone tied around the neck and be thrown into the sea." *Mark 9: 38-43, 45, 47-48*

"For whoever is not against us is for us."

True faith

Many people have noticed that Christianity often is practised better by people who deny it in *word*.

I think of many of the early communists and union leaders who sacrificed their possessions, their security and sometimes their lives for a cause that would bring an end to injustice. They sought God – even as avowed atheists – and they named God by their *actions* rather than their words. How could they be against us?

The film, *Motorcycle Diaries*, shows a scene of the Argentinian revolutionary Che Guevara at a Peruvian leper colony. Was his stay there not Christian?

**Lord, help me get beyond the words of faith
to its real presence.**

An argument broke out among the disciples as to which one of them was the greatest. Jesus knew what they were thinking, so he took a child, stood him by his side, and said to them, "Whoever welcomes this child in my name, welcomes me; and whoever welcomes me, also welcomes the one who sent me. For the one who is least among you all is the greatest."

John spoke up, "Master, we saw a man driving out demons in your name, and we told him to stop, because he doesn't belong to our group." "Do not try to stop him," Jesus said to him and to the other disciples, "because whoever is not against you is for you."

Luke 9: 46-50

> "Whoever welcomes this child in my name…"

Seeing the person

These words sound great from the pulpit: "The least among you all is the greatest!" Then I leave church and drive home. I go past people sleeping on the street and squeegee kids pressing me to give them money. So many people with so many needs. How can I possibly "welcome" them all?

Jesus' words are so easy to agree with, but so hard to live. The demands of life seem to conspire to make us treat each other like objects.

Every Saturday morning I stop for coffee. I'm usually part of a long lineup, but the woman behind the counter treats each of us with genuine good humour and kindness. In her own way she shows me the truth: recognize and treat others as persons, just like me.

Lord, help me stop and consider my actions.
Have I forgotten that people, indeed, come first?

thank you, Lord, with all my heart;
I sing praise to you before the gods.
I face your holy Temple,
bow down, and praise your name
because of your constant love and faithfulness,
because you have shown that your name
and your commands are supreme.
You answered me when I called to you;
with your strength you strengthened me.
All the kings in the world will praise you, Lord,
because they have heard your promises.
They will sing about what you have done
and about your great glory.

Psalm 138: 1-5

"With your strength you strengthened me."

In times of need

A winter of illness had drawn me to the point of despair. Unable to attend to the roles and responsibilities that had long defined my life, I felt worthless. There was little left to give me a sense of purpose or meaning. Hopelessness and helplessness became my daily companions.

Into that pocket of despondency drifted a memory of God's promise of constant love. Despite my emptiness, this memory touched my heart and delighted me. With it came the reassurance that I did not have to rely on my own strength, but that I could trust God's strength. God's love and faithfulness are constant.

Initially, I felt overwhelmed. Then, as I opened myself to God's promise, hope surged through me, bringing me to life again.

Lord, may I always turn to you,
especially when I feel weak and without hope.

A man said to Jesus, "I will follow you wherever you go." Jesus replied, "Foxes have holes, and birds have nests, but the Son of Man has no place to lie down and rest." He said to another man, "Follow me." But that man said, "Sir, first let me go back and bury my father." Jesus answered, "Let the dead bury their own dead. You go and proclaim the kingdom of God." Someone else said, "I will follow you, sir; but first let me go and say good-bye to my family." Jesus said, "Anyone who starts to plow and then keeps looking back is of no use for the kingdom of God."

Luke 9: 57-62

"...then keeps looking back..."

Don't look back

I am a serious lap swimmer, with a secret desire to swim competitively. In order to improve my stroke, I read training manuals as well as motivational material. One of my favourite articles, "The Twenty-One Top Laws of Swimming," summarizes the entire sport for me.

Some rules are difficult to implement, such as generating power from the hips and torso, and maintaining body stability with the legs. But I have no problem with Rule Number 17: "Never look back." This makes sense to any swimmer intent on reaching the goal as quickly as possible. Looking back produces counter-productive movement, creating what is known as drag.

When I read Jesus' harsh words in today's gospel, this analogy comes to mind. Jesus is describing what a single-minded commitment to his kingdom involves. No drag allowed.

Holy Spirit, strengthen my will so I can witness to your truth.

The Lord chose another seventy-two men and sent them out two by two, to go ahead of him to every town and place where he himself was about to go. He said to them, "There is a large harvest, but few workers to gather it in. Pray to the owner of the harvest that he will send out workers to gather in his harvest…. Don't take a purse or a beggar's bag or shoes; don't stop to greet anyone on the road. Whenever you go into a house, first say, 'Peace be with this house.' If someone who is peace-loving lives there, let your greeting of peace remain on that person; if not, take back your greeting of peace. Stay in that same house, eating and drinking whatever they offer you, for workers should be given their pay."

Luke 10: 1-12

"…first say, 'Peace be with this house.'"

Travelling light

In my early 20s, I went backpacking in Northern Ireland for several months. I met people of peace who opened their homes and hearts to me. I met others torn apart by the division, the hatred and the violence they experienced. In one hostel, a woman pushed another woman down the stairs because of their differing religious affiliations!

As a visitor, I brought none of that baggage of sectarian hatred with me. And so my new friends seemed to find a few hours of peace talking to me. I could simply sit with them and listen to their stories without prejudice.

Travelling light, without prejudgments, enabled me to meet others with openness and simplicity. I hope I'll remember that in my day-to-day reality, here at home.

**God, may I remember to "travel light" today,
to rely on the strength that lies within.**

The disciples came to Jesus, asking, "Who is the greatest in the kingdom of heaven?"

So Jesus called a child to come and stand in front of them, and said, "I assure you that unless you change and become like children, you will never enter the kingdom of heaven. The greatest in the kingdom of heaven is the one who humbles himself and becomes like this child. And whoever welcomes in my name one such child as this, welcomes me....

"See that you don't despise any of these little ones. Their angels in heaven, I tell you, are always in the presence of my Father in heaven."   *Matthew 18: 1-5, 10*

> "...whoever welcomes in my name one such child..."

Listening

I was having a great time with the parents, but my daughter was having problems getting along with their child. I wasn't very sympathetic. "Be more understanding!" I said. "She's probably behaving like that because she lacks self-confidence!" My daughter was downcast, and I was about to go back to my friends, but something made me turn back.

When I took her in my arms and asked to hear more, she burst into tears. Once she had poured out her heart – and I had listened without imposing my own diagnoses or prescriptions – it was *she* who came up with the best ideas for resolving the problem.

I've learned Jesus' lesson about listening to children over and over, but it seems I forget it over and over, too.

Lord, you are faithful to your children.
Help me be worthy of the trust given me by others.

Saturday | OCTOBER 3

The seventy-two men came back in great joy. "Lord," they said, "even the demons obeyed us when we gave them a command in your name...." Jesus was filled with joy by the Holy Spirit and said, "Father, I thank you because you have shown to the unlearned what you have hidden from the wise and learned....

"My Father has given me all things. No one knows who the Son is except the Father, and no one knows who the Father is except the Son and those to whom the Son chooses to reveal him."

Then Jesus turned to the disciples and said, "How fortunate you are to see the things you see! I tell you that many prophets and kings wanted to see what you see, but they could not, and to hear what you hear, but they did not."

Luke 10: 17-24

> "How fortunate you are to see…"

Seeing and hearing

Yes, I guess the disciples were fortunate – they were actually there with Jesus.

I think back to times when we played the game "Who would you like to meet from history?" Usually it came down to Jesus. I, too, would like to see what his followers saw, and hear what they heard.

But I have a suspicion Jesus might ask me about what I see and hear today. The geese calling to me on fall mornings. My children's banter around the table. The voice coming from the scarred, whiskered face asking for spare change.

Yes, I would dearly love to sit and talk with Jesus. For now, I guess I need to pay close attention to what I do see, what I do hear all around me.

**Dear God, help me to see and hear you
in all of your creatures.**

Some people brought children to Jesus for him to place his hands on them, but the disciples scolded the people. When Jesus noticed this, he was angry and said to his disciples, "Let the children come to me, and do not stop them, because the kingdom of God belongs to such as these. I assure you that whoever does not receive the kingdom of God like a child will never enter it." Then he took the children in his arms, placed his hands on each of them, and blessed them.

Mark 10: 2-16

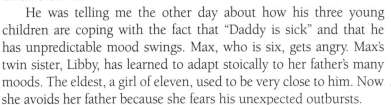

"Then he took the children in his arms..."

Comfort the children

My cousin has a brain tumour. The condition affects his ability to keep his emotions on an even keel.

He was telling me the other day about how his three young children are coping with the fact that "Daddy is sick" and that he has unpredictable mood swings. Max, who is six, gets angry. Max's twin sister, Libby, has learned to adapt stoically to her father's many moods. The eldest, a girl of eleven, used to be very close to him. Now she avoids her father because she fears his unexpected outbursts.

I think of how Christ would have gathered these children to himself and comforted them. I ask the Lord to help us put loving, consoling arms around them – and all children in pain – today.

Lord, I believe that you care for the little ones of this world. Increase my faith.

"In my distress, O Lord, I called to you,
and you answered me.
From deep in the world of the dead
I cried for help, and you heard me.
You threw me down into the depths....
But you, O Lord my God,
brought me back from the depths alive.
When I felt my life slipping away,
then, O Lord, I prayed to you,
and in your holy Temple you heard me....
But I will sing praises to you;
I will offer you a sacrifice
and do what I have promised.
Salvation comes from the Lord!"

Jonah 2: 2-9

"In my distress, O Lord, I called to you..."

A reason to praise

This reading reminds me of the long, painful months when my parents were dying of cancer. My sisters and I were helping them in this final stage of their lives: one of us was always at their home to do whatever was needed.

Often I felt as though I was living in a strange new world. Every detail of life was important, and each moment had a fearsome intensity. Sometimes this world was wonderful, sometimes it was terrifying. But I could never leave it, no matter what I wished.

When it was over and I returned to the "old" world, everything was different. I hadn't realized it, but God had been with me all that time, teaching me that life was unspeakably precious.

**Lord, I have learned that there is only one prayer,
the prayer of gratitude. Thank you.**

A s Jesus and his disciples went on their way, he came to a village where a woman named Martha welcomed him in her home. She had a sister named Mary, who sat down at the feet of the Lord and listened to his teaching. Martha was upset over all the work she had to do, so she came and said, "Lord, don't you care that my sister has left me to do all the work by myself? Tell her to come and help me!"

The Lord answered her, "Martha, Martha! You are worried and troubled over so many things, but just one is needed. Mary has chosen the right thing, and it will not be taken away from her."

Luke 10: 38-42

> "You are worried and troubled…"

Too busy

Last year I was in a car accident that left me with a fractured pelvis. I was off work for three months, and suddenly I found myself having to learn to ask for help.

The accident not only broke a few bones, it broke through the layers of busyness I'd created to shield myself from letting people get too close to me. When I was confined to my room, people came to visit and to share a cup of tea with me. People drove me to my appointments, and we had good conversations in the car. I had time to read, pray and listen to music.

I rediscovered the place of Mary – sitting at Jesus' feet and listening to him. Now that my physical strength has returned, I want to remember the value of Mary's quiet, listening stance.

**Lord, help me to create a space
where I can listen to you in my busy life.**

One day Jesus was praying in a certain place. When he had finished, one of his disciples said to him, "Lord, teach us to pray, just as John taught his disciples."
Jesus said to them, "When you pray, say this:
'Father: May your holy name be honoured;
may your kingdom come.
Give us day by day the food we need.
Forgive us our sins,
for we forgive everyone who does us wrong.
And do not bring us to hard testing.'"

Luke 11: 1-4

"...for we forgive everyone who does us wrong."

Wanting to forgive

She'd heard that I visited sex offenders in prison, and she wanted to talk to me. "What he did to me comes back almost every time I am with my husband. I was only a little girl at the time; my folks drank a lot, and he seemed like such a gentle, friendly uncle. He used to take me for drives in his car, and one thing just led to another. Marriage brought the whole issue out.

"At his trial I found out that he had done the same thing to all of my sisters. Now we talk about it; we cry, we pray, and we try to forgive. We know that just *wishing* will not make it better; that *working* at forgiving is what is needed. But there are times…."

**O God, the gift of forgiveness does not come easily.
Help me to forgive.**

Jesus said to his disciples, "I say to you: Ask, and you will receive; seek, and you will find; knock, and the door will be opened to you. For those who ask will receive, and those who seek will find, and the door will be opened to anyone who knocks. Would any of you who are fathers give your son a snake when he asks for fish? Or would you give him a scorpion when he asks for an egg? As bad as you are, you know how to give good things to your children. How much more, then, will the Father in heaven give the Holy Spirit to those who ask him!"

Luke 11:5-13

> "Ask, and you will receive…"

Keep knocking

"Daddy, look! Daddy, watch this!" No matter how tired or busy I am, and despite my body language that may say, "Don't bother me!" my children keep on seeking my attention. They keep knocking at the door. They seem to have an unquenchable faith in me – a stronger faith than I have in myself!

I grew up thinking a father had to be the strong, distant, silent type. Now that I'm a father, I'm trying to change this image – both for myself and as I seek an ever-attentive and caring God.

When God seems silent in my life, I tend to stop asking. I stop knocking at the door. If only I could have the kind of faith in God that my children have in me.

Dear God, give me the faith to keep on knocking at the door, even when you seem silent.

" **A**nyone who is not for me is really against me; anyone who does not help me gather is really scattering.

"When an evil spirit goes out of a person, it travels over dry country looking for a place to rest. If it can't find one, it says to itself, 'I will go back to my house.' So it goes back and finds the house clean and all fixed up. Then it goes out and brings seven other spirits even worse than itself, and they come and live there. So when it is all over, that person is in worse shape than at the beginning."

Luke 11: 15-26

"...that person is in worse shape..."

Dark times

Psychiatrist Kay Redfield explains in her book *Touched with Fire* that there is a strong link between creativity and depression. This is certainly the experience of John Bentley Mays, whose stark autobiography of depression he entitles *In the Jaws of the Black Dogs*. Author Andrew Solomon calls depression *The Noonday Demon*, and explores it as a scientific and cultural phenomenon.

All three writers share not only a common subject; they also write from personal experience. Each describes how depression is their constant companion: treatable, but rarely overcome – the visitor who keeps their promise to return. The melancholic in me has certainly experienced this familiar guest.

There is deep wisdom in these words of Jesus. Once graced with his blessing, we become decidedly more vulnerable.

Dear God, I know that, with your help, my moments of darkness do recede, even though they often return.

When Jesus had said this, a woman spoke up from the crowd and said to him, "How happy is the woman who bore you and nursed you!". But Jesus answered, "Rather, how happy are those who hear the word of God and obey it!"
Luke 11: 27-28

> "...happy are those who hear the word of God..."

True nurture

What is this woman in the crowd really saying? And why doesn't Jesus allow Mary, his mother, these few words of praise?

Jesus seems to be saying that it's not just the physical act of bearing and nursing a child that matters. What matters in my parenting is how I hear the word of God: in my children's questions and their searching. In their anger, sadness and hurt. In what they say and what they leave unsaid. In their eyes that plead for understanding. In their tight, angry bodies that need to be hugged and comforted.

Giving birth and caring for the physical needs of my children has come fairly easily to me. Nurturing their spirits – by hearing and responding to their deeper needs – is proving much harder.

**God, grant me the strength to recognize your word
as it is spoken today. May I respond with love.**

A man asked Jesus, "Good Teacher, what must I do to receive eternal life?"

"Why do you call me good?" Jesus asked him. "You know the commandments: 'Do not commit murder; do not commit adultery; do not steal; do not accuse anyone falsely; do not cheat; respect your father and your mother.'"

"Teacher," the man said, "ever since I was young, I have obeyed all these commandments." Jesus looked straight at him with love and said, "You need only one thing. Go and sell all you have and give the money to the poor, and you will have riches in heaven; then come and follow me." When the man heard this, gloom spread over his face, and he went away sad, because he was very rich.

Mark 10: 17-30

> "...what must I do to receive eternal life?"

By the rule

When I was young, life was mostly a series of rules – rules at school, at home, at church. Life was simple: just follow the rules. I liked it (for the most part) because the world was mysterious to me then, and knowing and following the rules made this mystery less frightening.

Today, I have to admit, I'm still attracted to that way of being in the world. Like the rich young man, I want to be told the Answer, the one Big Rule.

But I've been around long enough to have learned the lesson Jesus was teaching: the Answer is not what you expect. In fact, the Rule makes life harder, not easier. And even if you think you can, it's impossible to follow it on your own.

Lord, what is impossible for me alone is possible with you.
Help me to follow you more closely today.

Jesus said, "How evil are the people of this day! They ask for a miracle, but none will be given them except the miracle of Jonah. In the same way that the prophet Jonah was a sign for the people of Nineveh, so the Son of Man will be a sign for the people of this day. On the Judgment Day the Queen of Sheba will stand up and accuse the people of today, because she travelled all the way from her country to listen to King Solomon's wise teaching; and there is something here, I tell you, greater than Solomon. On the Judgment Day the people of Nineveh will stand up and accuse you, because they turned from their sins when they heard Jonah preach; and I assure you that there is something here greater than Jonah!"

Luke 11: 29-32

> "They ask for a miracle, but none will be given..."

Too wonderful

When I taught drama, one play always grabbed the hearts and minds of my students. *Our Town* is Thornton Wilder's portrait of Grover's Corners, where children grow and parents age, and illness and death lie waiting. Wilder said the play was his attempt "to find a value above all price for the smallest events in our daily life."

Like the people in today's reading, I often look to some distant horizon for exciting signs and portents of God's presence. I have to make a conscious effort to look for the richness of God's grace beneath my feet and in everyone around me. Only then can I say, as Emily does at the end of the play, "Oh earth, you're too wonderful for anybody to realize you."

God, may I discover something about you in all I do today.

How clearly the sky reveals God's glory!
How plainly it shows what he has done!
Each day announces it to the following day;
each night repeats it to the next.
No speech or words are used,
no sound is heard;
yet their message goes out to all the world
and is heard to the ends of the earth.
God made a home in the sky for the sun.

Psalm 19: 1-4

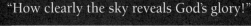

"How clearly the sky reveals God's glory!"

God's glory

The sky speaks, in a special way, to people who live on the prairies, to sailors and to anyone lucky enough to have some outdoor open space – sunrises and sunsets that range from the tranquil to the wildly melodramatic. Deep velvet night skies packed with glittering jewels in motion. Richly textured sunlit clouds that invite the imagination to stroll on their tops like great mountains. Low, raking sunlight casting a deep magenta glow, and sharp shadows under retreating black clouds. And sundogs, comets and breathtaking moon appearances – all here for a brief moment, and then gone.

"Come, look!" we say. And in a moment, it has vanished and a new wonder is on its way. God's glory? How can it be anything else?

My God, you write across the heavens with such beauty.
I love your style.

"How terrible for you Pharisees! You give to God one tenth of the seasoning herbs, such as mint and rue and all the other herbs, but you neglect justice and love for God…. You love the reserved seats in the synagogues and to be greeted with respect in the marketplaces. How terrible for you! You are like unmarked graves which people walk on without knowing it."

One of the teachers of the Law said to him, "Teacher, when you say this, you insult us too!" Jesus answered, "How terrible also for you teachers of the Law! You put onto people's backs loads which are hard to carry, but you yourselves will not stretch out a finger to help them carry those loads."

Luke 11: 42-46

> "You love the reserved seats in the synagogues…"

Just love!

Passing judgment, creating laws and punishing transgressors is an obvious way to deal with things that aren't going right in the world. And there is a place for laws.

But when things in our house aren't going the way I'd like them to, it's usually because I'm comparing us to some other family. "Their" children read more, play more music, are more popular or more athletic. My reaction is often to make sarcastic comments, and then to create some new rule or other. Inevitably, the result is not improvement but resistance!

But Jesus says, Stop! Stop judging. Look around you. Just love.

Lord, fill my heart with your love so there's no more room for comparisons and judgments.

"How terrible for you! You make fine tombs for the prophets – the very prophets your ancestors murdered. You yourselves admit, then, that you approve of what your ancestors did; they murdered the prophets, and you build their tombs. For this reason the Wisdom of God said, 'I will send them prophets and messengers; they will kill some of them and persecute others.' So the people of this time will be punished for the murder of all the prophets killed since the creation of the world, from the murder of Abel to the murder of Zechariah.... How terrible for you teachers of the Law! You have kept the key that opens the door to the house of knowledge; you yourselves will not go in, and you stop those who are trying to go in!"

Luke 11:47-54

"You make fine tombs for the prophets..."

True to my ideals

When Jesus speaks this way to the religious leaders of his day – in anger, about punishment and accountability – I am glad he is not speaking to me. Then again, maybe he is.

I start to think about ways that I "murder the prophets" and then make fine tombs for them: buying cheap imported goods and then being indignant about child labour and poor working conditions in developing countries; wasting food and resources and then wondering why some people in the world have so little; arguing with a family member and then asking why our society cannot live in peace.

The ideals that I hold up for the world to see often shine much brighter than the realities I live each day.

Lord, help me make my actions each day mirror what I claim to believe.

Jesus said to his disciples, "Be on guard against the yeast of the Pharisees – I mean their hypocrisy. Whatever is covered up will be uncovered, and every secret will be made known. So then, whatever you have said in the dark will be heard in broad daylight, and whatever you have whispered in private in a closed room will be shouted from the housetops.

"I tell you, my friends, do not be afraid of those who kill the body but cannot afterward do anything worse. I will show you whom to fear: fear God, who, after killing, has the authority to throw into hell....

"Aren't five sparrows sold for two pennies? Yet not one sparrow is forgotten by God. Even the hairs of your head have all been counted. So do not be afraid; you are worth much more than many sparrows!"
Luke 12: 1-7

> "Whatever is covered up will be uncovered..."

Towards the light

A friend of mine is in a coma. For months, Dan has been lying in a hospital bed, being fed through a tube. Always an elusive man, now he's a complete mystery. Does he hear our words? And if not, who is this lying here, and where is the Dan we knew?

Dan was the best listener. He knew how to weave the scraps of a person's life into a beautiful pattern and hand it back to them, transformed by light. He now carries the confidences of many people with him.

Perhaps, with his silence, he is asking us to repossess our secrets and learn to weave. Perhaps he is still listening, still weaving. When he goes, he will carry all those dark secrets with him into the light.

Lord, thank you for all who shine your light into our darkness.

W hen God promised Abraham and his descendants that the world would belong to him, he did so, not because Abraham obeyed the Law, but because he believed and was accepted as righteous by God....

And so the promise was based on faith, in order that the promise should be guaranteed as God's free gift to all of Abraham's descendants – not just to those who obey the Law, but also to those who believe as Abraham did.... So the promise is good in the sight of God, in whom Abraham believed – the God who brings the dead to life and whose command brings into being what did not exist. Abraham believed and hoped, even when there was no reason for hoping.

Romans 4: 13, 16-18

"...even when there was no reason for hoping."

Reason to believe

It's easy to believe in God or trust that God loves me when things are going well, but that isn't always the way life is. There have been times when I have experienced intense sorrow, pain or disappointment, times when I thought God had abandoned me or no longer loved me.

Abraham is called our "father in faith." He left his family and homeland to go to an unknown land God had promised him. And although he and his wife were well past childbearing years, they trusted God's promise of countless descendants.

I have a long way to go before I have that kind of faith. Still, I draw hope from people like Abraham and Sarah. They are proof that such faith is humanly possible.

**Lord, may I trust you in bad times as well as in good.
Give me the gift of faith.**

James and John, the sons of Zebedee, came to Jesus. "Teacher," they said, "when you sit on your throne in your glorious kingdom, we want you to let us sit with you, one at your right and one at your left." Jesus said, "You don't know what you are asking for...."

When the other ten disciples heard about it, they became angry with James and John. So Jesus called them together and said, "You know that those who are considered rulers of the heathen have power over them.... This, however, is not the way it is among you. If one of you wants to be great, you must be the servant of the rest.... For even the Son of Man did not come to be served; he came to serve and to give his life to redeem many people."

Mark 10: 35-45

> "...you must be the servant of the rest..."

Gentle service

The Grade Six students at my son's school, having reached their final year of primary school, tend to behave as if they have nothing left to learn. For some, this translates as bullying the younger students; for others, it's a general attitude of disrespect.

This year the teachers tried something new: the Grade Six students were required *to earn* their position of privilege. They could choose to volunteer in any number of activities: from coaching the younger students' sports teams to refereeing their games, from answering the phone in the office to helping the janitor clean the classrooms.

Now, instead of "lording it over" the other students, the Grade Sixers are serving the school community. Everyone seems much happier, and the school has become a kinder and gentler place.

**Lord, when I want things to go my way,
help me to see that I may be missing the big picture.**

Jesus told this parable: "There was once a rich man who had land which bore good crops. He began to think to himself, 'I don't have a place to keep all my crops. What can I do? This is what I will do,' he told himself; 'I will tear down my barns and build bigger ones, where I will store the grain and all my other goods. Then I will say to myself, Lucky man! You have all the good things you need for many years. Take life easy, eat, drink, and enjoy yourself!' But God said to him, 'You fool! This very night you will have to give up your life; then who will get all these things you have kept for yourself?'"

And Jesus concluded, "This is how it is with those who pile up riches for themselves but are not rich in God's sight."

Luke 12: 13-21

> "This very night you will have to give up your life…"

Walking the talk

We've all *heard* the lesson in today's reading many times. *Living* it is the hard part. How can I take care of material concerns without being possessed by them?

My friend is a director in a hospital. A week ago, one of her young nurses went home from work and died, without warning. This sudden loss, of course, hit everyone very hard.

For my friend and me, it has meant conversations in which the usual comments are made about "living in the moment," and "not getting caught in the rat race." Genuine, heartfelt sentiments, but then life starts up again: bills to pay, cars to fix.

It is hard to remember what is important – moment by moment, day by day. Living it is even harder.

**Lord, help me keep my eyes
and heart fixed on what is important.**

Y ou do not want sacrifices and offerings;
you do not ask for animals burned whole on the altar
or for sacrifices to take away sins.
Instead, you have given me ears to hear you,
and so I answered, "Here I am...."
In the assembly of all your people, Lord,
I told the good news that you save us.
You know that I will never stop telling it.
I have not kept the news of salvation to myself;
I have always spoken of your faithfulness and help.
In the assembly of all your people I have not been silent
about your loyalty and constant love.
Lord, I know you will never stop being merciful to me.
Your love and loyalty will always keep me safe.

Psalm 40: 6-11

> "...you will never stop being merciful to me."

In need of mercy

Regrettably, there are times when my words and actions do not "speak of God's faithfulness and love." Anticipating a potentially difficult meeting at work, I snarl at my children at the breakfast table. When they're finally out the door and on the school bus, silence fills the house. I take a deep breath and realize that I've blown it... again. How I long to take back some of the harsh words I've uttered. How I wish I'd started our day with kind and loving words instead.

Today's reading assures me that God "will never stop being merciful to me." I find myself straining to receive that mercy and love. In turn, I hope to be more merciful and loving to my children... starting today.

God of mercy, fill my heart with your loving kindness.

[J esus said], "Who is the faithful and wise servant? He is the one that his master will put in charge, to run the household.... How happy that servant is if his master finds him doing this when he comes home...! But if that servant says to himself that his master is taking a long time to come back and if he begins to beat the other servants..., then the master will come back one day when the servant does not expect him and at a time he does not know. The master will cut him in pieces and make him share the fate of the disobedient....

"Much is required from the person to whom much is given; much more is required from the person to whom much more is given."
Luke 12: 39-48

> "Who is the faithful and wise servant?"

Knowing what to do

Today's reading reminds me of the difference between knowing what to do... and actually doing it.

A group of us walking home from school began teasing a girl who was tall – taller than any of us. Even at the age of twelve, I had a knack for instant songs and rhymes. I can still remember the song that came to me that morning. Even as I sang the hurtful words, I could hear my mother's voice in my head, saying, "You know better!" And, yes, I did know better.

You can say it was just one kid teasing another. But that experience taught me something about the misuse of gifts, whether they are cleverness, money or power. Yes, I knew what to do. I just didn't do it.

Lord, help me know my gifts and use them to do "for" others, not "to" them.

"I came to set the earth on fire, and how I wish it were already kindled! I have a baptism to receive, and how distressed I am until it is over! Do you suppose that I came to bring peace to the world? No, not peace, but division. From now on a family of five will be divided, three against two and two against three. Fathers will be against their sons, and sons against their fathers; mothers will be against their daughters, and daughters against their mothers; mothers-in-law will be against their daughters-in-law, and daughters-in-law against their mothers-in-law."

Luke 12: 49-53

> "Do you suppose that I came to bring peace to the world?"

Beyond division

Years ago, before my husband and I were married, I had a terrible disagreement with his mother. It was a very painful experience.

Last Mother's Day, my husband gave his mother and me a series of painting classes. It has offered us many surprises that at one time seemed impossible. I see now that the disagreement long ago was important because it eventually taught us that we both have a passionate sense of justice.

I was thinking about this last week as my mother-in-law and I sat laughing over a set of watercolours. Years ago, standing up for what I believed was right caused division in our family. But with time and God's grace we've come to respect and enjoy each other.

God, help me to trust that with time and with your grace, out of division can come new gifts.

know that good does not live in me – that is, in my human nature. For even though the desire to do good is in me, I am not able to do it. I don't do the good I want to do; instead, I do the evil that I do not want to do….

So I find that this law is at work: when I want to do what is good, what is evil is the only choice I have. My inner being delights in the law of God. But I see a different law at work in my body – a law that fights against the law which my mind approves of…. Who will rescue me from this body that is taking me to death? Thanks be to God, who does this through our Lord Jesus Christ!

Romans 7: 18-25

> "I don't do the good I want to do…"

Faced with a choice

"Lord knows I didn't intend to have an affair with him," she began. "It's just that…." "But Lynn, you knew he was married when you met him," I responded. "I know," she said. "It goes against everything I believe in. And I don't want to hurt his wife or his children. How did I ever let this happen?"

Lynn was being brutally honest with herself, agonizing over her predicament. She wasn't trying to justify or rationalize her actions. But how could she reconcile the two desires within her: the desire for an intimate relationship and the desire to do what she believes is right?

Paul says that God, through Jesus, can help in this struggle. But, in moments of deep loneliness, it's hard to find comfort in prayer alone.

Lord, when I look for love in the wrong people or places, strengthen my desire to live by your law of love.

J esus told them this parable: "There was once a man who had a fig tree growing in his vineyard. He went looking for figs on it but found none. So he said to his gardener, 'Look, for three years I have been coming here looking for figs on this fig tree, and I haven't found any. Cut it down! Why should it go on using up the soil?' But the gardener answered, 'Leave it alone, sir, just one more year; I will dig around it and put in some fertilizer. Then if the tree bears figs next year, so much the better; if not, then you can have it cut down.'"

Luke 13: 1-9

> "Leave it alone, sir, just one more year…"

Left alone to grow

I transplanted a tree once. Soon, however, it looked quite dead. I kept watering it, but then I stopped. The next spring, what did I see? New growth! It needed time, some nutrients – sometimes it takes a while for fertilizer to work.

People can be like that, too. My friend Harry teaches a young woman. She's had a tough life. Not one high school credit. Lots of piercings, though: ears, nose – you name it. Not many smiles, either. But boy, can that kid write. She's just finishing her high school. I saw her this morning and she smiled. She really did. And said she wants to be a journalist.

Many people had "cut her down," given up on her. Harry? He gave her a little time… and some fertilizer.

**Dear God, when I see people who appear to be dead,
don't let me cut too quickly.**

Every high priest is chosen from his fellow-men and appointed to serve God on their behalf, to offer sacrifices and offerings for sins. Since he himself is weak in many ways, he is able to be gentle with those who are ignorant and make mistakes. And because he is himself weak, he must offer sacrifices not only for the sins of the people but also for his own sins. No one chooses for himself the honour of being a high priest. It is only by God's call that a man is made a high priest – just as Aaron was.

In the same way, Christ did not take upon himself the honour of being a high priest. Instead, God said to him, "You are my Son; today I have become your Father."

Hebrews 5: 1-6

> "...he is able to be gentle with those who... make mistakes."

Remembering when...

My phone rings and I cringe. Please don't let it be her again. How does a bright, beautiful, successful woman like her end up with a mean, two-timing boyfriend? What will she tell me tonight? Are they together (again)? Broken up (again)?

For many months, I've tried so hard to listen and help. Tried everything from tact to brutal honesty. She still doesn't get it – and yet, she still calls me for advice....

My phone rings, and I cringe. But this time I cringe because I remember all the rambling, tearful late-night phone calls I've made to my friends... friends who kept listening and loving me, problems and all. And remembering when I've been "weak in many ways" reminds me to be "gentle with those who... make mistakes."

God, help me open my arms
and my heart to struggling people just like me.

One Sabbath Jesus was teaching in a synagogue. A woman there had an evil spirit that had kept her sick for eighteen years; she was bent over and could not straighten up at all. When Jesus saw her, he called out to her, "Woman, you are free from your sickness!" He placed his hands on her, and at once she straightened herself up and praised God.

The official of the synagogue was angry that Jesus had healed on the Sabbath, so he said, "There are six days in which we should work; so come during those days and be healed, but not on the Sabbath!"

The Lord answered him, "You hypocrites! Here is this descendant of Abraham whom Satan has kept in bonds for eighteen years; should she not be released on the Sabbath?"

Luke 13: 10-17

> "...so come during those days and be healed..."

Office hours

Our family is lucky to have a wonderful doctor. She works long hours. Her waiting room is usually crowded – often with cranky, sick people who are irritated with the wait. Yet, on more than one occasion, she's made time to fit me in when my child's fever is running high. She's efficient and effective. What strikes me most about our doctor is her ability to listen – really listen – to her patients' needs.

Of course, there are days when her office is closed. But unlike the synagogue official, she doesn't simply slam the door. On those days, her machine gives us several options of where to go if we need help. She truly is a healer. God, bless her and all who are called to heal.

God, give strength and wisdom to all who care for the sick.

Jesus asked, "What is the kingdom of God like? What shall I compare it with? It is like this. A man takes a mustard seed and plants it in his field. The plant grows and becomes a tree, and the birds make their nests in its branches."

Again Jesus asked, "What shall I compare the kingdom of God with? It is like this. A woman takes some yeast and mixes it with a bushel of flour until the whole batch of dough rises."

Luke 13: 18-21

"What is the kingdom of God like?"

Concealed meanings

Such simple metaphors: the kingdom of God is like a mustard seed, like some yeast mixed into flour....

People today have trouble with metaphors. They're suspicious of all figures of speech, as if they were flights of fancy rather than trustworthy truth. When I teach workshops on Jesus' parables, engineers often have the most difficulty. "But the kingdom of God can't be just a mustard seed," they protest.

That's the whole point. Metaphors draw together two unlike things, two things that can't be the same. And like overlapping images, sometimes you suddenly see relationships that weren't in either image before. Like a ship plowing the ocean. Or fish jumping like popcorn.

Either you see it, or you don't.

Thank you, God, for giving me a mind that can seek and find meanings in metaphors.

How clearly the sky reveals God's glory!
How plainly it shows what he has done!
Each day announces it to the following day;
each night repeats it to the next.
No speech or words are used,
no sound is heard;
yet their message goes out to all the world
and is heard to the ends of the earth.
God made a home in the sky for the sun.

Psalm 19: 1-4

> "...the sky reveals God's glory!"

God's energy

I work in a room without windows. I've tried to make what was once a storage room into an inviting place. Bright posters, fake plants and a desk lamp do wonders. Most days I get wrapped up in my work and have no idea what's happening outside.

But by the end of the day I usually have little energy. Heading outside I am greeted by a horizon that stretches over a chain-link fence and telephone poles. It is remarkable how quickly I am renewed by this first glimpse of the sky.

My relationship with God can be like this. My little world often keeps me from pausing to acknowledge God's awesome presence. Today I will make time to connect with God.

God, I look into the sky and see your vast gift of hope.

f God is for us, who can be against us? Certainly not God, who did not even keep back his own Son, but offered him for us all! He gave us his Son – will he not also freely give us all things? ... Who, then, can separate us from the love of Christ? Can trouble do it, or hardship or persecution or hunger or poverty or danger or death?

No, in all these things we have complete victory through him who loved us! For I am certain that nothing can separate us from his love: neither death nor life, neither angels nor other heavenly rulers or powers, neither the present nor the future, neither the world above nor the world below – there is nothing in all creation that will ever be able to separate us from the love of God which is ours through Christ Jesus our Lord.

Romans 8: 31-39

> "If God is for us, who can be against us?"

Speaking out

"If God is with us, who can be against us?" Can there be a stronger argument for living to conscience – not bound by conscience – but living *to* it?

Helen Prejean, the nun who was the subject of the movie *Dead Man Walking*, travels from city to city, to hundreds of venues during the course of a year, to speak in public. She speaks out against America's morally corrupt practice of state-sanctioned revenge: the death penalty.

Not everyone is pleased with her message, but she goes on, enjoying that freedom, taking that risk, speaking to whoever will listen.

**Lord, give heart and courage to those
who seek to live their lives in your presence.**

I am speaking the truth; I belong to Christ and I do not lie. My conscience, ruled by the Holy Spirit, also assures me that I am not lying when I say how great is my sorrow, how endless the pain in my heart for my people, my own flesh and blood! For their sake I could wish that I myself were under God's curse and separated from Christ. They are God's people; he made them his children and revealed his glory to them; he made his covenants with them and gave them the Law; they have the true worship; they have received God's promises; they are descended from the famous Hebrew ancestors; and Christ, as a human being, belongs to their race. May God, who rules over all, be praised forever! Amen.   *Romans 9: 1-5*

> "…my own flesh and blood!"

God's people

I remember walking home from elementary school when two sixth-grade bullies leaped out from behind a sycamore tree, trying to scare me. They succeeded: I was terrified!

They had badgered me all week and now were intent on carrying out their threat to thrash me. However, before the first blow fell, someone came rushing from across the street. It was my cousin, stepping in to take my place.

Many people have strong family ties and are willing to put their lives at risk for one of their relatives. Some will do the same for citizens of their own country. But who would wish to be separated from God's love for the sake of others?

In today's reading, Paul declares his love for his own people – which is only a fraction of God's love for each one of us.

Lord, may I bring your love to all your people.

J esus went to eat a meal at the home of one of the leading Phari-sees…. He noticed how some of the guests were choosing the best places, so he told this parable: "When someone invites you to a wedding feast, do not sit down in the best place. It could happen that someone more important than you has been invited, and your host would have to come and say to you, 'Let him have this place.' Then you would have to sit in the lowest place. Instead, when you are invited, go and sit in the lowest place, so that your host will come to you and say, 'Come on up, my friend, to a better place….' For those who make themselves great will be humbled, and those who humble themselves will be made great." *Luke 14: 1, 7-11*

"Come on up, my friend, to a better place…"

The way of humility

When my kids were young, I often sounded like a broken record: "Don't boast. Let what you do speak for you." I'm sure my kids were sick of hearing it, too. It's a tough one, though. Everything in society says, "Me first!" "Look out for Number One." "It's a dog-eat-dog world."

It's hard to resist joining those voices. After all, what parents don't want their child to be successful, to have a secure place in the world? And what if your child listens to you, takes the lower place, and then is not seen?

That's the risk, I guess – living life believing that even if your worth is unnoticed at the wedding feast, God recognizes and values you way down at the table by the kitchen door.

**Lord, teach me the way of humility
and give me the courage to live it.**

J esus began to teach: "Happy are those who know they are spiritually poor; the kingdom of heaven belongs to them! Happy are those who mourn; God will comfort them! Happy are those who are humble; they will receive what God has promised.... Happy are those who are persecuted because they do what God requires; the kingdom of heaven belongs to them! Happy are you when people insult you and persecute you and tell all kinds of evil lies against you because you are my followers... for a great reward is kept for you in heaven."

Matthew 5: 1-12

> "Happy are you when people insult you..."

Hurt into blessing

While having supper at a friend's house, my young daughter asked if we could sing grace. Hoping my friend (who is an atheist) would not begrudge a four-year-old's request, we began singing. But my friend mocked us – loudly singing a nonsense version of our grace – until we fell silent.

That night I lay awake feeling angry and hurt. Then I realized that it was God's business to be hurt, not mine.

I struggled to remember the last beatitude but I couldn't remember how it went. All that resounded in my head were the words, "Happy... happy... happy...." Suddenly the words themselves became God's own peace, filling my heart and washing the hurt away.

Thank you, Lord, for the mysterious way in which you take my hurt and transform it into blessing.

How I wish that someone would remember my words
and record them in a book!
Or with a chisel carve my words in stone
and write them so that they would last forever.
But I know there is someone in heaven
who will come at last to my defence.
Even after my skin is eaten by disease,
while still in this body I will see God.
I will see him with my own eyes,
and he will not be a stranger.

Job 19: 23-27

"…I will see God."

Beyond illness

A friend of mine is in the midst of cancer treatments. It would be easy for her to get bogged down in the relentless worry, the erratic schedule of doctors' appointments, the treatments, the fatigue.

And yet, she knows that her illness is not the whole story. No matter what happens down the road, she is sure that God is with her and that, whenever her life ends, she will see God. What's more, they will know each other well, and neither will be a stranger.

I can learn a lot from her hopeful vision and full heart.

**Lord, when I am afraid, help me remember
that death is a passage to new life in you.**

Love must be completely sincere. Hate what is evil, hold on to what is good. Love one another warmly as Christians, and be eager to show respect for one another. Work hard and do not be lazy. Serve the Lord with a heart full of devotion. Let your hope keep you joyful, be patient in your troubles, and pray at all times. Share your belongings with your needy fellow Christians, and open your homes to strangers.

Ask God to bless those who persecute you – yes, ask him to bless, not to curse. Be happy with those who are happy, weep with those who weep. Have the same concern for everyone. Do not be proud, but accept humble duties. Do not think of yourselves as wise. *Romans 12: 9-16*

"Work hard and do not be lazy."

Work as holy

From this list of Christian principles, I am drawn to the ones about *work*. The sacred nature of work is a tenet of the Shaker community, a religious sect that no longer exists. Because I live in the area where Mother Ann Lee first established the Shakers, I've learned about them through many local initiatives set up to preserve their heritage.

I recently attended a performance by a local group that plays Shaker music. The violinist explained that the Shakers played as hard as they worked, enjoying music and often dancing far into the night. They sought balance and order in what they produced and how they produced it.

To them, work was a meeting of the human and divine. Their motto was "Put your hands to work, and your hearts to God."

Lord, help me to savour my daily tasks
and to share them with you.

"Those who come to me cannot be my disciples unless they love me more than they love father and mother, wife and children, brothers and sisters, and themselves as well. Those who do not carry their own cross and come after me cannot be my disciples. If one of you is planning to build a tower, sit down first and figure out what it will cost, to see if you have enough money to finish the job. If you don't, you will not be able to finish the tower after laying the foundation; and all who see what happened will make fun of you. 'You began to build but can't finish the job!' In the same way," concluded Jesus, "none of you can be my disciple unless you give up everything you have."

Luke 14: 25-33

> "…unless you give up everything you have."

Costing everything

I can imagine Jesus looking around at the enthusiastic crowd. He knows many of these people will soon abandon him. They don't realize how hard it will be to stay! Jesus is the one who eats with tax collectors and prostitutes, stares down the religious authorities, and makes demands of his followers. If you plan on following me, Jesus says, be aware that it will cost.

It can cost a lot when an outsider comes up to me and my friends and I want to turn away. When the gossip starts in the staff room. When a homeless person freezes sleeping on a grate – while my government closes psychiatric hospitals and cuts funds to shelters.

A poet writes, "Never say love is a gentle thing."

**Dear God, help me find the courage and strength to live
what I believe, even when the cost is high.**

T he Pharisees and the teachers of the Law started grumbling, "This man welcomes outcasts and even eats with them!" So Jesus told this parable: "Suppose one of you has a hundred sheep and loses one of them – what do you do? You leave the other ninety-nine sheep in the pasture and go looking for the one that got lost until you find it. When you find it, you are so happy that you put it on your shoulders and carry it back home... and say, 'I am so happy I found my lost sheep. Let us celebrate!' In the same way, I tell you, there will be more joy in heaven over one sinner who repents than over ninety-nine respectable people who do not need to repent."

Luke 15: 1-10

> "...more joy in heaven over one sinner who repents..."

Boring respectability

I almost get the feeling that respectable people *bore* God. That heaven only gets excited over sinners who repent and likely sin again, and repent again, and so on.

It is troubling to think of myself as "respectable." But then it dawns on me that I am hardly respectable. There may be the suggestion of respectability, but things are not necessarily as they seem. I look at myself – from the inside out, rather than the outside in – and discover that I am a sinner!

Heaven can enjoy my comeback. And though I don't want to admit it – more, way more, than once.

**Lord, give me the ability to recognize the sinner in me,
and to turn to you.**

"The rich man was told that the manager was wasting his money. 'Turn in a complete account of your handling of my property....' The servant said to himself, 'My master is going to dismiss me from my job. What shall I do...? I know what I will do! Then when my job is gone, I shall have friends who will welcome me in their homes.' So he called in all the people who were in debt to his master. He asked, 'How much do you owe my master?' 'One hundred barrels of olive oil,' he answered. 'Here is your account, sit down and write fifty.' Then he asked another, 'How much do you owe...?'

"The people of this world are much more shrewd in handling their affairs than the people who belong to the light."

Luke 16: 1-8

> "My master is going to dismiss me..."

Trust in God

Whether the shrewd actions of the manager in Jesus' story were commendable or not, the sense of desperation beneath them haunts me.

As someone currently looking for work, I struggle daily with the same strong feelings of fear, rejection, shame and desperation. Conscious of these feelings, I strive to reach beyond them, to find a deeper trust in God's sustaining care for me and my family.

Being dismissed from work is an experience that I share with many people in our time. It is a painful experience of rejection and isolation. How can I transform it into an experience of solidarity with others who suffer in the same way?

Faithful God, help me to trust in your abundant grace rather than my own shrewdness.

E very day I will thank you;
I will praise you forever and ever.
The Lord is great and is to be highly praised;
his greatness is beyond understanding.
What you have done will be praised
from one generation to the next;
they will proclaim your mighty acts.
They will speak of your glory and majesty,
and I will meditate on your wonderful deeds....
All your creatures, Lord, will praise you,
and all your people will give you thanks.

Psalm 145: 2-5, 10-11

"...I will meditate on your wonderful deeds."

Looking for the miracle

Did you know that the DNA in a single human cell, if stretched out, would measure three metres? That humpback whales catch their food in "nets" made of bubbles?

A recent song asks, "Where have all the cowboys gone?" At times I find myself asking, "Where have all the miracles gone?"

I remember an autumn afternoon, digging potatoes with my four-year-old son, as clouds rolled and Canada geese passed overhead. An inward stirring, a magic moment, surrounded by the wondrous works of the Creator.

How often I thirst for something to carry me out of myself, when all the while I'm in the midst of a garden of wondrous works. The miracles are right here. I just have to look.

Dear God, remind me to appreciate your creation today, and every day.

As Elijah came to the town gate, he saw a widow gathering firewood. "Please bring me a drink of water," he said…. "And please bring me some bread, too."

She answered, "All I have is a handful of flour in a bowl and a bit of olive oil. I came here to gather some firewood to take back home and prepare what little I have for my son and me. That will be our last meal, and then we will starve to death."

"Don't worry," Elijah said. "Go on and prepare your meal. But first make a small loaf from what you have and bring it to me…. For this is what the Lord, the God of Israel, says: 'The bowl will not run out of flour or the jar run out of oil before the day that I, the Lord, send rain.'"

The widow did as Elijah had told her, and all of them had enough food for many days. *1 Kings 17: 10-16*

> "…please bring me some bread…"

True generosity

I love it when friends drop by, but I rarely invite them because my house is often messy and I have no interesting food to offer. By setting my standards so high, I limit my opportunities to enjoy their company.

Recently I visited a village in Tanzania where the land was parched and the crops were dying. In the middle of these desperate circumstances, the villagers gathered to prepare a feast of *ugali* (a porridge-like dish), cabbage and goat meat for us. Though they didn't know where their next meal would come from, they lived as the widow in today's reading did – joyfully serving us what they had, trusting God to provide for tomorrow.

In their poverty, they taught me a great lesson in generosity.

Lord, give me the spirit of generosity.

J esus went to Jerusalem. There in the Temple he found people selling cattle, sheep and pigeons, and also the moneychangers sitting at their tables. So he made a whip from cords and drove all the animals out of the Temple, both the sheep and the cattle; he overturned the tables of the moneychangers and scattered their coins; and he ordered those who sold the pigeons, "Take them out of here! Stop making my Father's house a marketplace!" His disciples remembered that the scripture says, "My devotion to your house, O God, burns in me like a fire."

The Jewish authorities came back at him with a question, "What miracle can you perform to show us that you have the right to do this?" Jesus answered, "Tear down this Temple, and in three days I will build it again." *John 2: 13-22*

> "My devotion… burns in me like a fire."

Living what is

I think of how the disciples must have wondered, "Who is this guy? One minute it's 'Turn the other cheek. Love your enemy.' Now he's whipping people in the Temple!"

Can you imagine being Jesus' PR person? "You're going to have to be more consistent, Jesus." In my life I want everything to be consistent, with all the loose ends tied up. But is life consistent? Does it always make sense?

What draws me to Jesus is his disregard for packaging, for making everything easily understood. Sometimes I need patience, other times burning devotion. To fight injustice when I can't win; to believe when there are so many reasons not to believe; to hope when it doesn't make sense; to follow this fierce and gentle, wild and peaceful man.

Lord, let devotion burn in me, as it did in you.

"**S**uppose one of you has a servant who is plowing or looking after the sheep. When he comes in from the field, do you tell him to hurry along and eat his meal? Of course not! Instead, you say to him, 'Get my supper ready, then put on your apron and wait on me while I eat and drink; after that you may have your meal.' The servant does not deserve thanks for obeying orders, does he? It is the same with you; when you have done all you have been told to do, say, 'We are ordinary servants; we have only done our duty.'"

Luke 17: 7-10

"…we have only done our duty."

Doing my duty

After my little ones finally drift off to sleep, I often head towards the thankless tasks of managing the household… with a scowl on my face. Clean up the supper dishes, sort the mountain of dirty (or are they clean?) clothes, wade through the flotsam and jetsam of toys, chase the cat hair that roams the house like a nomad, feed the cat (if we still have one)…. Sometimes I think Sisyphus had an easier job.

Perhaps it would be better if I stopped hoping someone would thank me for every little task I do.

I know I make a difference in our home. I know my family is thankful. And I know their thanks will come in time.

Dear God, may I learn to serve others with loving hands rather than a grumbling heart.

As Jesus made his way to Jerusalem… along the border between Samaria and Galilee… he was met by ten men suffering from a dreaded skin disease. They stood at a distance and shouted, "Jesus! Master! Have pity on us!" Jesus said to them, "Go and let the priests examine you."

On the way they were made clean. When one of them saw that he was healed, he came back, praising God in a loud voice. He threw himself to the ground at Jesus' feet and thanked him. The man was a Samaritan. Jesus spoke up, "There were ten who were healed; where are the other nine? Why is this foreigner the only one who came back to give thanks to God?" Jesus said to him, "Get up and go; your faith has made you well."   *Luke 17: 11-19*

> "…who came back to give thanks to God?"

Blessed by God

I have security, education and meaningful work. Most of the time I don't think much about my good fortune – or about people who have no home, no security and no way of earning their daily bread.

The other night a news program featured a young Somali immigrant. Escaping from war, hunger and the danger of rape, this young woman had miraculously found her way to safety and a new life. Now she has become a citizen of our country. She spoke about her profound gratitude to our nation for the freedom it has given her.

What a contrast between her attitude and mine! She knows how to value the blessings she's received. She teaches me to be grateful, to say "thank you" to God more often!

**O God, thank you for your gifts
that I so often take for granted.**

learned things that were well known and things that had never been known before, because Wisdom, who gave shape to everything that exists, was my teacher.

The spirit of Wisdom is intelligent and holy. It is of one nature but reveals itself in many ways. It is not made of any material substance, and it moves about freely.... It loves what is good. It is sharp and unconquerable, kind and a friend of humanity. It is dependable and sure, and has no worries. It has power over everything, and sees everything. It penetrates every spirit that is intelligent and pure.... Wisdom moves more easily than motion itself; she is so pure that she penetrates everything. She is a breath of God's power – a pure and radiant stream of glory from the Almighty.   *Wisdom 7: 21 – 8: 1*

> "...a pure and radiant stream of glory..."

In search of Wisdom

I was in my mid-teens when I was smitten with philosophy. What I thought of as the best part of me – my mind – was enchanted and seduced. Philosopher, Lover of Wisdom: that was me.

Everything – previous beliefs, long-held opinions, respect for the thoughts of others – was swept away. The antiseptic, razor-sharp and non-sentimental world in which I now lived had no room for such foolishness.

The passion lasted for many years, but eventually my ardour cooled. The Wisdom I was keeping company with was not the Wisdom I longed for. My soul needed more.

These days Wisdom's caresses are somewhat different: now I feel them in the unfathomable moments I experience, in this astonishing world God has created.

Thank you, Lord, for the gift of your Wisdom that embraces my restless spirit with constant tenderness.

As it was in the time of Noah so shall it be in the days of the Son of Man. Everybody kept on eating and drinking, and men and women married, up to the very day Noah went into the boat and the flood came and killed them all. It will be as it was in the time of Lot. Everybody kept on eating and drinking, buying and selling, planting and building. On the day Lot left Sodom, fire and sulfur rained down from heaven and killed them all. That is how it will be on the day the Son of Man is revealed....

Those who try to save their own life will lose it; those who lose their life will save it."

Luke 17: 26-37

> "...fire and sulfur rained down..."

Motivation to change

The last time we had a smog alert in our city, my son and I were driving down a crowded highway. On the radio they were discussing how cars and fossil fuels are the main reason for the pollution.

"Do you think we're ever going to change our ways?" I asked. "We know what we're doing is wrong, and yet we keep on doing it." My son replied, "I think people need to feel pain before they'll change. As long as they're still comfortable, there's no reason to change."

From the mouths of babes! How comfortable I am: not only regarding social issues, but in my faith life, also. I pay attention when I'm hurting; when I'm comfortable, I go on automatic pilot.

**Lord, draw me out of my complacency.
Inspire me to action and growth.**

Jesus told his disciples a parable to teach them that they should always pray and never become discouraged. "In a certain town there was a judge who neither feared God nor respected people. And there was a widow in that same town who kept coming to him and pleading for her rights.... For a long time the judge refused to act, but at last he said to himself, 'Because of all the trouble this widow is giving me, I will see to it that she gets her rights. If I don't, she will keep on coming and finally wear me out!'"

And the Lord continued, "Listen to what that corrupt judge said. Now, will God not judge in favour of his own people who cry to him day and night for help? Will he be slow to help them? I tell you, he will judge in their favour and do it quickly."

Luke 18: 1-8

> "...always pray and never become discouraged."

Keep going

Artists are not born with an innate ability to draw. Like many other things, it's a learned skill requiring discipline and perseverance.

First attempts usually yield results that are oversimplified; students simply stop too soon. Their trees have too few branches, their portraits too few shades of grey. I tell them to keep going for at least an hour after they think they're finished. That way they will have the opportunity to discover treasures they might otherwise never know.

As with the persistent widow, if there's something I really want, I need to keep working towards it, even if it seems like there's nothing left to do. She was rewarded for her efforts, and I will be, too.

**God, help me to keep going,
especially when I feel like quitting.**

The angel wearing linen clothes said, "At that time the great angel Michael, who guards your people, will appear. Then there will be a time of troubles, the worst since nations first came into existence. When that time comes, all the people of your nation whose names are written in God's book will be saved. Many of those who have already died will live again: some will enjoy eternal life, and some will suffer eternal disgrace. The wise leaders will shine with all the brightness of the sky. And those who have taught many people to do what is right will shine like the stars forever."
Daniel 12: 1-3

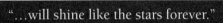
"...will shine like the stars forever."

Shining stars

Now that I am a parent, I see the truth in the statement "It takes a village to raise a child." As I watch my son grow up surrounded by loving relatives, dedicated teachers and other supportive adults, I know that their caring and guidance are helping to shape and mould him into the person God created him to be.

When I look back through my own life, I see grandparents, aunts, teachers, friends, co-workers and others whose wisdom and love have influenced me along the way.

When the day of judgment comes, I picture each one of these people from my journey shining like the stars forever. Even now, the light they cast on my path leads me into faithfulness and love.

**Lord, help me to recognize those
whose wisdom guides me like a shining star.**

There was a blind man sitting by the road, begging. When he heard the crowd passing by, he asked, "What is this?" "Jesus of Nazareth is passing by," they told him. He cried out, "Jesus! Son of David! Have mercy on me!" The people in front scolded him and told him to be quiet. But he shouted even more loudly, "Son of David! Have mercy on me!" Jesus stopped and ordered the blind man to be brought to him. Jesus asked him, "What do you want me to do for you?" "Sir," he answered, "I want to see again." So Jesus said to him, "Then see! Your faith has made you well." At once he was able to see, and he followed Jesus, giving thanks to God. When the crowd saw it, they all praised God.

Luke 18: 35-43

> "I want to see again."

True sight

At l'Arche, I share a house with Helen, who doesn't speak at all. Helen doesn't engage in conversation in an attempt to get to know me. Yet I feel she has an intuitive, heart-to-heart knowledge of who I am. She knows me through eyes and touch, laughter and time spent together.

The blind man who sat by the road was not able to see physically, yet he saw clearly who Jesus was, better than many others. He knew and trusted that Jesus was the Son of David, who would be merciful and heal him.

Those who are "off-side," marginalized, pushed to the edges of our culture, often have a wisdom that can teach me who God really is.

Jesus, teach me to see clearly with the wisdom of those at the side of the road.

have so many enemies, Lord,
so many who turn against me!
They talk about me and say,
"God will not help him."
But you, O Lord, are always my shield from danger;
you give me victory
and restore my courage.
I call to the Lord for help,
and from his sacred hill he answers me.
I lie down and sleep,
and all night long the Lord protects me.
I am not afraid of the thousands of enemies
who surround me on every side.
Psalm 3: 1-6

> "I have so many enemies, Lord…"

So many enemies…

I have never known war first-hand, so I cannot relate fully to the experience of today's psalmist: "I have so many enemies…." I realize, however, that I *can* relate to the underlying emotions of the psalm.

The enemies in my life are not so much "people" as they are "voices." They seem to lie in wait, attacking me when and where I am most vulnerable. When I am overwhelmed by the demands of home and work, they goad me into giving up. When I feel lonely, they tell me that I am unlovable. When I worry about making ends meet, they remind me that poverty lurks just around the corner.

But my experience shows that these voices cannot defeat me: God's love fills me, giving me victory over my fears.

**Dearest God, when my fears threaten to overwhelm me,
remind me that you are with me through it all.**

While the people were listening, Jesus continued and told them a parable. He was now almost at Jerusalem, and they supposed that the kingdom of God was just about to appear. So he said, "There was once a man of high rank who was going to a country far away…. Before he left, he called his ten servants and gave them each a gold coin and told them, 'See what you can earn with this while I am gone….'

"The man was made king and came back. At once he ordered his servants to appear before him, in order to find out how much they had earned…. 'I tell you that to those who have something, even more will be given; but those who have nothing, even the little that they have will be taken away from them.'"

After Jesus said this, he went on in front of them towards Jerusalem.   *Luke 19: 11-28*

> "…he went on in front of them towards Jerusalem."

Difficult encounter

One day, nearing the end of my two-year practicum, my supervisor interrupted me. "No!" she said sharply. "You must listen!" I felt rebuked, and although I realized my mistake, I was taken aback by the severity of her response. It didn't seem to fit with the person I knew. But my supervisor knew that our time together was growing short, and there were lessons that I still needed to learn.

I wonder if Jesus felt the same way as my supervisor. As he turned towards Jerusalem, he knew the seriousness of what was going to happen. He knew he would not be with his disciples much longer, and they needed to understand the importance of using their gifts, and of not being afraid.

**God, give me humility and openness to hear you,
and the courage to act.**

He came closer to the city, and when he saw it, he wept over it, saying, "If you only knew today what is needed for peace! But now you cannot see it! The time will come when your enemies will surround you with barricades, blockade you, and close in on you from every side. They will completely destroy you and the people within your walls; not a single stone will they leave in its place, because you did not recognize the time when God came to save you!"

Luke 19: 41-44

"...he wept over it..."

Caring enough to cry

Tears of compassion? Tears of frustration?

Time and again, Jesus' followers just don't get it. How frustrated he must have been. But his tears did not dry up; he did not become cynical. His tears are the sign that he still cares.

I'm a teacher and a parent. Both roles bring tears of frustration and of compassion. Sometimes, as a teacher, it's difficult not to become cynical – about governments, difficult students, parents. And yes, as a parent, to be cynical about teachers.

It's so hard to keep caring. But I must. I must preserve my compassion – for those students who don't understand, for those parents who are, above all, concerned for their children, and don't know whom to trust.

I must preserve my tears.

Dear Lord, help me care enough to be frustrated, and to love enough to show compassion.

T here in front of the whole assembly King David praised the Lord. He said, "Lord God of our ancestor Jacob, may you be praised forever and ever! You are great and powerful, glorious, splendid and majestic. Everything in heaven and earth is yours, and you are king, supreme ruler over all. All riches and wealth come from you; you rule everything by your strength and power; and you are able to make anyone great and strong."

1 Chronicles 29: 10-12

"...may you be praised..."

Prayers of praise

One summer, when I was young, a Jewish boy invited me to his house for a meal. His father began the grace: "Blessed are you, O God, creator of the universe, for you bring forth good things from the earth...." It's a traditional pattern – King David used a similar formula, more than 25 centuries ago.

I was accustomed to camp graces, which were sometimes little more than "Rub a dub dub, Thanks for the grub, Yaayy, God!"

I was also surprised to hear a human bless God. I thought God was supposed to bless us, usually with things we wanted. As a child, I was more likely to pray for a red bicycle. As an adult, I might ask for a promotion at work, a loyal friend, a stronger faith....

Someone called them "Gimme" prayers. On reflection, I prefer the Jewish tradition.

Blessed are you, Lord God, for you continually remind us how to pray when we forget.

"Teacher, Moses wrote this law: 'If a man dies and leaves a wife but no children, that man's brother must marry the widow....' Now, on the day when the dead rise to life, whose wife will she be...?"

Jesus answered them, "The men and women of this age marry, but the men and women who are worthy to rise from death and live in the age to come will not then marry.... They are the children of God, because they have risen from death. And Moses clearly proves that the dead are raised to life. In the passage about the burning bush he speaks of the Lord as 'the God of Abraham, the God of Isaac, and the God of Jacob.' He is the God of the living, not of the dead, for to him all are alive."

Luke 20: 27-40

> "...the God of the living, not of the dead..."

The life within

As November days darken, my garden becomes tangled with reminders that this is a season of decay. Like the Sadducees, I am concerned about the details of death – what plants will survive the snow? Which ones will be killed by a harsh winter? What can I do to ensure that most will survive?

It is hard to trust that there is a rhythm and wisdom to this season, hard to believe there is a spark of life hidden in this decaying garden. It is difficult to wait for the signs of life that will appear again next spring.

As the chill and dark increase, I'll try to remember Jesus' promise: that our God is the God of the living. The promise of life is always present.

**God of life, as November days grow short,
help me see the spark of life in all things.**

P ilate asked Jesus, "Are you the king of the Jews?" Jesus answered, "Does this question come from you or have others told you about me?"

Pilate replied, "Do you think I am a Jew? It was your own people and the chief priests who handed you over to me. What have you done?" Jesus said, "If my kingdom belonged to this world, my followers would fight to keep me from being handed over to the Jewish authorities. No, my kingdom does not belong here!"

So Pilate asked, "Are you a king, then?" Jesus answered, "You say that I am a king. I was born and came into the world for this one purpose, to speak about the truth. Whoever belongs to the truth listens to me."

"And what is truth?" Pilate asked.   *John 18: 33-38*

"...or have others told you about me?"

What is truth?

I like a good, juicy piece of gossip as much as the next person. And, on more than one occasion, I must admit, I've stood sure and smug, ready to condemn someone on the basis of rumour and hearsay.

Like Pilate, I can be swayed by the sentiments of the crowd. And life certainly seems simpler when there's a clear villain to blame or, for that matter, when there's an obvious hero to praise. Jesus' question, about whether Pilate's accusation is based on hearsay, is a tough one; I notice that in today's reading, Pilate has no reply for it.

The next time I'm ready to condemn another person based on the opinions of others, I'll try to remember Jesus' question. I hope I'll stop to answer it.

**Lord, help me to approach others today
with compassionate questioning.**

Jesus looked around and saw rich people dropping their gifts in the Temple treasury, and he also saw a very poor widow dropping in two little copper coins. He said, "I tell you that this poor widow put in more than all the others. For the others offered their gifts from what they had to spare of their riches; but she, poor as she is, gave all she had to live on."

Luke 21: 1-4

"She, poor as she is, gave all she had…"

True giving

While walking to work each morning, I see street people and to be honest, I don't know what to do. Many, of course, have psychiatric disabilities and are victims of what today we call "restructuring" of health care programs.

One morning, a "regular" was in his usual spot. Many people passed by. Some, coming out of a trendy coffee shop, dropped coins into his hat. Then another street person stopped and, taking from his pocket his own meagre coinage, painstakingly sorted it and gave some. And me? Sadly, I admit that I did not give anything.

Who was the most alive, the most transformed by this gift? I don't know, but the one with a look of serenity was the man who gave when it hurt, who truly gave of himself.

**Lord, let me remember
I always have something to give.**

Some of the disciples were talking about the Temple, how beautiful it looked with its fine stones and the gifts offered to God. Jesus said, "All this you see – the time will come when not a single stone here will be left in its place; every one will be thrown down."

"Teacher," they asked, "when will this be? And what will happen in order to show that the time has come for it to take place?"

Jesus said, "Watch out; don't be fooled. Many men, claiming to speak for me, will come and say, 'I am he!' and, 'The time has come!' But don't follow them. Don't be afraid when you hear of wars and revolutions; such things must happen first, but they do not mean that the end is near."

Luke 21:5-11

"...not a single stone here will be left..."

Home or temple?

My friend was as I remembered her: light-hearted, full of laughter and energy. It had been years since we'd seen each other. By chance, we met one another in a restaurant.

"Oh yes," she added – as we ended our list of births, deaths and marriages – "then there was the house fire. We lost everything. But thank God no one was hurt."

Later, as I entered my own home, I remembered her words and was humbled. While I like being surrounded by beautiful things, today's reading and my friend's words give me pause. Have I built a home, or a temple of things that I cannot imagine losing?

God, let my faith in you be the foundation for all that I build.

"Before all these things take place, however, you will be arrested and persecuted; you will be handed over to be tried in synagogues and be put in prison; you will be brought before kings and rulers for my sake. This will be your chance to tell the Good News. Make up your minds ahead of time not to worry about how you will defend yourselves, because I will give you such words and wisdom that none of your enemies will be able to refute or contradict what you say. You will be handed over by your parents, your brothers, your relatives, and your friends; and some of you will be put to death. Everyone will hate you because of me. But not a single hair from your heads will be lost. Stand firm, and you will save yourselves."

Luke 21: 12-19

> "Not a single hair from your heads will be lost."

A steadfast faith

I know a woman of great faith. After she'd raised five children, her husband left her for another woman. For years, her adult children took advantage of her generous nature. Now, older and working for low wages, she not only supports herself, she also helps a friend with multiple sclerosis. Unwavering in her faith, she trusts in God.

When Jesus speaks of persecution, he speaks of arrest, trial and prison for his sake. But persecution can also mean the pain of this woman who gave generously in her youth only to experience rejection and loss as she grew older.

Jesus assures me that not a single hair of her head will be lost. Standing firm in her faith, she has found peace and meaning in her life.

O God, strengthen me in times of loss and loneliness.

"When you see Jerusalem surrounded by armies, then you will know that it will soon be destroyed. Then those who are in Judea must run away to the hills; those who are in the city must leave, and those who are out in the country must not go into the city. For those will be 'The Days of Punishment,' to make come true all that the Scriptures say....

"There will be strange things happening to the sun, the moon and the stars. On earth whole countries will be in despair, afraid of the roar of the sea and the raging tides. People will faint from fear as they wait for what is coming over the whole earth.... Then the Son of Man will appear, coming in a cloud with great power and glory. When these things begin to happen, stand up and raise your heads, because your salvation is near."

Luke 21:20-28

> "On earth whole countries will be in despair..."

Hope for the planet

People have doubtless been applying these warning signs to their own times for the past 2,000 years. But now, I'm tempted to say, it's *really* relevant. Jerusalem is crawling with soldiers, refugees worldwide are "running away to the hills," climate change is accelerating, and environmental catastrophes seem to be on the increase.

What hope we can pass on to our children? It's easier to be cynical, or to give in to fear. I don't find Jesus' words, "raise your heads, because your salvation is near," all that helpful. Don't bury your head in the sand: okay. But what is this liberation?

Jesus submitted to the destructive forces of the world and died on the cross. But love was even stronger. Could the resurrection apply to our beloved planet, too?

Lord, sometimes I'm overwhelmed by the world's problems. Give me the courage to act, and the faith to trust you.

Then Jesus told them this parable: "Think of the fig tree and all the other trees. When you see their leaves beginning to appear, you know that summer is near. In the same way, when you see these things happening, you will know that the kingdom of God is about to come.

"Remember that all these things will take place before the people now living have all died. Heaven and earth will pass away, but my words will never pass away."

Luke 21: 29-33

"...all these things will take place..."

Seeking the truth

Jesus – both human and divine. In today's reading, it would seem he's acting a little too human. Overdoing it a bit. Perhaps I'm being sacrilegious? I don't know. But if you read the whole passage, it seems that things haven't turned out exactly as Jesus said they would.

I have a friend who sometimes goes to extremes – like when he's holding forth about the depravity of our consumer society. Okay, it's not a friend; it's me. But I know that if I'm a bit over the top at times, the essence of what I'm saying is true. Maybe that's the case with Jesus. Maybe he's just being human.

But if you listen to the whole story of what he's saying, Wow! He speaks the truth, and in spades.

Lord, help me listen to your truth, clearly and with openness.

"Be careful not to let yourselves become occupied with too much feasting and drinking and with the worries of this life, or that Day may suddenly catch you like a trap. For it will come upon all people everywhere on earth. Be on watch and pray always that you will have the strength to go safely through all those things that will happen and to stand before the Son of Man."

Luke 21: 34-36

"Be on watch…"

Live in the moment

The message in today's reading is clear: Be ready! Live each day as if it were the only one you have.

We all nod in agreement, but then we go to work on Monday and wish for Friday. Or we do things on Friday to help us forget Monday. It is so hard to live in the moment. To be where we are. Right now.

To feel the breath of God in the biting November winds. To recognize the face of God in the elderly person on the bus, or in the pierced, tattooed teenager on the sidewalk. To hear the voice of God in the words of our students, co-workers and loved ones.

Stop. Drink each moment in. See God in his creation. Live your life so that God can be seen in it.

Dear God, help me be conscious
of each moment of each day.

The Lord said, "The time is coming when I will fulfill the promise that I made to the people of Israel and Judah. At that time I will choose as king a righteous descendant of David. That king will do what is right and just throughout the land. The people of Judah and of Jerusalem will be rescued and will live in safety. The city will be called 'The Lord Our Salvation.'"

Jeremiah 33: 14-16

"That king will do what is right and just..."

Doing what is right

I've been working on a municipal issue that could have a huge impact on our neighbourhood and our city. As a result of my involvement, I've come to learn more about how decisions are made and how politics work. It's hard not to be cynical.

I don't have the stomach for the deal-making and strategizing. I don't understand why the decision-makers don't just "do the right thing." I try to keep informed, write letters, attend a protest here and there, and remain optimistic.

Today's reading reminds me to add prayer to my list of things to do. Instead of being cynical, I need to find a quiet place to simply pray for someone to "do what is right and just." In the busy work of making a better world, where is the room for faith?

**God, grant our leaders wisdom and insight –
to do what is right and just.**

As Jesus walked along the shore of Lake Galilee, he saw two brothers who were fishermen, Simon (called Peter) and his brother Andrew, catching fish in the lake with a net. Jesus said to them, "Come with me, and I will teach you to catch people." At once they left their nets and went with him.

He went on and saw two other brothers, James and John, the sons of Zebedee. They were in their boat with their father Zebedee, getting their nets ready. Jesus called them, and at once they left the boat and their father, and went with him.

Matthew 4: 18-22

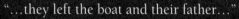

"...they left the boat and their father..."

Wildcat walkout

Somehow I suspect that Zebedee was not pleased. He's getting ready to go fishing – the way he earns a living to support his family – and his two sons drop everything and abandon him!

It's like a wildcat walkout at an auto plant. Everything grinds to a standstill. Especially revenues.

"Wait a minute!" he might yell. "You haven't finished…." And then, as the four young men and their new leader fade out of sight, he might call after his boys, "Are you coming back…?"

Later events suggest he did not disown his sons. Perhaps, when they did return, he ran to meet them. I'd like to think that maybe Zebedee was the model for the father in Jesus' parable of the Prodigal Son.

**Lord, when I hear you calling, give me the courage
to drop everything and follow you.**

J esus was filled with joy by the Holy Spirit and said, "Father, Lord of heaven and earth! I thank you because you have shown to the unlearned what you have hidden from the wise and learned. Yes, Father, this was how you were pleased to have it happen.

"My Father has given me all things. No one knows who the Son is except the Father, and no one knows who the Father is except the Son and those to whom the Son chooses to reveal him."

Then Jesus turned to the disciples and said to them privately, "How fortunate you are to see the things you see! I tell you that many prophets and kings wanted to see what you see, but they could not, and to hear what you hear, but they did not."

Luke 10: 21-24

> "…you have shown to the unlearned…"

Blind to the truth

What does this passage really mean? Am I to stop thinking? Is it better to be ignorant? And yet….

An old professor once told me that he saw an advertisement for bus drivers. It said that applicants *must not* possess a driver's licence. Why not? I suppose it meant the bus company wouldn't have to undo all the driver's bad habits.

This story helps me understand what Jesus is saying in today's reading. How my learned attitudes sometimes blind me to the truth. How I need to examine them to see if they are still valid.

I have to remind myself that sometimes I, too, am blind and don't see the true path… when it's right there in front of me.

Dear God, help me to see with new eyes
– eyes not blinded by self-righteousness.

Jesus said, "I feel sorry for these people, because they have been with me for three days and now have nothing to eat. I don't want to send them away without feeding them, for they might faint on their way home."

The disciples asked him, "Where will we find enough food in this desert to feed this crowd?" "How much bread do you have?" Jesus asked. "Seven loaves," they answered, "and a few small fish."

So Jesus ordered the crowd to sit down on the ground. Then he took the seven loaves and the fish, gave thanks to God, broke them, and gave them to the disciples; and the disciples gave them to the people. They all ate and had enough. Then the disciples took up seven baskets full of pieces left over.

Matthew 15: 29-37

> "...the disciples gave them to the people."

Sharing ourselves

When I was in university, the campus ministry organized a cross-country ski outing. As few people knew one another, small groups tended to set off separately on the trails.

When we reached the warm-up hut, I noticed two guys off by themselves. As I pulled my lunch from my pack, I realized that they didn't have any food. I offered them some of my lunch, and others in the group did the same. As food was shared, conversation flowed. It turned out to be quite a celebration, with lots of food left over!

We shared more than the food in our packs. We shared our very selves. I hope I'll remember this experience of giving and receiving this Christmas season – and long after the tinsel is down.

**God, help me to reach out to those around me
who are in need.**

344

A day is coming when the people will sing this song
in the land of Judah:
Our city is strong!
God himself defends its walls....
You, Lord, give perfect peace
to those who keep their purpose firm
and put their trust in you.
Trust in the Lord forever;
he will always protect us.
He has humbled those who were proud;
he destroyed the strong city they lived in,
and sent its walls crashing into the dust.
Isaiah 26: 1-6

"A day is coming when the people will sing this song..."

Past, present and future

Learning a new language is always a challenge. Invariably, I have to figure out what tense I'm in, and the tense I am trying to use – before I can apply myself to the mundane demands of grammar. It's why I love language.

Isaiah presents a song in the present tense, but stresses that it is something to be sung at some unspecified time in the future. For the residents of Judah, security and peace were only future promises; they certainly were not their present experience.

I'm challenged to find comfort in the God of all my tenses: past, present and future, even though my most compelling need is decidedly in the here and now.

God of the present, the past, and of my future,
may I discover you now and for always.

As Jesus walked along, two blind men started following him. "Have mercy on us, Son of David!" they shouted…. Jesus asked them, "Do you believe that I can heal you?"

"Yes, sir!" they answered. Then Jesus touched their eyes and said, "Let it happen, then, just as you believe!" – and their sight was restored.

Jesus spoke sternly to them, "Don't tell this to anyone!" But they left and spread the news about Jesus all over that part of the country. *Matthew 9: 27-31*

"Jesus spoke sternly to them…"

Seeing the truth

I know that, in today's reading, Matthew is writing about the extraordinary power of faith. But that's not the part of the story that touches me. I delight in the small detail at the end where Jesus, after performing this amazing miracle, sternly admonishes the two men to keep his gift a secret.

Brimming with gratitude, the men, just like kids who have found a puppy under the Christmas tree, run off and tell absolutely everyone they meet about Jesus – in spite of his admonition.

This could only have happened if the newly sighted men could see the deep compassion behind the stern words.

Who among us could keep such a secret?

Lord, give me eyes to see your love.

P raise the Lord!
It is good to sing praise to our God;
    it is pleasant and right to praise him.
The Lord is restoring Jerusalem;
he is bringing back the exiles.
He heals the broken-hearted
and bandages their wounds.
He has decided the number of the stars
and calls each one by name.
Great and mighty is our Lord;
his wisdom cannot be measured.

Psalm 147: 1-6

> "He heals the broken-hearted..."

Blue Christmas

I know several people for whom the
Christmas season becomes more of an
ordeal each year. It's not just the excessive
consumerism that gets them down; it's the cheery Christmas carols
and songs that trigger their reaction. For one, Christmas is inseparable
from painful memories of his father's drunken rampages. For another,
it's the memory of being eleven, facing the horror of her mother's
death on Christmas Eve.

These people still feel the need to mark the birth of Jesus, and
to celebrate the God who heals their broken hearts, and who gently
bandages their wounds. So they've started attending "Blue Christmas"
events – those low-key, reflection-filled gatherings for people who find
traditional Christmas celebrations painful and, at times, distressing.

**Lord, this Christmas, let me encounter you anew,
rather than relive memories of the past.**

t was the fifteenth year of the rule of Emperor Tiberius; Pontius Pilate was governor of Judea, Herod was ruler of Galilee…. At that time the word of God came to John, son of Zechariah in the desert. So John went throughout the whole territory of the Jordan River, preaching, "Turn away from your sins and be baptized, and God will forgive your sins." As it is written in the book of the prophet Isaiah:

"Someone is shouting in the desert: 'Get the road ready for the Lord; make a straight path for him to travel! Every valley must be filled up, every hill and mountain levelled off. The winding roads must be made straight, and the rough paths made smooth. The whole human race will see God's salvation!'" *Luke 3: 1-6*

"The whole human race will see God's salvation!"

What endures

I wonder if there were any Roman soldiers listening? Not knowing, as we do now, that their universe would someday be turned upside down? And in our own time: the Berlin Wall, the Soviet Union, the British Empire…. What seems so permanent to us now will change so radically! It seems that only change is the true constant.

John the Baptist challenges us to look within. He counsels preparation for the event that will utterly displace the way things are. We need to take the time to see what is at the basis of our lives, what is really true and valuable – our families, our friends, our beliefs – so that when change comes, we will be focused on what endures.

Lord, may I be given the vision to see what is really constant and never-changing: your truth and love.

The teachers of the Law and the Pharisees began to say to themselves, "Who is this man who speaks such blasphemy! God is the only one who can forgive sins!"

Jesus said to them, "Is it easier to say, 'Your sins are forgiven you, or to say, 'Get up and walk'? I will prove to you, then, that the Son of Man has authority on earth to forgive sins." So he said to the paralyzed man, "I tell you, get up, pick up your bed, and go home!"

At once the man got up, took the bed he had been lying on, and went home, praising God. They were all completely amazed! Full of fear, they praised God, saying, "What marvellous things we have seen today!"

Luke 5: 17-26

"What marvellous things we have seen today!"

The miracle of love

Several years ago I sat with the parents of a gravely ill young man. Together we prayed that if it were God's will, their son would get better. In the following days there were visible signs of improvement; a month later he was discharged from hospital.

In these times of change and uncertainty, our faith constantly is being put to the test. The remarkable stories of faith of these parents, or the people who brought the paralytic to Jesus, rarely make headlines.

How important it is to pause to reflect on the many small miracles that have occurred in our own lives, especially the miracle of God's unconditional love for us. And to consider the remarkable people who inspire us – courageous people whose faith has been tried and tested many times.

**Lord, strengthen my faith so that I believe
in your loving presence, even when I feel far from you.**

G od sent the angel Gabriel to a young woman promised in marriage to a man named Joseph. Her name was Mary. The angel said, "Peace be with you! The Lord is with you and has greatly blessed you!"

Mary was deeply troubled by the angel's message, and she wondered what his words meant. The angel said, "Don't be afraid, Mary; God has been gracious to you. You will become pregnant and give birth to a son, and you will name him Jesus...." Mary said to the angel, "I am a virgin. How, then, can this be?" The angel answered, "The Holy Spirit will come on you, and God's power will rest upon you...."

"I am the Lord's servant," said Mary; "may it happen to me as you have said." *Luke 1: 26-38*

> "...may it happen to me as you have said."

God's choice

I feel I spend much of my life trying to control how other people see me: will this person choose me as their friend? Will that magazine choose to publish my story? Does my partner love me? Ensuring the answer is "yes" takes up a lot of my energy.

Why God chooses me, and chooses to love me, is quite beyond my control. It doesn't seem to make sense. There is only one way to respond to this love – one that Mary shows me. She doesn't try to earn it, or waste time being anxious about losing it. She accepts it, enters into the mystery of it, and lives it to the full.

**Loving God, dispose my heart to give up control,
and to accept your love with joy.**

"Come to me, all of you who are tired from carrying heavy loads, and I will give you rest. Take my yoke and put it on you, and learn from me, because I am gentle and humble in spirit; and you will find rest. For the yoke I will give you is easy, and the load I will put on you is light."

Matthew 11: 28-30

"...the load I will put on you is light."

The load

How can Jesus, who tells people to give away everything they own, and to turn the other cheek, actually say that his yoke is easy? What's he talking about?

I think of the students I'm trying to help. Often they are wound so tight from trying to remember all the details and rules that they paralyze themselves. So stressed by it all, they can't think.

What did Jesus see? Rules, rules, rules. Don't do this, now; don't do that, then. How do you stickhandle through all these rules? Jesus offers a commandment of love. Difficult to follow, for sure, but life-giving, clear and freeing. This "easy yoke" allows me to focus on what's really important, rather than trying to memorize a manual.

**Lord, give me enough strength to carry
this light load you give me.**

"I assure you that John the Baptist is greater than anyone who has ever lived. But the one who is least in the kingdom of heaven is greater than John. From the time John preached his message until this very day the kingdom of heaven has suffered violent attacks, and violent men try to seize it. Until the time of John all the prophets and the Law of Moses spoke about the kingdom; and if you are willing to believe their message, John is Elijah, whose coming was predicted. Listen, then, if you have ears!"

Matthew 11: 11-15

"...if you are willing to believe their message..."

Beyond appearances

When I was in university there was a homeless man who often wandered about in our neighbourhood. He had bird's-nest tangled hair and wild eyes. Even in the summer he wore a long winter coat tied tight around his waist with a leather belt. Some of us called him the "wild man." We gave him plenty of space and avoided him whenever we could.

But one of my housemates called him "JB" or "the prophet." She felt he was probably closer to God than most of the preachers on television. How easily most of us had dismissed him!

John the Baptist was also known for his wild appearance. I wonder if I would have dismissed him as "just another one of those crazies." Sometimes God's messengers come in surprising packages.

**God, teach me to listen to your messengers –
no matter how they might appear.**

"Now, to what can I compare the people of this day? They are like children sitting in the marketplace. One group shouts to the other, 'We played wedding music for you, but you wouldn't dance! We sang funeral songs, but you wouldn't cry!' When John came, he fasted and drank no wine, and everyone said, 'He has a demon in him!' When the Son of Man came, he ate and drank, and everyone said, 'Look at this man! He is a glutton and wine drinker, a friend of tax collectors and other outcasts!' God's wisdom, however, is shown to be true by its results."

Matthew 11:16-19

> "God's wisdom is shown to be true by its results."

God's own time

One of my favourite memories is of my husband sitting in his workshop surrounded by wood shavings as he fashioned a canoe paddle for me. After his death I found myself unable to sort through his workshop and, for years, it sat gathering dust and clutter. My more orderly minded friends despaired at this piece of "unfinished business" in my life.

One weekend, almost seven years after my husband's death, my teenage sons helped to sort through and tidy up his workshop. While we were clearing off the workbench, the boys found an unfinished project of their dad's. They were excited with their find and asked if they could finish it.

I realized then why I hadn't cleaned the workshop earlier!

Lord, bear with me when I am slow to trust your wisdom, your sense of order and your timing in my life.

Mary got ready and hurried off to a town in the hill country of Judea. She went into Zechariah's house and greeted Elizabeth. When Elizabeth heard Mary's greeting, the baby moved within her. Elizabeth was filled with the Holy Spirit and said in a loud voice, "You are the most blessed of all women, and blessed is the child you will bear! Why should this great thing happen to me, that my Lord's mother comes to visit me? For as soon as I heard your greeting, the baby within me jumped with gladness. How happy you are to believe that the Lord's message to you will come true!" Mary said, "My heart praises the Lord; my soul is glad because of God my Saviour, for he has remembered me, his lowly servant! From now on all people will call me happy, because of the great things the Mighty God has done for me."   *Luke 1: 39-47*

> "...that my Lord's mother comes to visit me?"

The qualities of friendship

If I put myself in either Mary's or Elizabeth's position, I'm sure my reaction would have been different. Mary is young, unmarried and pregnant, and has just been told that the father of her child is God! Who will believe her? But there is never a hint of self-pity or doubt.

Elizabeth knows the child she is carrying is special, but when Mary arrives, she knows that Mary's is even more special. There is no hint of jealousy, only awe and gratitude. They have come together – not to compete or commiserate – but to celebrate.

Neither friend presents any obstacles to the Holy Spirit, who fills both of them, sweeping them up in a surge of joy and wonder at their shared physical intimacy with God.

Lord, let my friendships be invaded by the Holy Spirit.

T he people asked John the Baptist, "What are we to do, then?" He answered, "Whoever has two shirts must give one to the man who has none, and whoever has food must share it."

Some tax collectors came to be baptized, and they asked him, "Teacher, what are we to do?"

"Don't collect more than is legal," he told them.

Luke 3: 10-18

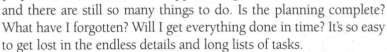

"Teacher, what are we to do?"

Christmas questions

Celebrations take a lot of planning and preparation. Christmas is fast approaching, and there are still so many things to do. Is the planning complete? What have I forgotten? Will I get everything done in time? It's so easy to get lost in the endless details and long lists of tasks.

But the people in today's reading are not lost. And they remind me not to get lost, too. Their one question is also mine: "What am I to do?" And the answer is definitely not "Remember to get cranberry sauce," or "Make sure the downstairs gets vacuumed."

The answer may not be simple or obvious, but if I don't remember to ask the question, I'll never hear the response.

Lord, this is a busy time.
Help me slow down so that I might hear you.

The chief priests and the elders came to [Jesus] and asked, "What right do you have to do these things? Who gave you such right?"

Jesus answered, "I will ask you just one question, and if you give me an answer, I will tell you what right I have to do these things. Where did John's right to baptize come from...?" They started to argue among themselves, "If we answer, 'From God,' he will say, 'Why, then, did you not believe John?' But if we say, 'From human beings,' we are afraid of what the people might do, because they are all convinced that John was a prophet." So they answered Jesus, "We don't know." And he said, "Neither will I tell you, then, by what right I do these things."

Matthew 21: 23-27

"What right do you have to do these things?"

Open to new ideas

I often find myself sympathizing with the chief priests and elders. Yes, they had their own axe to grind, their own position to protect, but then I realize how I can be a lot like them at times.

My children are growing up; they are beginning to see things in their own way. And they challenge my limits! On occasion, when I have to exert my authority, I say "No" before I've taken time to think. It's just a reflex action.

The chief priests and elders were so concerned about "who's the boss around here?" that they didn't even hear the message. When I read about them, I sometimes get embarrassed. It's hard to preserve what's good in the old ways while remaining open to what's good in the new.

Lord, I will try today to hear the question completely, and to think before I respond.

"There was once a man who had two sons. He went to the older one and said, 'Son, go and work in the vineyard today.' 'I don't want to,' he answered, but later he changed his mind and went. Then the father went to the other son and said the same thing. 'Yes, sir,' he answered, but he did not go. Which one of the two did what his father wanted?"

"The older one," they answered.

Jesus said, "The tax collectors and the prostitutes are going into the kingdom of God ahead of you. For John the Baptist came to you... and you would not believe him; but the tax collectors and the prostitutes believed him. Even when you saw this, you did not later change your minds and believe him."   *Matthew 21:28-32*

"...but the tax collectors and the prostitutes believed him."

A hard lesson to learn

This is a lesson I have to learn over and over and over. How easy it is to say what I know I am supposed to say, what people want to hear.

Why did the second son not go into the vineyard? The answer appears so obvious, so easy to grasp when we *read* it. Sometimes it is so difficult to *live* it – when life is full, hectic and complicated.

Certainly it is easy to see who only paid lip service, but much harder to remember when I am at work, hoping for the same promotion as Sheila in the next cubicle. Or at high school, talking to some nerd when my cool friends come along. When the "work in the vineyard" seems so hard, and who will notice anyway?

**Lord, help me to ensure that my actions flow
from my good intentions.**

do this so that everyone
from one end of the world to the other
may know that I am the Lord
and that there is no other god.
I create both light and darkness;
I bring both blessing and disaster.
I, the Lord, do all these things.
I will send victory from the sky like rain;
the earth will open to receive it
and will blossom with freedom and justice.
I, the Lord, will make this happen.

Isaiah 45: 6-8, 18, 21-25

"I create both light and darkness…"

Celebrating the seasons

As these winter nights continue to grow longer, I'm tempted to curse the darkness. How I long for those glorious summer days when there is plenty of light – long after the dinner dishes have been cleared away!

And, yet, I know there is wisdom in God's plan. Long winter evenings give our days a rhythm with more quiet time after sunset. We enjoy candles at suppertime more often, and linger around the table. Some nights we all camp out in front of the fireplace and enjoy watching the shadows, the play of light and darkness.

The winter solstice is around the corner. Soon we will celebrate the slow shift towards more sunlight. I welcome the light, but also give thanks for the gifts that come during this season of darkness.

Thank you, God, for both light and darkness.

This is the list of the ancestors of Jesus Christ…. From Abraham to King David: Abraham, Isaac, Jacob, Judah and his brothers; then Perez and Zerah (their mother was Tamar), Hezron, Ram, Amminadab, Nahshon, Salmon, Boaz (his mother was Rahab), Obed (his mother was Ruth), Jesse, and King David.

From David to the time when the people of Israel were taken into exile in Babylon: David, Solomon (his mother was the woman who had been Uriah's wife), Rehoboam, Abijah, Asa, Jehoshaphat, Jehoram, Uzziah, Jotham, Ahaz, Hezekiah, Manasseh, Amon, Josiah, and Jehoiachin and his brothers.

From the time after the exile in Babylon to the birth of Jesus: Jehoiachin, Shealtiel, Zerubbabel, Abiud, Eliakim, Azor, Zadok, Achim, Eliud, Eleazar, Matthan, Jacob, and Joseph, who married Mary, the mother of Jesus, who was called the Messiah.

Matthew 1: 1-17

> "This is the list of the ancestors of Jesus Christ…"

Families

This list of Jesus' ancestors sounds so illustrious, and so orderly! But what of those of us whose family ancestry is not so "perfect"?

A friend introduced me to the concept of a "family of choice." He described how sometimes a gay person's family rejects them because of their sexual orientation. To compensate for the lack of their own family, close friends create a network of love and support, becoming that person's "family of choice."

We all need a family to give us a sense of belonging. Though messy and imperfect at times, families – of origin or of choice – embody God's love for us.

Loving God, you have given me much love and support through my friends and family. Thank you.

This was how the birth of Jesus Christ took place. His mother Mary was engaged to Joseph, but before they were married, she found out that she was going to have a baby by the Holy Spirit…. An angel of the Lord appeared to [Joseph] in a dream and said, "Joseph, descendant of David, do not be afraid to take Mary to be your wife. For it is by the Holy Spirit that she has conceived. She will have a son, and you will name him Jesus – because he will save his people from their sins."

Now all this happened in order to make come true what the Lord had said through the prophet, "A virgin will become pregnant and have a son, and he will be called Immanuel" (which means, "God is with us").

Matthew 1: 18-24

"…and he will be called Immanuel."

God-with-us

The gospel writers pack so much into such a short phrase, to capture the meaning of the entire Christmas season in the word "Immanuel." If, at Jesus' birth, "God is with us," then we have reason to rejoice and sing and celebrate. God is not far away, perched on some celestial throne with hosts of angels around, but rather, "God is with us."

So when I clean the house, shovel the snow, put up the tree, bake for friends and family, God is with me in everything I do. Sometimes I forget, but God doesn't forget. God is always present. In preparing for Christmas, let me recall that "God is with us" and let me live my life in God's presence.

Dear God, help us be aware each day of the ways you are "with us." Help us remember "Immanuel."

S overeign Lord, I put my hope in you;
I have trusted in you since I was young.
I have relied on you all my life;
you have protected me since the day I was born.
I will always praise you....
I will go in the strength of the Lord God;
I will proclaim your goodness, yours alone.
You have taught me ever since I was young,
and I still tell of your wonderful acts.
Now that I am old and my hair is grey,
do not abandon me, O God!
Psalm 71: 3-6, 16-18

"I have trusted in you since I was young."

Secure in God

The electronic outer door of the home remains shut until the inner door closes. This prevents confused residents from wandering into the street. Visitors, too, are caught momentarily between these doors. Sitting in this lobby when I'm visiting my mother-in-law, I notice the stress on the faces of visitors as they experience this momentary entrapment.

Residents, those still able to walk or drive their scooter-chairs, wander by seemingly oblivious to the door's existence or purpose. This home is certainly a secure shelter. My mother-in-law's needs are met, even though she can barely articulate them now.

My wife and I look to this institution, as the psalmist once looked to God, for security and protection. Not for ourselves, but for someone who no longer has the words to pray.

Dear God, when I have no words to express my need for you, may your love still pour down on me.

Mary said, "My heart praises the Lord; my soul is glad because of God my Saviour, for he has remembered me, his lowly servant! From now on all people will call me happy, because of the great things the Mighty God has done for me. His name is holy; from one generation to another he shows mercy to those who honour him. He has stretched out his mighty arm and scattered the proud with all their plans. He has brought down mighty kings from their thrones, and lifted up the lowly. He has filled the hungry with good things, and sent the rich away with empty hands. He has kept the promise he made to our ancestors, and has come to the help of his servant Israel. He has remembered to show mercy to Abraham and to all his descendants forever!"

Luke 1: 39-56

"My heart praises the Lord…"

Light and shadow

Mary's outpouring of words sounds like a poem of praise – and of course it is – but when I read it carefully, I see many references to the shadows of life.

In the young Mary's world, kings still hold onto their thrones with violence, the powerful and their plans remain secure, the rich still have their hands full. Meanwhile Mary knows what it's like to be a lowly servant – perhaps even a hungry servant. No wonder her cousin Elizabeth thinks Mary deserves congratulations for believing in the Lord's message!

Like Mary, I experience the shadows – even when it seems I should rejoice. I hope I will find strength to sing Mary's song of faith – even when the shadows threaten to overwhelm me.

Lord, give me faith to believe in your promises, and strength to work towards their fulfillment.

I hear my lover's voice.
He comes running over the mountains,
racing across the hills to me….
My lover speaks to me.
Come then, my love;
my darling, come with me.
The winter is over; the rains have stopped;
in the countryside the flowers are in bloom.
This is the time for singing….
Let me see your lovely face
and hear your enchanting voice.

Song of Songs 2: 8-14

"This is the time for singing…"

With eyes of love

The whole world looks different when you're in love!

I remember a warm autumn day: I was sitting on a rock by the river with my new girl. With her at my side, the colours seemed brighter and I felt that wonderful feeling of being truly alive. Being in love made me realize how beautiful the world really was!

Now, when the world seems grey, it's usually me that has changed. If only I could see with the eyes of one newly in love… every day. If only I could recognize the beauty of all that I'm given… every day.

And that "new girl" of mine? Well, that was 27 years ago, and we still sit on that rock, and it's still a beautiful river.

**Dear God, open my heart to new love every day,
and open my eyes to the beauty that surrounds me.**

"**N**o one is holy like the Lord; there is none like him, no protector like our God…. For the Lord is a God who knows, and he judges all that people do…. The people who once were well fed now hire themselves out to get food, but the hungry are hungry no more…. The Lord kills and restores to life; he sends people to the world of the dead and brings them back again. He makes some people poor and others rich; he humbles some and makes others great. He lifts the poor from the dust and raises the needy from their misery. He makes them companions of princes and puts them in places of honour. The foundations of the earth belong to the Lord; on them he has built the world."

1 Samuel 2: 1-8

> "…and raises the needy from their misery."

A song of praise

How I resonate with today's hymn of praise! Like Hannah, my heart sang for joy as I gazed at my newborn son, Daniel. It's easy enough to rejoice, sing, even jump for joy at a birth – especially a long-awaited, much-longed-for one like Samuel's. But, putting today's reading in its context, doesn't it strike you as odd that Hannah sings at the very moment she is offering up her precious son to God?

Even though she would one day lose Jesus to death on a cross, Mary sang her *Magnificat* using words similar to Hannah's, rejoicing that God's love would be revealed through him.

Cuddling my baby close, I acknowledge that he is not really mine, but God's. And every day, I try to remember to "offer up" Daniel to God's loving service.

Lord, I offer you this child whom you have given to me.
May he grow to reveal your love to others.

When the baby was a week old, they came to circumcise him, and they were going to name him Zechariah, after his father. But [Elizabeth] his mother said, "No! His name is to be John." They said to her, "But you don't have any relative with that name!" Then they made signs to his father, asking him what name he would like the boy to have. Zechariah asked for a writing pad and wrote, "His name is John." How surprised they all were! At that moment Zechariah was able to speak again, and he started praising God…. Everyone who heard of it thought about it and asked, "What is this child going to be?"

Luke 1: 57-66

> "No! His name is to be John."

Speaking up

Naming a child can be a tricky business. With the birth of our first child, my husband and I soon learned that traditions and strong feelings run deep in family circles. Like Elizabeth, we had to contend with a great number of opinions.

I like this reading because of Elizabeth's ability to speak with her heart – in the face of the arguments around her. I can hear her humble but firm "No!" rising above the protests. I admire her courage.

It's not easy to stick to what you know is right when opinions differ. I'm often distracted by what people might think before I've even tried to acknowledge my own feelings. Elizabeth reminds me that there are times when it's good to think things through, to stand firm.

God, help me hear your voice when I try to find what is in my heart.

Thursday | DECEMBER 24

John's father Zechariah was filled with the Holy Spirit: "Let us praise the Lord, the God of Israel! He has come to the help of his people and has set them free. He has provided for us a mighty Saviour....

"You, my child, will be called a prophet of the Most High God. You will go ahead of the Lord to prepare his road for him, to tell his people that they will be saved by having their sins forgiven. Our God is merciful and tender. He will cause the bright dawn of salvation... to shine from heaven on all those who live in the dark shadow of death, to guide our steps into the path of peace."

Luke 1: 67-79

"You, my child, will be called a prophet..."

A father's love

I guess a lot of fathers prophesy great things for their children. Children are our ultimate sign of hope. And this prophecy is so joyful. But I wonder if Zechariah, the dad, saw the other side – the twisted Herod handing Herodias his son's head on a plate.

Like Zechariah, I see such great promise in my children. And I pray and hope that they will not have to suffer too much to find their place in the world.

I wonder what Zechariah did to help his son prepare to give his gift to the world. Each day I try to help my children learn to accept what comes to them, and to give to the world what is theirs to give... even when it costs.

**Lord, help me teach my children well.
Help me let go when it's time.**

n the past God spoke to our ancestors many times and in many ways through the prophets, but in these last days he has spoken to us through his Son. He is the one through whom God created the universe, the one whom God has chosen to possess all things at the end. He reflects the brightness of God's glory and is the exact likeness of God's own being, sustaining the universe with his powerful word. After achieving forgiveness for the sins of all human beings, he sat down in heaven at the right side of God, the Supreme Power.

The Son was made greater than the angels, just as the name that God gave him is greater than theirs. For God never said to any of his angels, "You are my Son; today I have become your Father."
Hebrews 1: 1-6

> "...he has spoken to us through his Son."

Show and tell

When I was young, I wondered what language God spoke. Was it English in Ontario, French in Quebec? Now I wonder how God speaks to infants, before they have learned any language. Or to people with senility, who can no longer handle language.

One day I realized that the language doesn't matter, because we all share one thing, regardless of the language we speak. We have all had the experience of being human.

And so, instead of lecturing us through prophets and visionaries, God decided to show us the true nature of God. Perhaps God got tired of our quibbling, our arguments, our misinterpretation of second-hand words. God became the Word – a living, breathing person whom we could experience for ourselves, directly.

**Thank you, God. Thank you, Jesus. Thank you,
Spirit of holiness. Live in me, and may my life reveal you.**

"Watch out.... For my sake you will be brought to trial before rulers and kings, to tell the Good News to them and to the Gentiles. When they bring you to trial, do not worry about what you are going to say or how you will say it; when the time comes, you will be given what you will say. For the words you will speak will not be yours; they will come from the Spirit of your Father speaking through you. People will hand over their own brothers to be put to death, and fathers will do the same to their children; children will turn against their parents and have them put to death. Everyone will hate you because of me. But whoever holds out to the end will be saved."

Matthew 10: 17-22

"...do not worry about what you are going to say..."

Learning to speak

I love to swim. One day I injured my shoulder and thought I might have to give up my favourite sport. Soon, however, I discovered that I could swim *if* I didn't use any power or strength. "So why bother? I'll just quit altogether." Then I thought, "Well, if I start gently today, and then increase a bit each week, perhaps, in time, I'll be able to swim with greater strength and power."

Similarly, I recognize there are times when I say the right words, but that they lack intensity, power and conviction. Instead of getting discouraged and giving up, I realize I have a choice. If I try, each day, to speak with whatever conviction I can find within me, perhaps, in time, the Spirit of God will speak through me.

Lord, help me to be honest – with myself and with others – in the words that I speak today.

Every year the parents of Jesus went to Jerusalem for the Passover Festival. When Jesus was twelve years old, they went to the festival as usual. When the festival was over, they started back home, but the boy Jesus stayed in Jerusalem. His parents did not know this; they thought that he was with the group, so they travelled a whole day and then started looking for him.... On the third day they found him in the Temple.... His parents were astonished when they saw him, and his mother said to him, "Son, why have you done this to us? Your father and I have been terribly worried trying to find you."

He answered them, "Why did you have to look for me? Didn't you know that I had to be in my Father's house?"

Luke 2: 41-52

> "Son, why have you done this to us?"

Love and respect

Imagine the distress of Jesus' parents: "Where is our son?" And Jesus, beginning to move away from his family into the public forum, puzzled that his parents don't understand: "Why did you have to look for me?" Today this same process of letting go is still problematic, still fraught with worry.

But the answer remains the same: we need to try to see each other's perspective, to respect one another. For parents: to see their children as people with their own "business." For children: to listen to the experience of their parents and to learn from it. And for both: to trust, even when they don't understand one another. Jesus challenges us to discover new ways of relating to one another based in love and respect.

Dear God, help me to maintain the ties that connect me to my family, and accept each person in their own reality.

An angel of the Lord appeared in a dream to Joseph and said, "Herod will be looking for the child in order to kill him. So get up, take the child and his mother and escape to Egypt...."

When Herod realized that the visitors from the East had tricked him, he was furious. He gave orders to kill all the boys in Bethlehem and its neighbourhood who were two years old and younger....

In this way what the prophet Jeremiah had said came true: "A sound is heard in Ramah, the sound of bitter weeping. Rachel is crying for her children; she refuses to be comforted, for they are dead."

Matthew 2: 13-18

"...she refuses to be comforted, for they are dead."

The shadow of death

Every Christmastime, when images of "sweet baby Jesus" prevail, I struggle to suppress the images of horror provoked by today's reading: every boy under two executed, no exceptions.

These children were lost without a trace: no family albums, no videos, just the quickly fading memories of first words spoken, an unused cot in the corner.

Years later, their older brothers and sisters would struggle to remember something of the baby they knew for two years, before the soldiers arrived.

Across the joy of Jesus' birth falls the shadow of the violence that such light continues to provoke through time and space.

Dear Lord, your presence is often met with fear and violence. May I be a messenger of your peace.

There was a man named Simeon…. He was a good, God-fearing man and was waiting for Israel to be saved. The Holy Spirit was with him and had assured him that he would not die before he had seen the Lord's promised Messiah. Led by the Spirit, Simeon went into the Temple. When the parents brought the child Jesus into the Temple to do for him what the Law required, Simeon took the child in his arms and gave thanks to God: "Now, Lord, you have kept your promise, and you may let your servant go in peace. With my own eyes I have seen your salvation, which you have prepared in the presence of all peoples: A light to reveal your will to the Gentiles and bring glory to your people Israel."

Luke 2: 22-35

> "…you may let your servant go in peace."

Go in peace

Such peace in Simeon: "you may let your servant go in peace." I've heard it said that we die once we have accomplished that for which we are given life. Simeon accomplished his task: he saw and recognized the promised Messiah. And his response revealed the Messiah to others.

Throughout scripture, as in our lives, God is revealed in everyday life. The light – God's Word – reveals what is true and good in my world. However, there are forces that often obscure my path and throw me off track. The choices I make – the small decisions made each day – are choices for the light or for the dark. How will my life reveal the God of hope, of new possibilities in the decisions I make today?

**God, help me to recognize the true light in my life
and let it show me the way to truth and love.**

Wednesday | DECEMBER 30

P raise the Lord's glorious name;
bring an offering and come into his Temple.
Bow down before the Holy One when he appears;
tremble before him, all the earth!
Say to all the nations, "The Lord is king!
The earth is set firmly in place
and cannot be moved;
he will judge the peoples with justice."
Be glad, earth and sky!
Roar, sea, and every creature in you;
be glad, fields, and everything in you!
The trees in the woods will shout for joy
when the Lord comes to rule the earth.

Psalm 96: 4-12

"Be glad, earth and sky!"

God's temple

I like to describe it as a "piece of heaven": a small island in the river, connected to the shore by a long, floating dock.

I remember how I sat watching my children playing in the water: laughing, jumping, diving, splashing. And how I slowly became aware of the details of my surroundings: the forest floor, cushioned by years of fallen pine needles; the outcroppings of granite, laid bare by glacial action of long ago, now covered by lichen and moss; the blue of the summer sky and the bright sunlight glinting off the water.

I was filled with a deep sense of peace. In that temple of pine needles, granite and lichen, I sighed and said, "Thank you, God, for all that you have created!"

**Lord, may I remember to praise you
and give you thanks today, and every day.**

n the beginning the Word already existed; the Word was with God, and the Word was God. From the very beginning the Word was with God. Through him God made all things; not one thing in all creation was made without him. The Word was the source of life, and this life brought light to people....

The Word was in the world, and though God made the world through him, yet the world did not recognize him. He came to his own country, but his own people did not receive him. Some, however, did receive him and believed in him; so he gave them the right to become God's children.   *John 1: 1-18*

"In the beginning the Word already existed..."

The voice of God

"In the beginning, the Word already existed," says John. And now? Hurtling through the blackness of space, can we still hear the echoes of the Word? Still feel the vibrations?

Listen. You'll hear it. Each time the leaves rustle on a summer afternoon. You'll hear it.

Each time a mother sings lullabies to her child. You'll hear it.

Each time an old man looks with affection into the eyes of his lifelong beloved. You'll hear it.

Each time, amidst the insanity of this world's hatred, an act of kindness is done. You'll hear it.

Stop. Listen to the heartbeat of the universe, and you'll hear the voice of God.

Dear Lord, give me ears to hear your Word in all of creation.

List of Contributors

Mary Bastedo: 38, 156, 165, 200, 204, 217, 267, 287, 328
Rosalee Bender: 232, 245
Rick Benson: 50, 178, 218, 344
Louisa Blair: 25, 31, 69, 82, 91, 133, 142, 155, 162, 194, 195, 196, 207, 214,
    240, 266, 275, 283, 295, 297, 313, 338, 350, 354
Kevin Burns: 22, 29, 68, 81, 86, 116, 185, 202, 242, 258, 290, 293, 345, 347,
    361, 370
Dan Connors: 270
Mike Cooke: 16, 21, 33, 35, 45, 52, 61, 72, 80, 87, 90, 94, 98, 103, 105, 107,
    111, 112, 120, 139, 147, 157, 160, 177, 198, 205, 213, 216, 225, 227, 259,
    276, 279, 284, 300, 302, 305, 316, 319, 321, 331, 335, 339, 340, 343, 348,
    351, 356, 357, 363, 366, 369, 373
Regina Coupar: 153, 326
Jim Creskey: 12, 24, 75, 83, 84, 138, 146, 166, 180, 278, 294, 310, 317
Rebecca Cunningham: 9, 23, 44, 49, 54, 57, 79, 101, 104, 132, 145, 148, 152,
    159, 189, 190, 236, 237, 248, 260, 303, 307, 309, 322, 333, 334, 336, 341,
    352, 358, 365
Helga Doermer: 280
Karen Fee: 330
Tanya Ferdinandusz: 89, 364
Patrick Gallagher: 10, 19, 20, 34, 58, 70, 92, 115, 122, 136, 154, 161, 171, 183,
    188, 192, 223, 286, 292, 312, 324, 346, 355
George Gilliland: 51, 229
Barbara Green: 228, 360
Caryl Green: 18, 26, 40, 42, 53, 66, 71, 73, 95, 97, 102, 106, 113, 114, 124,
    135, 137, 168, 172, 173, 176, 209, 210, 220, 234, 264, 269, 272, 282, 291,
    299, 301, 304, 329, 353, 359, 368, 371, 372
Calvin Halley: 144, 167, 182, 241, 277
Maryanne Hannan: 37, 46, 63, 123, 125, 174, 208, 273, 274, 281, 315
Maura Hanrahan: 119
Charles Harrel: 311
Krystyna Higgins: 67, 164, 243, 250
Deirdre Jackson: 247
Phil Kelly: 14, 27, 74, 100, 110, 129, 150, 224, 233, 268, 288
Nancy Keyes: 13, 36

List of Photographers

J. Boutin: 13, 123, 215, 246, 373

D. Brunet: 5

Cérac: 230, 358

Cléo: 144

Comstock: 19, 32, 143, 259, 283, 295

Paul Dolphin: 278

Fotosearch: 315

Getty Images: 270

Ingram: 11, 23, 25, 33, 35, 49, 54, 73, 85, 93, 96, 102, 111, 121, 129, 157, 161, 181, 191, 199, 227, 232, 253, 263, 272, 277, 281, 314, 325, 339, 353, 355

iStockphoto: 290

JupiterImages (photos.com): 9, 17, 29, 37, 43, 59, 60, 64, 65, 67, 74, 76, 78, 83, 87, 90, 92, 98, 105, 108, 109, 115, 117, 119, 125, 131, 133, 137, 140, 142, 147, 149, 151, 154, 158, 159, 168, 174, 175, 177, 184, 185, 197, 205, 207, 211, 212, 218, 220, 221, 223, 226, 229, 235, 238, 241, 248, 255, 256, 262, 266, 275, 285, 289, 291, 298, 303, 305, 309, 322, 329, 331, 340, 341, 342, 346, 349, 351, 365, 368, 370

Gilles Larcher: 294

Mia & Klaus: 274

Mikilaaq Centre: 15, 57, 112, 319

Novalis: 21, 40, 72, 163, 182, 189, 196, 245, 251, 273, 332, 345, 352, 363

G. Plaisted: 68, 335

S. Skjold: 100, 104, 279

W. P. Wittman: 16, 30, 38, 70, 126, 134, 136, 153, 156, 169, 171, 186, 194, 198, 204, 219, 231, 243, 267, 269, 276, 287, 288, 308, 317, 327, 347, 348, 361, 366